Way Beyond Satire

Rowan Dean

WP

Published by:
Wilkinson Publishing Pty Ltd
ACN 006 042 173
Level 4, 2 Collins Street
Melbourne, Vic 3000
Ph: 03 9654 5446
www.wilkinsonpublishing.com

Copyright © Rowan Dean 2016.

All rights reserved. No part of this publication may be reproduced, stored in a retrieval system or transmitted in any form by any means without the prior permission of the copyright owner. Enquiries should be made to the publisher.

Every effort has been made to ensure that this book is free from error or omissions. However, the Publisher, the Author, the Editor or their respective employees or agents, shall not accept responsibility for injury, loss or damage occasioned to any person acting or refraining from action as a result of material in this book whether or not such injury, loss or damage is in any way due to any negligent act or omission, breach of duty or default on the part of the Publisher, the Author, the Editor, or their respective employees or agents.

National Library of Australia Cataloguing-in-Publication entry
Creator: Dean, Rowan, author.

Title: Way beyond satire / Rowan Dean.

ISBN: 9781925265873 (paperback)

Subjects: Political satire, Australian.
Australia--Politics and government--Humor.
Australia--Politics and government--21st century.

Jacket Photography and Design:
Matt Irwin

Interior Layout and Typesetting:
Daniel Goodrich

Typeset in Calibri

The Author

Rowan Dean is the *AFR Weekend*'s regular political satirist, as well as a columnist with the *Courier Mail*. He is also the Editor of *The Spectator Australia*, the Australian arm of the English language's oldest continually published political and cultural magazine.

Rowan regularly appears on shows on Sky News and the ABC: *The Bolt Report, Paul Murray Live, Viewpoint, The Drum*, and *Q&A*. In 2017, Mark Latham, Ross Cameron and Rowan will host their own show on Sky News, *The Outsiders*.

Acknowledgments

A satirist is only as good as the editor who allows him to say what he thinks. My gratitude for this book goes to Editor-in-Chief of the *Australian Financial Review* Michael Stutchbury, along with Kevin Chinnery, Luke Malpass, Mark Lawson and several confused and distraught sub-editors.

I would also like to acknowledge the many, many writers, friends, critics and readers who have encouraged, helped and inspired me: Andrew Bolt, Miranda Devine, Grace Collier, Tim Blair, Piers Akerman, Neil Brown, Paul Murray, Bill Leak, Vic Alhadeff, Mark Latham, Derek Hansen, Jeremy Jones, Chris Kenny, Tony and Margie Abbott, Sasha Dean, Claire Dean, John Wood, John and Janette Howard, Sandy Peacock, Dan Rosen, Tom Switzer, Janet Albrechtsen, Judith Sloan, Peta Credlin, George Brandis, Louise Clegg, Russel Howcroft, John Roskam, Ron Cutler, Peter Anderson, Rebecca Weisser, Bob and Ruth Magid, all my Twitter fans and that lovely person who came up to me in the street the other day and then couldn't remember my name.

**To Sarah
My Creative Director**

Contents

The Author & Acknowledgments iii

1968 — The Year of Inspiration 1

Introduction 5

2013 — The Year of Good Riddance 7

2014 — The Year of Living Decisively 22

2015 — The Year of Betrayal 88

2016 — The Year of Come Uppance 192

1968 — the Year of Inspiration

It was wonderful being the Teacher's Pet, what with all the perks. Such as being allowed to go and set up the TV monitor for the Moon Landing while the other kids did their maths tables. Or being given the day off with my fellow Teacher's Pet Virginia to go to Duntroon to shake hands with the Queen while the other kids had exams. But even that degree of power and privilege wasn't enough for my young self. In that long, hot, lazy Canberra summer of 1968 I went one better – I became the Headmaster's Pet. Now, Head's Pet; that meant real privileges. And real power.

At least once a day, as my classmates fidgeted irritably in our sweltering demountable classroom, I would receive the call over the classroom intercom and be summonsed to the Headmaster's office. Smirking with glee, I'd shove my books into my little wooden desk, slam it shut with a satisfying clunk, then head off to freedom as the rest of the class glowered at me with envy and anger.

My mission was to make the period of my absence from the classroom last as long as possible. I'd saunter slowly down the long, empty, brown linoleum corridors to the Head's Office. His door would be waiting for me, slightly ajar. See what I mean about privilege? I didn't even have to knock.

The Head (if he had a name it was never used and I certainly never heard it) was sitting at his desk, a frown on his face as he studied that day's sports and betting pages. He had a craggy, ruddy face; wore a white shirt with short sleeves, a tie, a pair of shorts, long white socks and black shoes as was the style of the day.

"Come over here," he'd say, beckoning me over to him. I'd slouch on over, in a cool, casual sort of way, hands stuffed deep into pockets, tie deliberately askew. After all, I had power and I had privilege. None of that snapping to attention nonsense for me. "Sure," I'd say. "What will it be today, sir?" (Every professional male was a 'sir' back then.)

Way Beyond Satire

The Head would sigh irritably, then start fumbling around in his pockets. "I'm not sure," he'd say, wheezing slightly. This would normally be followed by a loud, phlegmy cough from deep within his chest.

"Craven A?" I would suggest, helpfully. Craven A were the Head's favourite, but by no means only, brand of cigarettes. "Or," I might add, in order to impress him, "they've got Salems on special this week I think."

The Head would pull out a few shiny, new, recently-decimalised, weeny, little coins, then reach instead for his wallet and pull out a beautiful crisp dollar note instead. You beauty, I'd think to myself. "I'm fed up with all that healthy Menthol crap," the Head would snap. "It's all bullshit. Get me a pack of Craven A, or no, I tell you what, get me two, just in case I run out."

This was the real power of being Head's Pet. You got to hear swear words like crap and bullshit. Right in front of you. Bliss!

I would nod with a knowing, studious frown on my face. "Yes sir. Two packets of Craven A. I won't be long, sir."

The Head would give me a dismissive wave of his hand. "Just get back before the bell goes. And you can keep the change."

So off I'd go. Across the playground, over the oval, over the main road at the lights, past the Motel, down to the shops and into the local newsagent, where, with any luck, the Beatles would be playing on the radio. I'd angled for the Salems-on-special because that way I'd make a bit more cash, but still, I couldn't complain. A dollar minus two times Craven As at forty cents equals a hundred minus eighty equals twenty cents.

Add that to yesterday's twenty cents and I had forty cents.

Forty cents pure profit.

I'd hurry into the newsagent, and purchase the cigarettes, beautifully displayed for all to see with their glorious logos.

1968 — the Year of Inspiration

There was never any hassle (they knew me well in there, but even if they didn't, nobody stopped kids buying whatever they wanted in those halcyon days). Fingers crossed, I'd then scamper to the back of the shop where the slightly risqué magazines like *Playboy* were kept. And there, hopefully, it would be.

The latest *MAD* magazine.

For the next twenty minutes I was in heaven.

If there was any one literary item that shaped my formative years, it was the wonderfully irreverent, cruel, hilarious and ever-so-informative *MAD* magazine, along with its (very) poor cousin *CRACKED*.

These two comics were more important to me than all the Supermans, Batmans, Phantoms, Archies and Thors put together. *MAD* and *CRACKED* poked fun at the real world; at the madness of the sixties, the hypocrisy of the counter-culture, and the pomposity and hilarity of the establishment and the anti-establishment alike. In those well-thumbed pages, I fell in love with "The Lighter Side" and the myriad Roger Kaputnicks, I guffawed at the genius of *MAD*'s movie parodies, I revelled in the "What they say and what they really mean" side-by-side comparisons (the original and best lesson in the horrors of political correctness), I delighted in their advertising spoofs and I couldn't wait to get my hands on that inside back cover and fold it into three to see what it revealed. (A confession: Spy versus Spy always left me cold, alas. Try as I did every month, I just didn't find it funny.)

Still to this day, I find myself spotting allusions to the great *MAD* satire and gags in everyday life. *MAD* taught us to look behind the spin for the hidden meanings, to see humour and optimism in even the bleakest scenarios, to happily mock and ridicule pretention, pomposity and self-importance.

Best of all, I learned that politics and politicians were there for one simple reason. To entertain us.

Satire can hurt. Satire can also sit anywhere on the scale of hilarious through to bafflingly unfunny. But best of all, satire illuminates.

The kids of later decades may have had videos and DVDs, iPhones and Netflix, *The Simpsons* and *South Park*, *The Hangover* and *There's Something About Mary* or any of the myriad forms of entertainment that have come and gone. But we had the magazine with Alfred E. Neumann on the cover. Satire was the bedrock of our existence. How lucky were we.

I'd scurry back into the Head's office. The bell had already gone, of course, so I'd leave the two packs of Craven A on his desk and head out into the playground, clutching the latest *MAD* in my sweaty hand. Inspired.

Introduction

Late in 2013, not long after the launch of the first book of my satirical columns — Beyond Satire, which chronicled the madness of the extraordinary Rudd-Gillard-Rudd years — I was privileged to bump into the new Prime Minister, Tony Abbott. I can't actually remember what the event was, but I was astonished that Mr Abbott made a beeline for me. "Ma-ate," he said, in his distinctive and much mimicked drawl, "I just wanted to say, um, how much I have enjoyed your, ah, weekly columns. They're, um, very funny."

I was taken aback, assuming, like most writers do, that nobody actually ever reads their material. (Other than your Mum and your wife, and, if you twist their arms with enough force, other members of your family. Sometimes, of course, your friends will read your work, but only minutes before you turn up at their place for dinner clutching an ice cold chardy so they can say how much they love your work.)

"Well," I replied to Mr Abbott, struggling to think of some appropriately witty or scathing comment and failing abysmally. "It wasn't that hard. Rudd and Gillard make writing satire pretty easy." And then as an afterthought I added, "Mind you, it's pretty tough now... I hope you guys give me something decent to work with pretty soon! I've got to eat, you know." Even as I said the words, I cringed at my own sycophancy. Still, I was surprised by the immediate answer.

Turning away to greet another well-wisher, the Prime Minister smiled over his shoulder. "I wouldn't worry about that," he said with a smile. "We'll give you plenty to write about." As was so often the case, Tony Abbott was spot on the money.

2013 — The Year of Good Riddance

If the knifing of Kevin Rudd by Julia Gillard, in the depths of a cold Canberra winter three years earlier, had shocked and traumatised the nation, we soon got over it.

By 2013, it was crystal clear that Kevin Rudd had every intention, and would leave no opportunity unexplored, to literally wind back the clock and change the outcome of that particularly grisly (for him, not so much for the rest of us) event. So the first half of 2013 was all about Kevin. Yet again. Kevin plotting. Kevin getting even. Kevin sulking, scheming and manipulating.

Kevin was determined to do what Doctor Who, Marty McFly and every time traveller worth his time machine had always managed to pull off — to reverse his fate.

And on the fateful night of June 27, three years and three days after Gillard had knifed him, he knifed her. The Gods sat back, satisfied and amused.

But the real fun had just begun...

Having successfully waged a bloody three-year war against Julia Gillard, the woman who had knifed him in the back, Kevin Rudd had now been voted back in to lead the Labor party and defeat Tony Abbott at the federal election due in three months' time.

Regardless, the polls suggest Abbott will secure an easy victory against Rudd. As ever, lurking in the background, Malcolm Turnbull continues to excite interest from the left-wing media.

❖

Rolling Stone *magazine decides, somewhat controversially, to put Boston Marathon bomber Dzhokhar Tsarnaev on its front cover.*

Dzjoker Ruddkev

Financial Review
20/7/13

A popular rock 'n' roll magazine has been forced to defend its decision to put on its front cover a glamourous photograph of a baby-faced narcissist known to millions as "a dysfunctional psychopath".

The cover of this month's *Rolling PMs* magazine, which hit the newsstands at exactly 8pm three weeks ago, features a blurry 'selfie' of Dzjoker Ruddkev wielding a shaving razor with blood streaks clearly visible on his cherubic face.

"It's grotesque. They've portrayed him loik he's some koind of rockstar," said an unnamed childless single redheaded woman in Canberra. "Yet this man has brought untold misery to thousands of people. Moi in particular."

"The cover almost tricks you into thinking you're looking at someone normal," she said. "But none of it is real. Not the party reforms, not the ETS, not the Manus stuff. It's all a sham."

"Oi think the public will have trouble, loik me, making the association between here's the guy who stuck a knoife into my back and here's this cool guy on the cover of a rock 'n' roll magazine."

Speaking from his Gold Coast tree-house, well-known rock 'n' roll aficionado and unemployed economist Wayne was clearly off his rocker: "It's like so uncool, dude, that cover. Where's Bruce Springsteen? Where's the World's Greatest Class Warrior? At the very least the story should have been about all the traitors who survived. Shorty, Penny and Albo. Why are we glorifying a guy who created mayhem in the Labor party? I am going to be in touch with the public and tell them I want my job back."

The August issue of the magazine depicts Dzjoker (the 'Dz' is silent, apparently) Ruddkev patting down his short, wispy silvery hair with the headline: "The leader: How an unpopular PM was felled by his caucus, retreated to the back benches and became a monster."

Rolling PM's editors said in a statement that the story follows the noblest traditions of journalism. "We were allowed unfettered access to Ruddkev, so long as we gave the Labor party unfettered free advertising and unfettered favourable editorial content."

Contributing editor Janet Earwax spent three years interviewing childhood friends, teachers, neighbours and faceless men to piece together Ruddkev's early life.

In *Psycho's World*, Ms. Earwax reports that the young Ruddkev was so devout he regularly attended a Sunday prayer group at St. John's in Canberra. "He took his doorstop interviews very seriously."

"The fact that Dzjoker Ruddkev is self-obsessed to the point of narcissism, and in the same mental age group as many of our readers, makes it all the more important for us to examine the complexities of this issue and gain a more complete understanding of how a political disaster like this unfolded," *Rolling PMs* said.

Ruddkev is the only political survivor of the Gang of Four who set out to take over the Labor party in the mid-'90s, knocking off each successive leader one by one, himself included.

Ruddkev spent years in hiding planning his revenge which finally came just before the end of the three-year Gillard marathon on June 27 using a highly pressurised caucus meeting.

On the fateful day, a non-existent petition was circulated amongst three people before being tossed into a nearby bin, in the hope that terrified members of caucus would be spooked. Gillard was way behind in the race when the knives came out and her Prime Ministership imploded.

Dzjoker Ruddkev and his supporters plotted the caucus attack months in advance, journalists now claim.

Ruddkev, 55, looks fatter and older in the photo than when he appeared last week in a Townsville press conference where he claimed he only did what he did in order to "terminate" the carbon tax.

"I haven't read it, but I understand the substance of the article is invisible," said retail politician Tzony Abbottev.

Other retailers, such as the Greens shop, based about 8,000 kilometres from Reality in Marrickville, Tasmania, and Hunt's Direct Action Convenience Shop, said they will not put a price on the re-vamped issue.

The decision to put Ruddkev on the cover drew a wave of approval on social media, including Twitter. Parents of impressionable teenagers, however, remain appalled.

"It's setting such a bad example to our kids," said one distraught parent. "Not only did this bloke destroy a perfectly healthy economy and blow our surplus, he then sabotaged the 2010 election and left us with a minority government. On top of that, thanks to his policies thousands of people have drowned at sea and, as the coroner said, four young men died doing home insulation schemes."

Dzjoker Ruddkev has pleaded not guilty to everything.

❖

Desperate to win the election, Kevin Rudd decides to fix up the boat people mess he himself had created, and rushes off to Papua New Guinea. "From now on, any asylum seeker who arrives in Australia by boat will have no chance of being settled in Australia as refugees," he declares. Instead, asylum seekers will be shipped off to Manus Island.

Mantusy island

Financial Review
27/7/13

Excited fans have welcomed the unexpected return of the classic 1970s TV series *Mantusy Island* in a billion-dollar co-production deal signed last week between Papua New Guinea and the Australian taxpayer.

The series follows the original plotline, in which a smooth-talking, silver-haired psychopath known only as Mr. Rukk and his earnest, quirky sidekick Tatto'neill fulfil the fantasies of everyone who arrives as a guest on their tropical hideaway — at a price.

"Da plane! Boss! Boss! It's da plane" will continue to be the catchphrase that kicks off each new episode, as Tatto'neill spots an incoming planeload of desperate asylum seekers and rushes off to ring up the bill, which may run into the billions. (In later episodes, Tatto'neill himself can be seen whizzing around the island in his personal Ferrari, supervising the building of a new luxury day spa and massage parlour.)

The plane he is talking about is delivering new arrivals plucked out of the sea, each of whom has laid down a sizable sum of money to have their personal fantasies fulfilled.

The show's charismatic star, immaculately dressed in his flamboyant white suit and blue tie, is the enigmatic Mr. Rukk, who takes it upon himself to greet every new guest personally as they form a long queue outside his stunning residence, the Lodge. "Hi folks, I'm Mr. Rukk. Welcome to Mantusy Island," he says as he raises a glass and high fives the newcomers before posing for a selfie with them one by one. With a sly nod and a wink to his mischievous sidekick, Mr. Rukk then explains, usually with a cryptic comment that sounds amazing but on closer inspection makes little sense, how he intends to fulfil their fantasy. Before they can question him on the details, however, he magically disappears, saying he's "gotta zip".

Of course, being a supernaturally-empowered Trickster-Mentor character, Mr. Rukk very rarely allows his guests' fantasies to play out in the way that *they* expect them to.

Much of the drama of the series comes from the way Mr. Rukk manages to turn everything he touches to dust, with each episode predictably ending in a chaotic shambles of obfuscation and excuses.

Quite often, the fantasies themselves are ludicrously implausible — such as how to save the planet by sacking hundreds of car fleet managers or how to make caucus more democratic by making it impossible for them to ever vote you out again.

Invariably, the guest learns that it's all a charade and they have been conned all along.

Critics have long complained that very little thought or care goes into each new episode, with the plotline appearing to have been hastily scribbled down on the back of a beer coaster — in pidgin.

The source of Mr. Rukk's strange powers and the reason behind his popularity are never revealed, although it is implied that he is a supernatural force for Good Polls. Being the sole owner and proprietor of Mantusy Island, Mr. Rukk's personal beliefs and deeply-held convictions are a complete mystery to everyone, himself included.

However, there are some clues as to his true nature. In one uncut episode leaked onto YouTube, Mr. Rukk slams his fist onto his gilt mahogany desk screaming "aarrrgghhhh! this f---king dialogue!" before declaring that the guests who come to his island are all "dickheads". In another episode, Mr. Rukk tricks a woman into destroying herself via a petition, which also turns out to be a total fantasy. Throughout the new series Mr. Rukk gets to meet many seemingly-immortal beings on Earth, including Obama, Ban-Ki moon and others at the UN or the G20. Rukk even faces the devil, who has come onto the island in red speedos to tow back the boats.

There are constant hints throughout the series that Mr. Rukk thinks he himself is immortal, or sees himself as some kind of deity. Uncannily, he is able to appear to his guests in whatever guise they desire to perceive him. Yet Mr. Rukk's fantasies are certainly not without peril, and in some cases people are killed due to Rukk's own negligence, arrogance or undue haste in implementing them. Naturally, Mr. Rukk can never directly intervene when his fantasies go awry, nor accept any kind of blame or responsibility. For instance, when Tatto'neill is given his own hospital as a pre-election gift, which ends up with him being chased downriver by irate starving headhunters in canoes, Mr. Rukk zips off to a conference overseas, leaving the hapless Tatto'neill stewing (literally) in his own juices. Without exception, Rukk always makes it clear he is powerless to stop a fantasy once it has begun and that guests must suffer the disastrous consequences all by themselves. As well as pay the exorbitant price.

Industry experts say the budget for *Mantusy Island* is "uncapped", even though the show is expected to be axed within a few weeks.

❖

As the election campaign heats up, Kevin Rudd and Tony Abbott battle it out under the hot lights of a Sky News People's Forum Debate.

Meanwhile, as the world mourns the death of crime writer Elmore Leonard, rumours circulate of a few scraps of paper believed to contain the handwritten notes of his final novel.

Get Kevvie

Financial Review
22/8/13

When Kooky Kevvie first came to Bronco's Beach for the showdown, they were having one of their hot winters: twenty-six degrees the day he faced off against Negativity Tone for the big gabfest. Kevvie always knew he was hip; he had his bright yellow tie on, the one Therese had given him a year ago, when he was still scratching around on the backbenches trying to figure out how to kill the bitch that knifed him in the first place.

Kevvie hadn't changed much in the past three years. Still hated showing respect to people he thought were stupid, which was just about everyone. Still liked to talk his big mouth off for hours on end and wave his hands around.

Kevvie watched Tone come towards the make-up room and said to his friend the pollster, "I can do better'n him."

"Not these days," the pollster said.

Kevvie was in the chair when the barber woman came backstage and began to comment, telling him she could do a perm or something on his crazy quiff to stop it moving around. Maybe stick some gel on it. But Kevvie told her to cut the shit and just do precisely what he asked her to do or else she'd find herself stripping her clothes off at Scores nightclub.

"You really are a son of a bitch," she said. Then she ran out of the room bawling her eyes out. Afterwards she wrote a note on her Facebook page to remind herself what an asshole he'd been. Then she wiped it clean.

The sound guy pulled the microphone under Tone's shirt, and noticed his buffed physique. He said, "Today's the big day, big boy. You gonna nail him?" Tone just squinted, and flexed his pecs. On the other side of the room Kevvie struggled with his hairdo, swearing and cursing as he tried to tame his fringe with his fingers, one handful at a time.

"You guys are on," said a voice. Kevvie and Tone walked out into the crowded room like a couple of hard-ons.

"I think we need answers," Kevvie said, speaking first. "You gonna cut to the bone? You gonna cut, cut, cut? Tell me straight, where you gonna cut?"

So now it was up to Tone. He said. "You gotta stop telling these lies, Kevvie. I did not take the money from any hospitals. I did not." But Kevvie just stared at him. So Tone said, "Well, you know, the guy who did the job before me, you know, he made a slight adjustment, you know how it works. Slowed things down a bit, that's all. But not me. No way."

David 'the Speer' stood between the two men and tried to figure out who had shown disrespect to whom. The Speer always knew when to keep his mouth shut.

"Why don't you tell me where the money's gone, Kevvie," said Tone. "Pretty Boy Costello and Jonny Eyebrows left a shitload of moolah behind. Now it's all gone. You blew the lot. That's one big motherf---king debt you left us with."

But Kevvie was having none of it.

"I hear you want to give it free to all the pregnant mums, you sicko," Kevvie said. He pulled a five dollar note out of one pocket and a fifty dollar note out of the other and waved them around in the air.

Tone believed that if he concentrated really hard he'd remember what he was supposed to say next. "It's fully funded," he said. "The big end of town's gonna pay up big time." But Kevvie wouldn't leave it alone. "Some bitch's earning a million bucks," he said. "And you wanna give her seventy five gee for free?"

Tone wanted to smack him then and there, but Kevvie wouldn't let up. He said, "How many broads in this room earn 150G?" David 'the Speer' jumped to his feet. "Nobody's gonna tell ya that," he said. Kevvie ignored him. "We gotta know," he said.

Tone believed if he kept his eyes closed and quit listening the sound from Kooky Kevvie would eventually dry up and he'd get his turn to speak. But Kevvie kept pumping his fists. Kept running his fingers through his hair. Kept shouting dumb questions. Kept going on and on about the GFC and the GST, whatever they were.

Tone couldn't stand it any longer. He said, "Does this guy ever shut up?"

There was a deadly silence. The Speer stared at him. Tone felt a cold fear gripping him. He knew that this time he'd gone too far. Broken the rules. Lost his cool. Blown it. He saw the deadly glint in Kevvie's eyes.

And then, one by one, the crowd began to laugh.

❖

Tony Abbott wins the Prime Ministership in a landslide victory. Away from politics and at home in her new beachside pad, Julia Gillard signs a lucrative book deal and starts laying out the rough draft of her highly-anticipated autobiography.

Moi Choildhood

Financial Review
28/9/13

Chapter One
Moi choildhood. This will be all about how Oi was picked on at school boi all the boys but because Oi knew how to use my brines Oi overcame all the obstacles in moi path.
(editor's note: keep it brief please)

Chapter Two
Moi adolescence. This will be how Oi had to overcome misogyny and sexism wherever Oi saw it in order to get into Uni.
(ed's note: how about 'my first kiss' for cover of Woman's Weekly*?)*

Chapter Three
Moi early career. This will be how Oi studied to become a lawyer and got a job at Sloyter and Gordon and moved into a house with moi boyfriend Bruce and hung out with his mate little Ralphie. Great toimes and lots of larks like the toime Ralphie found a bag of money buried under the patio in the backyard and somebody

goive it to Bill the Greek to fix moi fence. Typical juvenile hoi-jinx Oi think we all agree.
(ed's note: might need to run this stuff past legal)

Chapter Four
Moi escape from betroyal. This will be a very pineful chapter to wroite, because it goes into the personal pine Oi felt when Oi was deeply hurt and betroyed boi moi boyfriend Bruce and so Oi had to quit moi job because Oi was so upset.
(ed's note: New Idea 'he broke my heart' spread?)

Chapter Foive
Moi dizzying roide to success. This is how Oi was talent-spotted boi the Upper Echelons of the Union movement as a person of great promise to lead the Labor party as a Potential First Femoil Proime Mininster of this country.
(ed's note: not sure we need this, thanks)

Chapter Six
Moi first day in Parliament. From Day One it was obvious that the Patriarchal System was stacked against me as Oi arroived in Canberra and was universally ignored boi everybody, thanks to flagrant Misogyny and Sexism.
(ed's note: can you recall what you wore that day? Lippy? Shoes? We could do a retro First Day Fashion Tips for Elle.*)*

Chapter Seven
Moi first troiumph. This is when Oi led the Labor Party to near-certain victory in the 2004 election but was sabotaged at the last minute boi Mark Latham and his aggressively masculine handshake which single-handedly destroyed moi chance to introduce moi Medicare Rolled Gold scheme which Oi desoigned all by moiself. Are we seeing a pattern here?
(ed: nope)

Chapter Eight
Moi second troiumph. This is where Oi help Kevin Rudd become Proime Minister against moi better judgment because that's the koind of caring and compassionate person Oi am. As usual, Oi did all the hard yards in the run up to the election which everybody

now agrees should have been the Julia '07 campaign but again Oi was thwarted by misogyny and sexism.
(ed: can we mock up J in a Julia '07 wet tee-shirt for Zoo?)

Chapter Noin
Third toim lucky! This is where the entire Labor Party come crawling into moi office on hands and knees begging for me to ditch Rudd and rescue the country from the doldrums because a good government has lost its way. This was entoirely unexpected and came as a great and humbling shock as Oi pointed out in the acceptance speech Oi wrote three weeks earlier.
(ed's note: maybe delete that last bit?)

Chapters Ten, Eleven, Twoilve
Camelot — or is it? This is moi favourite bit. Oi move into the Lodge with moi hairdress... er, Oi mean moi boyfriend and despoit a constant barrage of misogyny and voil sexism the loiks of which no woman in history has had to forbear, Oi still give the country a golden period of compassionate enloitenment including a carbon tax just loik Oi'd always said Oi would and which historians now agree was an oidyllic period of peace and prosperity as Oi inspired the entoire nation with moi visionary Gonski and Disability Care.
(ed's note: can we substantiate any of this stuff?)

Chapter Thirtoin
Unlucky for some! This is the bit where Oi am betrayed — yet again! — boi Bill, Penny, Albo, Bobby, Chris, Tanya and all the other misogynists who betroy me for purely personal gine.
(ed's note: need loads of 'How so-and-so stabbed me in the back' stuff for the Oz serialisation)

Chapter Fourtoin
Moi brilliant new career. This is where Oi become a University Professor just round the corner from moi new beach house so Oi can advoise moi good friends Michelle Obama and Hillary Clintoin how they can win the next election and become First Femoil President and First Femoil Voice-President of the United States just loik me.
(ed's note: what about some pics frolicking topless in the spa?)

2013 — The Year of Good Riddance

❖

When the Coalition decides to break its pre-election commitment on schools spending, the press attack Abbott's and Christopher Pyne's 'Gonski backflip'. Meanwhile, celebrity chef Nigella Lawson is seen being attacked by her husband in a restaurant. He accuses her of drug abuse.

Nigella Pyne

Financial Review
7/12/13

A tearful Nigella Pyne fronted the TV cameras this week to deny rumours that she was a habitual Gonski addict, although she did admit that she had snorted small amounts of the addictive education funding formula "from time to time".

"I'm not proud of the fact I have taken Gonski but that does not make me a Gonski addict or a regular user," she said.

"I did not have a funding problem, I had a political problem," she insisted to reporters yesterday. "I opened the cupboard and discovered someone had left a Gonski package there. It was all over the place."

It was the first public appearance of the famous 'Goddess of the Kitchen Cabinet' since the recent drama in which pictures surfaced of her being visibly throttled by an irate Tony Saabotchi. The incident — which was captured on mobile phones by stunned observers and made headlines around the world — occurred late last Sunday night outside a posh Canberra meeting place known as LNP HQ or 'The Panic Room'.

The photographs showed 'Pynella' (as she is known to her closest friends) and Saabotchi arguing passionately at their table. Tony is seen grabbing Pynella by the throat, twisting her spine roughly, snapping her lower vertebrae with both hands against her hips and forcing her to do a backflip.

Saabotchi denies reports that he was applying excessive force to his minister. "I wasn't trying to strangle Pynella, I was merely looking up her nose to see whether she'd been secretly sniffing out Gonski," he claimed.

"We were sitting in the party room having an intense debate about paying for everybody's children's education, and I twisted Pynella's neck repeatedly while attempting to emphasise my point. It was all perfectly friendly and has been misconstrued by the press."

Saabotchi admitted the backflip looked "incredibly painful" but claimed it was just his way of making his education minister see common sense. "There was no broken promise," he said. "In fact, there wasn't even a promise at all, just the promise that people thought we had made or the promise they would have liked us to make. It was all just a playful tiff. The pictures are horrific and give a far more drastic and violent impression of what actually took place.

"Pynella's tears were because we both hate stuff-ups, not because she had been comprehensively railroaded by me.

"We managed to kiss and make up by Question Time. The paparazzi were congregated outside Parliament house after the story broke, so I told Pynella to pretend to go along with the backflip till after MYEFO has come out and the dust has settled and then she can start slashing spending again."

Saabotchi and Pynella have been intimately involved in a hugely successful but often "turbulent" marriage of convenience since the sudden death of her previous paramour, Malcolm, whom many believe was the love of her life. Malcolm's leadership aspirations tragically died in late 2009, although Pynella is believed to still secretly hold a candle for him.

Pynella has denied keeping a stash of Gonski in a hollowed-out education budget in which she also stored her political reputation. Allegations have recently surfaced of a "dark secret" in her ten week relationship with the electorate, with suggestions of rolled-up banknotes coated with taxpayers' fingerprints being found stuffed in her handbag, reportedly worth over a billion dollars.

"I am a lot more puritanical about money than Tony is," a tearful Pynella explained. "I would never have thought it was the right idea to splash so much cash around in such a disgustingly socialist way."

An email was reportedly sent to Pynella from Tony in which he said the budget's bottom line was no longer a problem because the Treasurer was "so off his head" on abolishing the debt ceiling that ministers could "spend whatever they liked".

Pynella said she would rather be "honest and ashamed" than "bullied with lies" about her core libertarian beliefs.

Meanwhile, an anti-political violence organisation claimed that pollies from all sections of society can fall victim to abusive relationships, pointing out that backflips were a "massive political problem" which claimed dozens of victims every year.

"There are still so many myths and misconceptions surrounding this horrific practice. People often think that it only happens in a Labor caucus, but the truth is that backflipping affects pollies of all ages, parties and backgrounds.

"Backflippers are just as likely to be Coalition Prime Ministers, 'Age of Entitlement' Treasurers or National Party Deputy Leaders as they are spin doctors or ambitious backbenchers. Backflipping is all about retaining power and not losing control of the news agenda. It is a pattern of ruinous behaviour that often involves extreme reversals, humiliation and unbelievable physical contortions."

2014 — The Year of Living Decisively

The Year of Abbott. This was the year in which Tony Abbott attempted to restore to the country the sound governance and principles of the Howard era. After all, Abbott had been a hard-hitting conservative minister throughout the Howard years, and had once joked he was the love-child of conservative warrior Bronwyn Bishop and John Howard himself.

After a strangely muted reaction to winning his landslide victory against Kevin Rudd, Tony Abbott had opted for a low media profile over the latter part of 2013. For many commentators, "not much news" was a refreshing change to the endless media turmoil of the Rudd-Gillard-Rudd years. But, in what would prove to be his one and only entire year as Prime Minister of Australia, 2014 showed that rather than being fed up with leadership shenanigans, the media — and possibly even the public — craved for more. We'd become a nation addicted to turmoil.

The centrepiece of the year was of course Joe Hockey's 2014 Budget. Despite containing many sensible ideas for cutting government expenditure and starting the long trek back to a surplus, the major problem was that the groundwork had not been properly laid, many ideas were contradictory, and there was no clear sales pitch. And then of course, some bright spark decided to light up the cigars.

With the strike of a match, Tony Abbott's conservative, Howard-style government began to unravel.

❖

As the New Year dawns, and a scientific expedition studying global warming gets stranded in ice floes in the Antarctic, newspapers are full of predictions for the year ahead.

2014 Predictions

Financial Review
4/1/14

January: Efforts to free a group of climate change scientists marooned in the Antarctic due to an unprecedented amount of ice continue to be frustrated by the record-breaking cold weather. Speaking from the ship's icy bridge, the head of the expedition calls for urgent action on reducing dangerous carbon emissions: "W-w-w-w-e are at a t-t-t-ipp-ing p-p-point," he says. "The t-t-t-tip of my n-n-nose is about to f-f-freeze off."

Bill Shorten maintains that "hanging onto their jobs" will be the toughest challenge people face this year: "Me in particular."

Tony Abbott returns to work. Twitter goes into meltdown predicting the imminent collapse of the Abbott government.

February: At the Sydney Mardi Gras, a leading gay marriage advocate decrees gay marriage is "the defining issue of our times in which all of humanity can express their love and respect for every Australian, including those of a different persuasion". The speech is followed by the ritual burning of effigies of Tony Abbott, George Pell and Christopher Pyne.

Bill Shorten decrees: "I have no idea what gay marriage actually entails but I support it unequivocally."

March: Efforts to rescue a group of climate change scientists stranded in the Himalayas are hampered by record-breaking drifts of snow and "blizzard-like" conditions. Instruments designed to measure the catastrophic effects of global warming are ditched because they're "frozen solid".

April: Tony Abbott goes for a bike ride. Twitter erupts predicting Malcolm Turnbull will be Prime Minister "by Christmas".

Antony Albanese stars in an ABC special entitled "The Real Albo — an intimate portrait of the doting footy Dad who should be leading Labor".

May: A group of climate change scientists trapped in the Sahara due to excessive amounts of rainfall get swept away in floodwaters.

Joe Hockey releases "horror" budget. Minor cuts to health, education and welfare programs and scrapping of ineffectual climate change subsidies. Twitter goes into meltdown predicting the "end of civilisation".

June: Activists protesting outside the Parliamentary Midwinter Ball against the removal of the carbon tax are rushed to Canberra Hospital suffering hypothermia.

Tony Abbott and his cabinet go to Arnhem Land for a week to focus on Indigenous affairs. Twitter erupts claiming Peta Credlin will be PM "by spring".

July: A group of climate change scientists studying the devastating effects of global warming on plant growth become lost in the Amazon due to an unprecedented amount of jungle. Calling for help, the expedition leader tweets: "We're completely surrounded by all these huge trees and tangly stuff."

Carbon tax repealed by new senate. Twitter erupts predicting the extinction of the human species and that Barnaby Joyce will be Prime Minister "by year's end".

August: New Indonesian president vows to work closely with Australia to stop boats. Twitter silent.

September: A group of climate scientists monitoring the catastrophic effects of rising sea levels on an atoll in the Pacific don't need to be rescued when they don't get washed away.

Bill Shorten denies leadership is under threat, pointing out that new rules mean there can be no challenge before an election.

October: At the party conference, respected Labor elder John Faulkner releases long-awaited report: "Rebirth of Labor (version 13)." Delegates vote to change leadership rules back to "exactly how they were before Rudd stuffed it all up".

A group of climate experts heading to a climate change conference in Shanghai are unequivocal in their praise for China's new Five Year Carbon Reduction Plan, which envisages a new windmill farm in Guangzhou Province. Unfortunately, delegates can't see the windmill farm due to an "unprecedented" level of thick brown smog covering the entire nation.

November: No boat arrivals in six months.
Twitter manically depressed.

Chris Bowen goes on Sky to confirm: "There is no leadership challenge."

December: Bill Shorten steps down "in the interests of the party". Albo and Bowen anointed as Labor "dream team".
Twitter swoons.

Tony Abbott goes on Christmas hols. Twitter erupts predicting Scott Morrison will be Prime Minister "by Boxing Day".

A group of climate change scientists embark on a critical research mission to monitor the devastation wrought by melting glaciers in Iceland. (Update — cancelled due to extreme icy conditions.)

❖

An Australian entertainer is arrested in Britain, and goes to court.

Rolf Harris

Financial Review
18/1/14

Veteran entertainer Rolf Harris is believed to have pleaded not guilty to 12 counts of embarrassing a large amount of Australians.

The embarrassment charges relate to serial offences against good taste, Australian artistic credibility, rock music, national pride, Indigenous self-esteem, cartooning and painting and occurred over a period from the late 1950s until quite recently.

One elderly witness complained how he arrived in Britain in 1960 to escape the parochialism of rural Australia. "It was excruciating. The first thing that greeted me was this odd song about somebody tying up — or was it tying down? — a kangaroo. On top of that, everybody insisted on calling me 'sport'. I've never been so embarrassed in all my life."

Victim groups said the embarrassment was not limited to the music and chorus of the song, with many complaining of the toe-curling, cringe-making fourth verse: Let me abos go loose, Lew/ Let me abos go loose/ They're of no further use, Lew/ So let me abos go loose.*

However, others claim to have suffered even greater embarrassments and indignities as Harris set about grooming the entire British nation to view him as the pinnacle of Australian musical talent and artistic achievement.

"You've got to remember, this was the era of Bob Dylan, the Stones and the Beatles," lamented one victim of repeat embarrassment. "Artists and rock musicians were radically transforming an entire generation, with cool, hip songs about the sexual revolution, civil rights and drugs. Yet turn on *Top of the Pops* in the mid-'60s and the major contribution you heard from

2014 — The Year of Living Decisively

Australia was Rolf Harris prancing around with a third appendage strapped to his waist singing 'I'm Jake the Peg diddle-um diddle-um with his extra leg diddle-um diddle-um' or warbling on about 'Two Little Boys with Two Little Toys'. It was awkward, to say the least."

Harris initially faced only three charges of embarrassing Aussie street cred throughout the '60s and '70s by indecently assaulting the hit parade. Then last year he was charged with another count of performing a tasteless act upon the Led Zeppelin opus 'Stairway to Heaven' in the early '90s. Footage recovered from YouTube clearly shows Harris dressed in a hideously kitsch jacket of white clouds on a sky blue background wearing an akubra hat and deliberately violating the credibility of one of rock's greatest all-time songs.

"That was the song I grew up to," said one distraught victim. "'Stairway to Heaven' meant the world to me. I knew every word and I even knew how to play the opening chords. Yet now I can hardly bring myself to listen to it without mental images of Rolf flooding back to haunt me. He stole my teenagehood. He sullied my love of *Led Zep IV* for all time."

A similar complainant alleges she never recovered from hearing Rolf Harris's late '90s re-recording of the Alanis Morissette classic feminist anthem 'Hand In Pocket', and recalls with horror the manner in which Harris manipulated the lyrics to include this hideously embarrassing line: I've got one hand in my pocket / and the other one is fingering my didgeridoo'.* "I was struck dumb. I just couldn't speak about it. To anyone," she recalls.

Harris was originally questioned under caution last year by the good taste taskforce working on Operation Gumtree, an investigation into the abuse of Aussie artistic credibility abroad. A string of victims are believed to have contacted the taskforce regarding Harris's so-called invention of the wobble-board. "Talk about embarrassing! Of all the great musical achievements we Australians should have been able to boast about on the international stage, the only thing anybody overseas ever mentions is Rolf Harris and his bloody wobble-board. It's not even a musical Instrument!" said one classically-trained muso, struggling to control his rage even after all these years.

Further charges relate to "offences against language, tasteful humour, and all-round coolness" which are believed to have been generated by several complaints against Harris's longtime habit of engaging in quickie, one-handed self-portraits (described by witnesses as 'Rolfaroos') and teasing his viewers by splashing large dollops of paint on a gigantic canvas and excitedly yelling "Can you tell what it is yet?"

For many, the painful memories of seeing Rolf perform his one-man show, which included lamentable clichés at the expense of Aussies as well as irritating ditties played on the didgeridoo and Stylophone, have never gone away.

"It was the era of Brett Whitely, Sidney Nolan and Arthur Boyd, yet the only Aussie painter ever mentioned on UK TV was Rolf Harris. Worse, his artistic catchphrase was beyond embarrassing to struggling Aussie paint manufacturers: 'Trust British Paints? Sure can!'"

Mr. Harris has denied all charges.

*original lyrics R. Harris

❖

Tony Abbott resists calls for his government to bail out a host of failing or struggling businesses. As the government successfully stops the boats, the ABC claim a group of asylum seekers were forced to hold onto burning hot pipes. Meanwhile, the NSW government decides to shut down late night boozing in the centre of Sydney.

Australia Day

Financial Review
25/1/14

Australia Day means something different to everyone in this culturally rich, diverse nation of ours. This year, we urge you to Celebrate Your Way! But what does that actually mean? Here's a handy guide to those festivities you might otherwise have missed.

Professor T's Australia Day Ice Sculpture Exhibition: a real treat, these exquisite ice sculptures were hand-crafted by the Professor's talented climate change crew whilst stranded in the Antarctic ice. Highlights include amazing life-like ice-busts of Al Gore and Tim Flannery; an impressive gigantic hockey-stick ice-graph; and the heart-breaking ice-sculpture of a polar bear devastated by climate change floating out to sea on a melting ice cap.

Enterprise Bargain Breakfast Bonanza: Join Qantas trolley-dollies, SPC tin-packers, Holden hubcab-welders and a host of greedy union officials as you stuff your face on our EBA 'all-you-can-eat' Oz Day smorgasbord. You'll feel sick as a dog afterwards when your firm goes bankrupt, but don't worry, you can always ask the taxpayer for more!

Christmas Island Boat Float: Unfortunately, this highly popular event has been cancelled this year due to a lack of any boat arrivals in the last five weeks.

Al-Kidsi Weekend: We Aussies have always fought for what we believe in so this weekend why not give the kids a chance to find out for themselves what self-sacrifice really feels like? Join fun-loving Sheik Abu Aussie (aka Yusuf Mustafard-Gas) and celebrate the Australian way of life by sending your offspring to experience first-hand a martyr's death in the Syrian Civil War. Tickets available from Lakemba Kiddies Bookshop include complimentary pre-packed backpack and one-way ticket to Aleppo.

Way Beyond Satire

Barry's Booze-free Binge-Up: Avoid the normal colourful crowds of steroid-fuelled murderous thugs who traditionally roam our world-famous city and come and visit the empty clubs and bars of Kings Cross, Darlinghurst and the Rocks instead. Watch tumbleweeds roll down George Street as everyone who fancies a festive drink or two heads anywhere other than the Sydney CBD.

ABC Workshop: In this imaginative re-enactment of traditional asylum seeking practices, devotees burn the palms of their hands on hot pipes and then send us the photos. Not for the faint-hearted.

Clairvoyants' Picnic: What better way to celebrate Australia Day than by seeing what the future holds? Join renowned mystic and psychic Billy Shortsighted as he wows the crowds with his extraordinary three-year predictions for the future. You'll be amazed! Learn how Tony Abbott will be a 'oncer', how the carbon tax is here to stay, and how Labor will win the next election. (*organisers take no responsibility for accuracy of predictions)

Ultimo Open House: Enjoy a warm, fuzzy inner glow at our special Groupthink-A-Thon this weekend and celebrate our disdain for the disgusting, repellent Australian way of life. Indulge yourself in a festive bout of self-loathing and victimhood, then take to Twitter and express our views all by yourself.

❖

The Abbott government announces a Royal Commission into the union movement. But who will run it?

Royal Commissioners Union

Financial Review
1/2/14

The Australian Royal Commissioners Union, one of the most powerful unions within the Australian royal commissions industry, today announced its support for a royal commission into the union movement.

2014 — The Year of Living Decisively

"Whilst we believe there are no grounds whatsoever for a royal commission into these isolated instances of trade union corruption, we nonetheless insist that if such a royal commission be commissioned then it be in compliance with the Australian Royal Commissioners Union's Enterprise Bargaining Agreement of 2013," said former royal commissions shop steward Fred Standover.

"As stipulated in our EBA, the final choice of Royal Commissioners selected to sit on the royal commission will be made by the Delegate Committee, led by, er, me."

They will include:

Craigie 'Play Misty for Me' Hardon, former boss of the HSU (Hookers and Strippers Union): An outstanding royal commissioner with first-hand experience in unsavoury work ethics and problems of memory loss within the sex industry and excessive book-keeping practices within the DVD hotel rentals market. Craigie is a fearless exponent of the rights of the individual to pursue a full and satisfactory work-leisure lifestyle balance via frequent visits to the Red Turbo Spa Room. (Note: in accordance with EBA sub-section 14, Craigie will require a Royal Commissioners Credit Card for the duration of the commission.)

Bill Michaelson, former union and Labor party boss (ret'd): An outstanding royal commissioner with extensive and valuable family contacts and an intimate knowledge of the environmentally-friendly use of eco-brown paper bags for funds dispersals within the printing industry. In line with royal commission EBA entitlements (append xiv), Bill will be available to attend all royal commission hearings at full pay plus penalty rates so long as they are held in the vicinity of Long Bay during normal visiting hours.

Julia Slayter-Gordonia, former paralegal adviser to the Australian Backyard Diggers Union (WA branch): An outstanding royal commissioner who brings to the Party intimate knowledge of reciprocal plumbing, fencing and backyard landscaping arrangements within the complex first-home buyers' home renovations industry. Julia has a keen eye for a tasteless brick wall and isn't afraid to call out a slush fund whenever she sets one up.

Bill Bonecrusher, former construction industry union heavyweight and Wild Riders Bike Club financial adviser/treasurer (ret'd): An outstanding royal commissioner with extensive experience in promoting productivity within the tattoo parlour industry and an expert in distribution and marketing within the home-based methamphetamine industry. Bill's ability to multi-task has seen his services frequently required in ongoing industrial disputes regarding the resolution of complex debt-restructuring plans throughout the Gold Coast region.

Bill Bangaroo, contract supplies agent specialising in sub-contracting arrangements within major infrastructure development projects requiring the allocating of union-approved subcontracts in accordance with incentive arrangements and other financial requirements that in no way reflect poorly on the parent construction company because as is standard practice in this industry, our, er, I mean their subcontractors may have questionable commercial arrangements with other entities with whom we, er, I mean they have nothing to do with whatsoever.

❖

Despite riding high in the polls before Christmas, Bill Shorten suddenly finds he is not so popular after all. Meanwhile, it's all downhill at the Winter Olympics in the Russian resort town of Sochi.

Bill Shochi

Financial Review
15/2/14

Jubilant opposition leader Bill Shochi last week picked up Silver in the Winter Olympics for the fastest ever downhill run by a Labor leader.

2014 — The Year of Living Decisively

Wiping tears from his eyes, an ecstatic Shochi declared a personal best of minus 9 points in a hair-raising four week slide from the top of the polls to the bottom.

"When I was riding high just before Christmas, everybody said I had peaked too soon," exclaimed the victorious Victorian. "And they were right!"

Shochi, known to his loyal fans and fellow team-mates as 'Shortpipe', said the spectacular finish made for one of the most pressure-packed competitions of his career.

"This one was really difficult. Perhaps like one of the hardest contests to lose that I have done in a while. After all, the government were on the nose and I had a clear run; all I really had to do was sit still and do nothing. But instead, I decided I'd beat them at their own game, and drop even faster in the polls than Abbott had done."

Shortpipe was referring to rival Speedo Skating Long Distance Champion Tony Abbott, and his legendary ability to skate along the bottom of the polls for months on end in minus five conditions but still sneak over the finishing line and win government.

"Obviously, I couldn't compete with that kind of performance," said a weary but delighted Shortpipe. "But I was determined to fall further and faster than any opposition leader in living memory. I knew I could easily improve on Brendan Nelson's impressive plummet, but I was convinced that if I really put my mind to it I could even beat Malcolm Turnbull's record-breaking fall in the 2009 Copenhagen games."

Shortpipe was referring to Malcolm Turnbull's dizzying fall from grace following his failed synchronised climate change performance with tandem loser Kevin 'ETS' Rudd.

Shortpipe began seriously competing in downhill poll racing back in September of last year, with an impressive loss at the Labor leadership trials where he was comprehensively trounced by long-term left-footer Anthony Alpine-ese.

Way Beyond Satire

"I really deserved to lose that one," exclaimed an exhausted yet ecstatic Shortpipe, "but obviously we were playing under the new Kevin Rudd rules so even though Alpo won by a country mile, the judges were still forced to pronounce me the winner."

Seasoned Olympians were quick to praise Shortpipe's losing strategy over the following summer, which saw his net satisfaction figures collapse by a staggering 17 points.

"I completely fumbled the whole carbon tax repeal thing. I should have done a one-eighty like everyone warned me but instead I chose to hang onto it. Now it's like a dead weight around my neck and I'm not sure I'll ever be able to shake it off. Then came all those ugly union moguls, but instead of sidestepping them I fell headfirst into a deep hole and I don't think I'll ever be able to dig my way out of it."

Observers were quick to point to Shortpipe's stiff bindings as being a key factor in his rapid slide. "In particular, you've got his bindings to the AWU; they're way too tight. When things start heating up there's a real danger he'll find himself in slushfundy conditions. He could come completely unstuck," said retired sports commentator Ralph Bagman.

Others blamed heel pressure. "The pressure he's under from those heels in the AMWU is immense."

Former team-mates criticised Shortpipe's notorious lack of team loyalty. "The trouble with Bill is his shifty front — one moment he's your best friend, the next he's spiking you in the back with a sharpened poll," complained veteran Women's Downhill Racing Champion Julia Skater-Gordon.

But there was plenty more excitement to come.

"Things got really sketchy when my fellow team-mate and freestyler 'Goofy' Howzat blindsided me with his Grand Compacted Snow routine. I had no idea it was coming, and no idea which way to turn," admitted a bewildered Shortpipe. "Finally there came all these calls for a royal commission into union thuggery and corruption. That's the moment I knew I was done for."

In what was another edge-of-the-seat performance from Shortpipe, the veteran loser crashed on his first run at opposing a royal commission and then laid down a ridiculous second effort with a late spin; something about leaving it all to the police to sort out. The punters weren't convinced.

"Conditions were below zero, which is exactly where my popularity has ended up," said the breathless opposition leader after his stunning turn-around performance.

"But I feel great. I feel like I won, even though — obviously — I lost again," he told reporters.

❖

Bill Shorten unveils his plans to revitalise his party.

Grand Designs

Financial Review
24/4/14

In this week's episode of *Grand Designs,* we take a close look at one of the most ambitious and optimistic renovation plans I've seen in a long time. Bill here wants to thoroughly modernise this derelict old artifice he quaintly calls his Labor Party, and replace it with an entirely different structure altogether — a modern New Labor Party.

But what a task he's set himself! The place is an absolute tip. Rotten floorboards, crumbling foundations. They've tried to paint over much of the recent damage but you can still see all this blood splattered on the walls from the previous occupants; a couple of dysfunctional psychopaths who lived together here under this very roof for six years despite stabbing each other in the back at any opportunity.

Way Beyond Satire

Bill's got a real job on his hands if he thinks he can patch this lot up in time, and on budget. He's given himself just over two years, which personally I think is ambitious.

I'm nervous about Bill's idea for widening the base of the structure. There's been a great deal of shrinkage, particularly among the members, and Bill hopes to change all that by allowing anyone to wander in "at the click of a button".

It all sounds very grand, but I'm not really convinced that Bill realises just how shaky his foundations are and just how deep the rot goes. Take a look at all these industrial wings, building unions, delegates and the like. I don't think Bill entirely appreciates that that's what's propping this entire façade up. Start pulling them out — and who knows? — the whole thing might simply collapse in one big heap of rubble.

Even as recently as last week, in the western wing over there, they were at it hammer and tongs. The builder who got the job done called the lesbian who didn't "a bloke with a sex change" and the lesbian called the builder a "right wing sexist thug". These sorts of petty disagreements can ruin the best laid plans, particularly when you're trying to give the place a facelift.

The trouble with Bill's blueprint is that nowhere does it show him getting rid of all the junk that clutters the place up, like the deadly pink batts in the rafters. Bill's even squibbed on the most crucial decisions: by hanging onto the carbon and mining taxes, he undermines his whole design. And he doesn't even attempt to replace the broken light at the top of the stairs, er, hill.

Bill assures me that what he's doing is just the first chapter of the platform, although it looks like a pretty wobbly platform to me. He's taken the highly unusual step of throwing open all the doors and inviting people from all walks of life to wander in and set up home. Frankly, I can't see that idea working before he completes a total clean-out and gets rid of all the current hangers-on. Not only has Bill gone and upset all the construction workers, who like to think they run the show, but more importantly there's nothing here that's even remotely attractive to, say, your average small business person or aspirational family. Worse than that, I can't help noticing a rather unpleasant stench lingering about the place that reminds me of an old bordello in Surry Hills, or a jail house on the central coast.

Then there's the costings. Bill assures me he's set up a slush fund especially to pay for all the renovations, although he's very coy about how much he's got and where it comes from. Funnily enough, I've noticed that whenever he needs some extra cash he simply strolls out into the back garden with a shovel and a hessian sack and comes back loaded.

Power is going to be a major problem in a re-build of this kind. Hanging onto it, at least. Bill seems to think that he can happily ignore all the branch-stackers and factional warlords, whom he seems to have forgotten actually own the joint, but I'm not so sure it will be all that easy. Between you and me, a few of these shop floor stewards and construction workers have made it perfectly clear they'll fight tooth and nail to keep things exactly as they are. Things could get pretty rough for poor old Bill.

The big question will be the pre-selections in the upper part of the house. Frankly, if nothing changes there then all the rest of Bill's ambitious plans will go out the top floor window. Along with Bill, too, I imagine.

Next week, we'll be back looking at an exciting north shore development, where handsome, young Manly surfers Tony and Mike will be working out how to rid their attractive new home of an unsightly and dangerous infestation in the lobby area. Can Mike get a decent price for his gold-plated poles and wires? Will the new neighbour, an overbearing mining magnate with extremely poor taste and a penchant for garden dinosaurs, ruin all their renovation plans? And did someone really just leave that expensive bottle of Grange lying in the cellar amongst all the rusty water pipes?

❖

As the 2014 Budget looms, the government hints at a special new tax levy.

Daftness Tax

Financial Review
3/5/14

In a shock move that stunned many of his cabinet colleagues, the Prime Minister today announced that in order to help reduce Labor's deficit a 'Daftness Tax' will be levied upon the daftest ideas coming out of Canberra.

"We always said everybody has to share the burden, and the beauty of a Daftness Tax is that it applies equally across the board," explained the PM. "Liberal, Labor, left or right, rich or poor, even Barnaby and that fat bloke in Queensland. Everybody who's ever had a daft idea pays equally."

When pressed for details, the Prime Minister admitted that his scheme meant that the dafter the idea was the higher the levy. "For example, the base level will be 1% of the cost of implementing the idea, rising by another percentage point for every category of daftness that the idea fits into. There may indeed be multiple levels of daftness in the one idea that will dramatically raise the size of the levy."

"Take my Paid Parental Leave scheme," he explained to a packed newsroom. "It was a daft idea to begin with, from an entitlements perspective, in that it's going to cost the taxpayer around $5 billion. So automatically it will incur the Daftness Tax under 'Section 1 (Middle Class Welfare)'. But it's even dafter than that because it also hits our most productive businesses with a higher tax rate than their competitors, which you'd have to admit fulfils the whacko criteria fair and square, so it will be liable for an additional 1% under 'Section 2 (Business Stuff)'. Add onto that the fact that it's also political lunacy, allowing the likes of Doug Cameron to run around banging on about millionaire's wives and so on, and you can see that it also falls into the 'Section 3 (Politically Daft)' category as well, which means it gets hit with another percentage point. That's 3% all up, out of just the one idea, which works out to around $150 million per annum, which will certainly help bring the deficit down. You can't say I'm not doing my bit."

The Treasurer was quick to offer his support for the idea. "Originally, I was skeptical, but when you look at the phenomenal revenue that a Daftness Tax is capable of raising, particularly amongst the current crop of parliamentarians, it's too good an opportunity to miss. I'm very confident that my colleagues across the entire spectrum are capable of offering up a plethora of daft ideas, all of which will fall into at least one or two categories."

When asked to elaborate on how he himself would be contributing to the Daftness Tax, the Treasurer pointed to his own recent pronouncements on ending the age of entitlements as a classic example of an idea that would fall under the new tax. "Imagine telling the electorate that I intended to stop giving them whatever money they wanted whenever they wanted it. You've got to admit, that was pretty daft."

Commentators were quick to point out that the Daftness Tax needn't just apply to economic activity. Speaking on strict condition of anonymity, the Commissioner for Human Rights and Gay Stuff Mr. Woodrow Wilson pointed to the recent contribution to the freedom of expression debate from his boss, the Attorney-General. "Just when we had this whole 18C thing in the bag, signed, sealed and delivered, up jumps bloody George and starts wanging on about how even bigots have the right to be, er, bigots. Ideas don't come any dafter than that. Now we're back to square one, so I don't see anything wrong with him being hit with the levy. Serves him right."

Economics experts are adamant that a Daftness Tax will not only be a boon to the budget, but should result in a sharp reduction in the number of daft parliamentarian ideas in future years.

Meanwhile, opposition leader Bill Shoringuphisleadership was at a loss for words. "I don't have any ideas, even daft ones, so I guess I'm pretty safe." Others within his party, however, disagreed. "The carbon tax was a daft idea from Day One. It's done sweet FA about stopping climate change and it's destroyed thousands of jobs, so that's 2% right away. On top of which, refusing to repeal it is plain daft. This could be a real cash cow for the government."

Speaking from his home on the Gold Coast, the World's Daftest Treasurer took off his headphones and pressed 'pause' before explaining that he was incensed by the actions of the new government. "How dare they suggest they thought of this idea first?" he told a room packed full of Bruce Springsteen posters. "I invented the mining tax and it didn't raise a brass razoo. Taxes don't come any dafter than that."

❖

Labor leader Bill Shorten and his colleagues pour scorn on the idea of a "budget emergency".

Crisis? What crisis?

Financial Review
10/5/14

Mount Vesuvius, September 13th, 79AD, 7pm: Speaking this evening to a large audience from his home in the quiet streets of Herculaneum, Praetor Bill Minimus 1st was quick to reassure the assembled crowds that repeated rumblings and earth tremors coming from the Pompeii district to the north were nothing to be concerned about. "This is a confected emergency. We are not buying this idea of some great crisis. Emperor Abbottitium has manufactured the entire thing. Now go back home and get some sleep."

London, September 2nd, 1666, 1am: Bakery shop-owner Billy Shortbread today reassured his nervous neighbours that "there is no crisis". Speaking from the burned out remnants of his bread oven, Mr. Shortbread was adamant that the flames engulfing the neighbouring homes and alleyways were of no major significance.

2014 — The Year of Living Decisively

"This is a false crisis," he explained to sweating reporters. "A fake emergency confected by rival bakeries such as that owned by Messrs Abbott and Hockey. More toast anyone?"

San Francisco, April 18th, 1906, 5.12am: Residents living in the vicinity of the San Andreas Fault were reliably informed by former community treasurer, Mr. Christopher Bowtie, that "there is no emergency". Mr. Bowtie denied reports that the entire Bay area was under risk of imminent collapse because it had been shoddily constructed over the past six years on faulty economics and loose fiscal planning designed by his former colleagues on the back of a beer coaster. "There is no looming crisis," he explained. "Both myself and my honourable predecessor Mr. Swansong left this place in tip top sh-sh-sha-a-aa-aaappp-e," he yelled as he lunged for the nearest lampost.

North Atlantic Ocean, 370 miles SSW of Newfoundland, April 15th, 1912: Speaking to a mob of angry and frightened people who happened to be sliding all over the upper deck of his luxury cruise liner, Captain's Mate Tony Iceburke has reassured passengers that "this is an entirely manufactured emergency".

"The truth is they wanted to confect an iceberg crisis because Mr. Abbott and Mr. Hockey want to cut your wages and hit you with new taxes and fuel excises," he told members of the Musical, Entertainment and Deckchair Re-arrangers Union: "This is a fake emergency. If it were a real emergency, then why on earth would Tony Abblobb-blob be blub-blubb and Joe Hobb-lobb-lobb..." (Transcript lost under bubbling sounds.)

From the Facebook page of Princess Tanya Pliberserb, July 28th, 1914: "Like, dudes, crisis? What crisis? They've made the whole thing up, guys! Like it's a fake. I mean, there is no emergency, or why would Abbott and... Hey, peeps, anybody else hear that? Sounded like a car backfiring."

Barcelona, January 30th, 1918: Addressing a packed newsroom today, renowned world epidemiologist and influenza expert Dr. Guillamo Shortsneeze, who has recently returned from a successful tour of duty on the western front, blew his nose before reassuring agitated onlookers and concerned citizens that "there is no emergency".

"We don't buy this confected idea of Señor Abbott's that the Spanish flu is some kind of dire pandemic emergency," he reassured his relieved followers. "What's a tickle in the back of the throat between friends? A few little germs never hurt... ah-ah-ahtchoo! ... anybody."

Lakehurst, New Jersey, May 6th, 1937: Speaking on the deck of his new airship, a buoyant Field Marshal Tony von Hindenburke reassured a group of nervous passengers that "das is nicht eine emergency!" Stroking his handlebar moustache, the General declared: "Mein entire financial airship vos designed on ze back of eine telegram by Herr Commandant Rudder-von-Gillardstein himself und filled mit pink batts. Vot could possibly go wrong?"

Tacoma Narrows strait, November 7th, 1940: Remarkable black and white footage has been recovered from the depths of the Tacoma straits showing proud local construction engineer Bill Shortspan offering a lift to anyone who wanted to travel across his brand new bridge. "We built this bridge to the highest standards, it's got a triple A rating, and the ratio of debt to wind speeds is among the lowest in the world. Every single rivet and nut and bolt was carefully planned down to the nth degree on the back of this envelope here. To say there's an emergency is a complete fabrication on the part of Mr. Abbott and his coalition of bridge-building alarmists. There is no emergency. Hop in. Oops! just lost my cap. Bloody windy today, isn't it?"

Canberra, May 9th, 2014: A fiery opposition leader Bill Shortsight today reminded his supporters "there is no budget emergency". Shaking his fist in the air, the leader of the opposition was unequivocal: "Crisis? What budget crisis? This is a fake budget emergency confected by Tony Abbott and Joe Hockey."

❖

2014 — The Year of Living Decisively

Tony Abbott makes the mistake of winking at his radio host during a talkback call from a sex worker.

Gloria's tips

Financial Review
24/5/14

Struggling to cope with life under Tony Abbott's budget and need to earn a little extra cash on the side? Why not take up talkback phone sex? Here's Glorious Gloria's secret tips on how to talk dirty on air and give even the most upstanding politician a call he'll never forget.

Talkback phone sex is just like role-playing; it's a titillating performance in which you have to choose your words carefully and remember — timing is everything! The main thing to remember is that instead of happening face to face (like a genuine exchange of ideas!) you are actually stimulating another person's responses via a telephone line connected to a talkback radio station; so I recommend using these five steps so you and your politician can feel like you really are rubbing each other up the wrong way while chatting live on air. Just be careful not to run up the phone bills!

Choose your identity: One of the best ways to start a talkback phone sex conversation is by choosing a tantalising fantasy identity; perhaps as a nurse or a teacher or a hospital worker. Give yourself a sultry name like Velma or Gloria. Imagine a whole backstory about your fantasy character, particularly how hard up you are. Remember, the politician can't see you so your fantasy self can be as "bogan" or as feral as you like. Speak in a husky voice, as if you smoke thirty a day! Make sure you have your finger on the button ready to dial as soon as the shock jock says "give us a call". Don't be fooled if a woman answers, she is just the producer. Say to her (as sweetly as you can): "I'd like to talk to the Prime Minister, please. I'm an ordinary Australian, and I'm a (fill this bit in yourself!) who is worried about the budget." Immediately she will put you on hold and before you know it you'll be having your very own talkback phone sex conversation.

Let the words come naturally: Now you are both on the phone together, say whatever comes to mind. It helps to have a few handy phrases jotted down, to get an instant reaction. (You can download these from your favourite union website, ALP brochure or Greens Twitter feed!) You want to build up slowly, toying with your politician as you slowly get him hot and bothered. You should never rehearse what you have to say because it will come across as scripted (which it is, of course!). But be careful or he might sense you have no idea what you're talking about! Remember, the only person you want to embarrass is on the other end of the line! Start off shyly to get him in the mood with, for example: "I'm an unemployed asbestos worker with five kids, two with learning allergies, two in prison, and one who takes after his Dad and wants to be a surfboard waxer in Ballina on the disability pension and it's tough trying to bring them up coz last week Mum was diagnosed with chronic dyslexia."

Use your imagination to the fullest: Think of what will really fire him up. The more personal the better! Talkback phone sex examples can be: "I've been lying here all day thinking about what you'll do to my benefits" or "tell me exactly what you want me to do to release my built up pension?" Or you can be very bold and say: "ooooh... I'll bet your cuts are really hard." By now his mind will be racing and he'll start breathing heavily.

Feed off what each other has to say: When you say one thing, pause teasingly so your politician exposes himself and then he will say or do something because he can't help himself! Once this happens, you need to be quick to turn the phone conversation into a proper newsworthy story full of smutty soundbites and innuendo.

Climaxing: At the point where you are both getting highly agitated, change your voice a little to make your politician squirm. Slightly whisper your questions and responses to him and, when the time is right, moan about the cost of living. By now, the shock jock should have at least one raised eyebrow. He, too, will be very aroused but he will completely deny it afterwards. Of course, let's not forget that the real purpose is to get the politician to have a really good wink; one he'll never forget! When this happens, tell him you are gagging for a Gonski and ask him if he's "leaking" votes. By the time the conversation ends, you will have lots to think about, and you won't be able to wait to see yourself splashed all over the evening news.

❖

Joining the ever expanding list of Labor literary talents, the former "World's Greatest Treasurer" releases his own book. And I start my own Agony Aunt column, Dear Rowena.

Nonplussed of Nundah

Financial Review
31/5/14

Dear Rowena,
I recently bought a house on the Gold Coast and when I was clearing out under the floorboards I was astonished to discover boxes and boxes crammed full of chunky, brick-like objects made of paper that were a complete mystery to me. Why were they there? What was their purpose? At first I presumed they must be one of those ridiculous eco-friendly building materials from the past, or some bizarre form of damp-absorbent foundations. But upon closer inspection I discovered that they were in fact thousands of copies of what I believe was once called a "book" — this one was a fantasy novelette entitled: "The Good Fight: Six Years, Two Prime Ministers and Staring Down the Great Recession" by an author I wasn't familiar with called, from memory, Wayne Goose. Please forgive my ignorance, but could you enlighten me as to what these objects are and if they may possibly serve any useful purpose around the home? Or indeed, are they of any value?

Dear Nonplussed of Nundah,
Don't apologise. You would be astonished how often this question arises; literally thousands of copies of this particular "book" still exist. It is known in the trade (ironically, I am sad to report) as "The World's Greatest Literary Treasure", which was clearly meant

tongue-in-cheek for even the most pristine copies — which most of them are — have no commercial value whatsoever. Usually they are found tucked away down the back of a sofa or in the furthest recesses of a garage and often appear to have been partially un-wrapped in Christmas paper. However, in answer to your second question, I have compiled a list of possible uses:

Insulation: Unlike the highly flammable pink batts, which also date from around the same period, these items you possess can be put to good use in any attic environment as year-round insulation, particularly if you have large numbers of them (as you clearly do!). In fact, there are several well-known bookshops and libraries that insulated their entire premises with them.

Retro Decor: If you're feeling in a naughty-noughties kind of mood, why not spray-paint one of the "books" a shiny black colour, and then leave it lying on top of your retro Bravia (available for $3.99 from Harvey Norman). Now you can tell everyone you're the proud owner of an original government financed $300 set-top box from 2011. Your friends will be soooo jealous!

Conduct a Séance: One of the crazy cultural habits of the past was to communicate with the dead via the medium of Australia Post. Indeed, there are rumours that the author you refer to was in the habit of frequently sending large amounts of money to beyond the grave, in the form of $900 cheques made out to corpses. Why not check it out for yourself? Get a group to sit around a table and all lay hands on a copy of the "book". Maybe one of you could even read aloud from one of the chapters ("How Peter Costello Stared Down The Great Recession and I Tried To Claim Credit" is a good place to start) and before you know it you'll all be in a strangely trance-like supernatural state (known as deep sleep).

Warm your home: Now that the science is well and truly settled and 95 per cent of respectable scientists agree global cooling is a proven fact, we all need to do our bit to warm the planet up. Indeed, why not take a tip from the highly respected Professor Flannelshirt from the Frozen Planet Institute, who has pointed out that there might never be a dry or warm spell again, and at this year's Bonfire Hour warm the cockles of Gaia's heart by taking all your boxes of the "book" outside, building a pyre and releasing all that precious carbon dioxide stored within them, just for one hour.

Fill in unsightly trenches: Most homes of your vintage have a large and unsightly trench running down the middle of the nature strip, straight across the front lawn and through what used to be the geranium bush. These are from the days before G6 wi-fi when people used to think (you won't believe this!) that broadband needed to literally be connected to every single home by an "optic cable" (another worthless collector's item from the period). Why not use all those books you were lucky enough to find and fill up your trench? Your garden will thank you!

Trivial pursuits: If you really want to trick your friends, ask them if they know which federal Treasurer designed a tax that raised no money? When they give up, tell them it was the same one who wrote the "book" that nobody read.

❖

A billionaire from Queensland sits in parliament, attempting to throw his weight around.

Professor Palmoff's Miracle Diet

Financial Review
7/6/14

Welcome to Professor Palmoff's New Miracle Diet. You'll be astonished how much credibility you can lose — and how fast! Your friends (not that you actually have any!) will hardly recognise you.

Introduction: It sounds too good to be true, and it probably is, but Professor Palmoff's New Miracle Diet can help you achieve a significant credibility loss without actually cutting down on your daily intake of food.

How much can I eat? The great thing about the New Miracle Diet is that you can eat as much as you want, whenever you want, and wherever you feel like. Indeed, we recommend that you take any and every opportunity to help yourself to a lavish meal, even if you've just had one. For example, a typical evening might see you leaving a slap-up dinner when a good friend texts you and invites you to go and chew over some leadership entrails followed by a caramelised banana split. Go for it! You've nothing to lose but your — and his — credibility.

The product: Most diets make you weak and apathetic but not this one. You'll feel fired up and hungry for power. Craving ever more and more popularity? Don't worry, you can gorge yourself on as much publicity — good or bad! — as you can get your hands on.

How does it work? By harnessing the body's immune-to-reason system, the diet encourages organs such as the liver and the gallbladder to generate as much bile and venom as possible. The beauty of Professor Palmoff's New Miracle Diet is that it disrupts everybody else's normal, healthy day-to-day routines whilst cleansing out your own digestive system via an excessive amount of verbal excretion. (Don't be alarmed if you make a bit of a mess! That's just nature doing her job. Maybe keep a few towels handy for those quick mop ups.) This way, you can burn off friendships and rid yourself of any cumbersome responsibilities in next to no time at all. And all that excess credibility literally just falls away.

What's new about the process? Professor Palmoff's New Miracle Diet is based upon the Professor's own unique (and patented!) economic and scientific principles, whereby you inject 70 billion calories directly into your system every three months instead of once a year. Every time this turns over in your stomach it will generate an extra 10 per cent of gaseous activity. This in turn will be re-ingested and regurgitated by at least three different people during the course of one year, thereby generating at least 21 billion calories of extra credibility loss.

The ingredients: It is worth remembering that the chief ingredients in Professor Palmoff's New Miracle Diet are extracted from the ground, and contain large traces of extremely expensive Chinese minerals. However, at some point the provider of these minerals may start asking where all the fat (which translates in Chinese as "cash") has disappeared to? At this awkward stage of the process it will probably be necessary to withdraw yourself entirely from your mineral consumption in order to lose the maximum amount of potential legal culpability — as well as credibility — as possible.

Anything else? Other ingredients in Professor Palmoff's New Miracle Diet include lashings of horse manure, large dollops of revenge (best served cold), a generous sprinkling of humbug and hypocrisy, all fueled by a deep inner rage.

Any side effects? Don't be surprised if you find yourself getting a bit lightheaded and your mind starts wandering into strange and dark places and your thoughts drifting into fantasy and self-delusion. This is called "daydreaming" and it is your brain's attempt to pretend you might one day be Prime Minister of Australia, or at least be the most powerful person in the land. Don't worry, this feeling will rapidly pass, as both your blood sugar levels and your poll ratings plummet. We suggest whenever you are in a place where you become overwhelmed by such fanciful thoughts, have a good lie down and maybe a quick snooze.

Measure your waste: The quickest way to lose maximum credibility is by over-indulgence. Some people think they can simply do the job all by themselves, but we recommend urgently getting some extra staff at taxpayers' expense and make excessive demands upon everyone around you.

How long does it last? The beauty of Professor Palmoff's New Miracle Diet is how speedily you can be shorn of every last ounce of credibility. Within a year or so everybody will recognise the real you that lurks beneath all that bluff and bluster. This is the final part in your journey, when BOTH your career AND your credibility entirely dissolve away to nothing.

We call this the Double Dissolution stage.

Way Beyond Satire

❖

War envelops the Middle East — and the Attorney General says land in the West Bank is "disputed" rather than "occupied".

Disputed, not occupied

Financial Review
21/6/14

The Middle East was plunged into a new crisis yesterday as a wave of protest convulsed the entire region following explosive revelations that Australia's Attorney General George Brandis had used the word "disputed" rather than the term "occupied" in a Senate estimates committee when describing the slope at the back of the hill between Morty's Chocolate Babke Cafe and Hazir's Halal Butcher Shop.

Speaking from his luxury bunker deep beneath the Aleppo hills, an incensed Syrian President Bashir Al Assad could hardly contain his outrage: "This is an absolute crime against humanity. Mr Brandis stands guilty in the eyes of the whole world of deliberately attacking his own people by using illegal adjectives against them."

Meanwhile angry crowds of protesters gathered in Egypt's Tahir Square overnight in scenes not seen since the overthrow of the Morsi government last July to protest against the provocative Australian actions. Carrying a gigantic banner that read "Check the dictionary, George, they're two different words!" a group of angry students held an all night vigil. Said one irate protester: "Mr Brandis must stand down immediately and admit that the correct word is "occupy", otherwise we will be forced to, er, occupy this square."

In the Libyan city of Benghazi, a flash mob of fully armed Al Qaeda terrorists spontaneously appeared outside the Australian embassy and overran it. Described by former U.S. Secretary of State Hillary Clinton as "a group of everyday Libyan citizens who just happened to be passing by and expressing themselves as is their democratic right", the terror organisation have declared they intend to teach Australia the very real difference between the words "occupy" and "disputed" via a collection of graphic YouTube videos.

Speaking on the ABC's *Lateline* to promote her new book "Why I want to be President to shove it up Bill", a fiery Ms Clinton was adamant that this latest fracas had its roots in the deliberate misogynistic policies of the Abbott government. "My good friend Julia Gillard explained to me that this sort of outrageous behaviour shouldn't be tolerated and is typical of the sort of sexism she suffered on a daily basis, whereby the Attorney General George — note that it's not Georgina! — Brandis feels at liberty to distort the language in the vilest ways imaginable in order to describe how badly Ms Gillard did her job."

Speaking from Isfahan University's elite Peace Studies and Conflict Resolution Centre, renowned Iranian nuclear physicist and peace activist Professor Ahma Geddon declared the use of such unstable language was the single biggest threat to world peace. "We are deeply concerned that Mr Brandis appears to have stockpiled numerous editions of *Roget's Thesaurus* deep under Capital Hill."

In Denmark, cartoons of George Brandis depicting him as a calm and unflustered politician appearing on the ABC's *7.30* program covered in a thin veil of perspiration caused waves of revulsion among viewers sickened by the abuse he suffered as he was ritually humiliated and tortured by the show's extremist presenter Sharia Ferguson.

Meanwhile, in Nigeria, the search continues for a group of schoolgirls who were kidnapped at gunpoint and are being sold into slavery for daring to look up the difference between "occupied" and "disputed" on an online dictionary so they could work out for themselves which term they felt was more appropriate in the current political context.

In the disputed tribal lands between Pakistan and Afghanistan, Pashtun tribesmen were keen to explain the subtler nuances between the two terminologies. Speaking through a translator who was blindfolded and held at gunpoint at the time, Abu bin Goatherd proclaimed: "I occupy this land now and have done so since last week. If you try to dispute this fact, I will occupy your head with this machete."

However, it has been reported that the words "occupied" and "disputed" are seen in an altogether different light throughout the wealthy oil-producing Gulf states. Speaking to an *Al Jazeera* news anchor from the back seat of his stretch Hummer (with personal helipad) limousine, Prince Ibn Bin Drinkin declared (between mouthfuls of caviar and champagne-drizzled-oysters): "If I see a parking space outside a shopping mall that I want to park my limos in and it is already occupied by one of my wives, then God help us all there will be one almighty dispute. That's why I don't let women drive."

Meanwhile, forces loyal to The Islamic State of Iraq and the Levant (ISIL) continued to behead anyone who gets in their way as they capture large swathes of territory on their way to establishing a Sunni caliphate. Said a spokesperson: "George is absolutely right. There won't be any more disputes at all once we occupy the whole of Israel and Palestine and butcher the lot of them."

❖

The Ebola virus ravages Western Africa.

The Granola virus

Financial Review
2/8/14

World health authorities have been put on major alert following an uncontrolled outbreak across Australia of the deadly Granola virus, a strain of radical left wing thinking that leads to unstoppable bleeding of the hearts. The Granola virus, or *elitus sophisticatus* to give it its proper name, is highly contagious and has been known to strike people from all walks of life and of all age groups, damaging their right frontal lobes and rendering them incapable of logical thought processes. Instead, sufferers of the disease find themselves becoming increasingly touchy-feely as they wander around in a fog of sanctimonious humbug excreting vast quantities of pinkish or greenish waffle from every orifice. There is no known cure.

The Granola virus is believed to have originated amongst a motley tribe of ex-communists and eco-warriors in the crowded, noisy cafes of Marrickville and Surry Hills, where Granola, yoghurt and fair trade organic soy lattes (flown in from Africa) are still a particularly popular form of early morning sustenance. From there the disease spread like wildfire throughout the crowded flat shares, terraces and university campuses of Australia's major cities, often passing from person to person via the handling of unhygienic copies of the *Sydney Morning Herald* or *The Age,* or by deliberately sharing tidbits picked up from the ABC. Epidemiologists believe the virus then moved along the intricate web of inner city bike paths leading directly into the fertile grounds of the inner west suburbs.

Medical authorities have identified some of the telltale symptoms of the onset of irreversible infection by the Granola virus:

Hot and cold sweats: You become susceptible to and neurotic about extremes of cold and heat, and become convinced that normal variations in weather patterns are due entirely to your own behaviour. On unusually hot days, you will be convinced that this is evidence of global warming, yet on unusually cool days you will also feel convinced this is evidence of global warming.

Inexplicable rash: You break out in a sudden rash of indignation about the fate of economic refugees from safe, democratic, law-abiding countries such as India, and develop a persecution complex on their behalf; believing well-educated citizens from such countries should be immediately granted Australian residency so long as they come ashore on a leaky boat.
Also known as Sarah Ferguson-Young syndrome.

Extreme lethargy: You find yourself completely incapable of getting up and looking for one job, let alone forty every month, and develop a deep-seated fear of the principle of work for the dole.

Delusional thoughts: You develop a severe and irrational hatred of Jews, which you try to hide by calling them "Israelis", convinced they are responsible for all the ills in the world. This bizarre condition, also known as *carltonitis,* sees you re-hashing anti-semitic cartoons and caricatures from the thirties and dressing them up as "progressive thinking". In this state, you start to believe that Hamas are a peace-loving group of guitar-strumming hippies with flowers in their hair whilst Israelis are the goose-stepping re-incarnation of the Third Reich.

Uncontrollable weeping: You find yourself extremely sensitive to any images whatsoever of Palestinian children, or parents, or schools, or hospitals, or teddy bears or anything else where Israelis may have injured or killed Muslims, yet you find yourself completely unmoved by the wholesale slaughter, beheadings, crucifixions, kidnappings, female genital mutilation and all the other butchery in Syria, Libya, Iraq, Somalia, Iran, Nigeria, Egypt and everywhere else on the planet where Muslims are busy slaughtering Muslims and Christians in record numbers.

Blurry vision: You develop severe *gonskiitis* in the left eye and become increasingly convinced that throwing as much money as possible at any and every school instead of firing all the crap teachers is the answer to our children's declining educational standards.

Severe bouts of nausea and vomiting: This occurs every time you open a copy of *The Australian* or accidentally switch on Channel Ten and catch *The Bolt Report.*

Dry wretching: You develop an antipathetic reaction to the following words; Abbott, Cory, Barnaby.

Fever: You become feverishly excited at the thought of Malcolm Turnbull leading the party. Any party.

Shorten-ess of breath (or shallow thinking): You convince yourself that Bill Shorten is capable of being Prime Minister.

Phantom pregnancy: Despite thinking Tony Abbott is the vilest misogynist on the planet you are extremely excited by the prospects of his Paid Parental Leave scheme (aka Doctor's Wives Syndrome).

If you are fearful that you may have come into contact with the Granola virus via any form of one-on-one discussion with anyone under 25, you should immediately seek refuge in the nearest leafy suburbs, preferably on the north shore.

❖

As part of his brilliant strategy to sell the proposed changes to Section 18C of the Racial Discrimination Act, the Attorney General points out in the Senate that bigots have rights too.

George Brandis

Financial Review
9/8/14

Having managed so spectacularly to sell the promised changes to 18C with his brilliant argument that "bigots have rights too", cabinet colleagues are urging George Brandis to put his unsurpassed communications skills to better use in another job.

But which job?

George Brandis, Orthopeadic surgeon: "Don't relax, because this will hurt quite a bit. In fact, it will hurt a lot more than just a bit. In fact this will be so bloody painful it'll feel like I've doused your nerve ends with capsicum spray. Ready?"

George Brandis, Minister for Immigration and Border Protection: "Well the whole point of Operation Sovereign Borders is to stop the boats because they're full of towelheads, obviously. Besides which, Nauru is such a shithole that with any luck they'll write home to their relos and tell them Timbuktu is paradise compared to offshore detention in Oz."

George Brandis, Pizza delivery guy: "It fell off the back of the bike and landed face down on the pavement in some dog-shit or whatever but I've smeared it all back on top and covered it with mozzarella and you'd never know it wasn't pepperoni."

George Brandis, Minister for Social Welfare: "Of course the unemployed have rights. They have the right to get off their fat arses, waddle over to the Bravia, switch it off for five minutes, and instead of driving down to McDonalds to get a $2 fat-laden deep fried breakfast for the whole family maybe actually take a walk down the street and buy some fruit and a newspaper? And while they're at, maybe, just maybe, they could stay off the grog long enough to actually open up that newspaper, turn to the back section — no, not the sports or the TAB, I mean the other back section — stub out their ciggie and take a long hard look in the classifieds under that rather large heading that says, in a neat, crisp, clean sans serif bold font I believe, the word 'Jobs'."

Brandis, Brandis and Brandis, divorce solicitors: "Listen you slut, you'll be lucky if we can get you a red bloody cent."

Brandis Blocked Drains, plumbers: "It's blocked with a repulsive mixture of your excrement, your dead hair and other cellular matter, wads of revolting tissues and probably some disgusting old tampon. Shall I have a look?"

George Brandis, Minister for Health: "Look, either we make you pay a miserable $7 or next time your Gran goes into hospital with a swollen ankle we'll just pull the plug and let her croak."

CEO J. Walter Brandis Worldwide Advertising: "Well of course we'd like your business so we can pay our staff but as for your brand and your product, well quite frankly there's no point trying to engage with the consumer because they're absolute rubbish."

George Brandis, Minister for Industrial Relations: "If anyone's going to have squillions of dollars of developer's money sloshing around in slush funds then we'd rather it was us than them."

Georgina Brandis, news anchor: "Nothing of any interest happened today. But there's a good movie on the other channel."

George Brandis, Minister for the Environment: "Look, we all know climate change is total crap but we want to keep Malcolm off our backs so we're going along with this whole Direct Action thing, whatever that means."

George Brandis, Treasurer: "Look, we all know this Paid Parental Leave scheme is total crap but I've got to keep Tony and Peta off my back so... whatever."

Brandis and Sons, butchers: "It's basically just dead animals, with chilli sauces and stuff on top."

L.J. Brandis, estate agents: "Well, obviously it's ludicrously over-priced but if you chop down a bunch of trees in the reserve — preferably after dark when no-one's looking — you might actually get a glimpse of the harbour. Then you can flog it for a fortune to the Chinese."

Giorgios Seafoods: "Of course they're fresh, but the mercury levels are off the Richter scale. God knows what toxic gunk they've been swimming in down there."

George Brandis, metadata analysist: "Apparently they've been looking at a bunch of kiddy porno sites and then building their own suicide vest out of garden fertiliser and, er, no, hang on, that's just the K-mart Spring Catalogue."

Archbishop Brandis: "What God?"

Brandis flakes, breakfast cereal: "They taste like cardboard and they make you crap."

Chez Georges: "Mais oui madame, I can assure you zat you will 'ave ze rudest waiters in town and ze smallest, most over-priced meals."

Dr. G. Brandis, Obstetrician: "What an ugly baby!"

Prime Minister George Brandis: "There will be no Section 18C under a government I lead."

Dr. George Brandis, proctologist: (er, unfortunately we've run out of space — editor)

❖

Meanwhile, the leader of the opposition is accused of bad behaviour in the past.

All over and done wiv

This article has not been published before.

The federal Labor leader has revealed that police have cleared him of an allegation that dates back nearly 61 weeks.

The leader of the Opposition and Canberra police both say the investigation has been finalised and no criminal charges will be laid.

The investigation reportedly relates to an allegation of serious asexual assault upon an anonymous red-headed woman.

The opposition leader said the allegations were made against him in a best-selling fantasy novel called *Moi Story* that is about to be released.

"Late last year I learned that a claim had been made about me, going back to when I was 46. It was made to a large, sobbing crowd of hysterical women in the Sydney Opera House. I will not go into details, except to say that the allegation was untrue and abhorrent. The allegation was made by someone I knew briefly at that time when she was Prime Minister of Australia."

The opposition leader said he had been thoroughly and vigorously investigated and had fully cooperated to clear his name.

2014 — The Year of Living Decisively

"The easy option would be to say nothing, but that is a word I have enormous difficulty pronouncing, as it keeps coming out as 'nuffink'. I have similar problems wiv the word wiv," he told a packed newsroom.

He went on to say the allegations had been deeply distressing and he was thankful for the love and support of his cabinet colleagues and his close friends (not to be in any way confused with each other).

"I have no intention of making any further comment," he said. "Wiv this announcement it is all over and done wiv."

The allegations first surfaced in a mysterious online posting on the Facebook page of former Prime Minister Kevin Rudd, which read:

> Dearest Kevin,
>
> I have known the opposition leader since we both hung out together in the '80s at a hip, cool joint called 'Slushfunds'. In 2010, after I had been unanimously elected Leader of the ALP by Paul Howes and Mark Arbib, I went to a Young Labor undergraduates camp somewhere under a hill in Canberra (which was laughably called a "cabinet meeting"). Imagine my surprise to see *he* was there.
>
> I tried my best to have as little to do with him as possible, but about 6pm one evening there was a knock at my door. He had been hiding in his office all week and I presumed I had his full support — but it was not to be! He pushed me into the corridor, up against a Sky News camera crew, pulled up my jacket and stabbed me repeatedly in the back. Without my permission! I don't expect you to read this and you probably get crazy messages all the time, but I remember that the ALP did this to you too.
>
> Yours, J.

The woman, who was believed to be drunk on power at the time, cannot be identified until her book is released in a major publicity tour in six weeks' time.

"How am I feeling?" she said yesterday. "Angry, really angry. I think that everybody who reads *Moi Story* (available soon from all good bookshops and the Opera House forecourt) will know who's telling the truth."

A Labor spokesman confirmed the allegation had been thoroughly investigated and the advice from the ALP thought police was that there was "no reasonable prospect of election".

"Nobody actually saw him do it," said the only cabinet colleague who agreed to speak up for him, "except the entire nation. So it's just her word against his."

Meanwhile, the Chinese government this week reacted angrily to an outburst by a populist maverick Australian politician on *Q&A*, in which the leader of the PUP party described the Chinese as "mongrels" and "bastards" who "shoot their own people".

"This is absolutely outrageous and a despicable slur against our government, our people, and our peaceful way of life," said a high-ranking spokesperson, Gang Ov Foh, from the Department of Peaceful Co-existence and World Domination. "This clown is clearly delusional. If he made those sorts of disgraceful and defamatory comments here in China he'd soon find himself up against a wall with a bunch of Falun Gongs and a blindfold round his head."

❖

As the leader of the opposition faces and denies certain accusations, his colleagues from the Gillard years are forced to explain the motivation behind 2013's so-called "blackest day in sport" doping scandal, whilst the Treasurer continues to defend his brilliant selling-the-budget strategy.

Auto Da-fé

Financial Review
23/8/14

A senior political figure held an explosive news conference this week in which he denied that an event that never occurred had ever occurred.

"The reason I am here today is to tell you that a line has been drawn under the event that never occurred, and therefore we can all agree that even though it never occurred it is now time to move on and put an end to any further gossip about an event that never took place in the first place," he told a crowded newsroom, before refusing to answer questions unless they didn't refer to the event that he had just announced.

"I refuse to be drawn on comments or speculation about events that never actually occurred, and which cannot have occurred because no action is going to be taken to determine whether or not they did occur, which they didn't. I am manning-up because that's the type of man I am and admitting that it's time to draw a line under this whole incident which never occurred," he said.

A senior colleague of the senior minister went on radio to offer his unequivocal support. "I believe every word he says," said the senior colleague. "It could never have happened because it never happened. What more proof do you need?"

Meanwhile, in the small coastal town of Salem, the Australian Salem Auto Da-fé Association (ASADA) and its close affiliate the Witches And Demons Authority (WADA) have put to death a number of witches who were found to be witches by the self-appointed Authority. "This was the blackest day in Salem," declared former Auto Da-fé Chief Inquisitor Jason de Torquemada. "Julia was on the ropes and being accused of being a witch who needed to be ditched because of the magic spells she had cast to make a huge pile of money disappear into a slush fund. The Salem government was in urgent need of a major distraction so Goody Lundy and I eagerly grabbed onto this one."

Asked to show what proof he had to back up his claims that the entire town was crawling with broom cheats and potion-takers, ASADA's chief executive Ben McDevil was unequivocal. "It was all very fair. We threw them one by one into a deep pond of adverse publicity. If they weren't witches their careers sank without a trace, but if they put up their hand and agreed to take a suspension we knew they were guilty and immediately burned them at the stake."

In other news this week, the Treasurer Joe Hockeysticks announced that it was time to re-boot his budget metaphors.

"Since I announced last week that poor people can't afford cars, the entire engine for selling my budget has been stuck in first gear," announced the Treasurer. "My car metaphor has been a huge success, allowing journalists to point out that my sales pitch has completely stalled."

When asked to explain which metaphors had already got through parliament, Mr Hockeysticks nominated the fire engine coming to the rescue as one of his successes. "The beauty of that particular metaphor is that it allows me to point out that it was Labor who burned the house down with all their outrageous entitlements and spending measures and that I am the bloke who's coming to pour more petrol on the, er, hang on, no that's not right, is it?"

Offered a cup of coffee, Mr. Hockeysticks was keen to point out the similarity between his budget measures and a cappuccino. "What you've got is the revenue side, which are the beans that go into the grinder. But not everybody has beans. So we add milk, which is the entitlements side, but then you have to add inflation, and it turns into froth. So the PPL, well, that's just the chocolate on top."

Senator Mathias Cormann was unavailable for comment, as he had a prior commitment on *Lateline* selling the budget.

❖

At yet another former Labor politician's book launch, former Prime Minister Paul Keating resorts to belittling his predecessor by referring to the size of his manhood.

Todgers in the Lodge

Financial Review
30/8/14

Australians were amazed and enlightened last week by Paul Keating's continuing sharp and powerful analysis of modern politics, seen through the unique prism of his frank and eagle-eyed assessment of prime ministerial manhood. The Keating Analytical Method, as it is known, was formulated during poolside cabinet meetings with his former boss, Labor's most popular post-war Prime Minister Bob Hawke, usually naked at the time.

However, we can now reveal that far from being an isolated incident, this unique method of assessing the acumen and skills of our most upstanding political figures will form the basis of Mr Keating's upcoming political treatise, *Todgers in the Lodge.*

Some sneak previews have been obtained by this column:

"They called him 'Little Johnny', so I always took that as a fairly accurate indication of the size of Howard's John Thomas, but imagine my complete surprise when I was invited to Kirri-willy House as I called it one day for cocktails on the lawn and there he was starkers in the backyard. Now, say what you will about Howard, and I never agreed with a bloody thing he said or did for the whole eleven years he ruled the roost, but let's be frank, this guy had staying power. Four elections in a row. Can't say fairer than that."

"First time I met Whitlam, way back before anybody knew who he was, he stuck out this great big hand at me and said 'Gough!' and for a moment I thought he wanted to squeeze my balls and check me for a hernia! Anyway, he invited me to share a sauna with him once and let me tell you there wasn't much room left on the bench next to him. But Gough knew a thing or two about todgers too. I once asked him what his biggest problem in the Senate was and he said Reg withers. I never found out who Reg was, but the Canberra winters can do that to a man."

"At least Abbott has the decency to keep his Speedos on when he goes for a dip, which is more than you can say about bloody Bob. But if you ask me any bloke that spends most of his spare time rushing around the bush with a great big hose in his hands is trying to make up for deficiencies in some other department."

"I never met the other Bob, Sir Robert that is — in his birthday suit or otherwise — but let's face it, any bloke whose nickname is Ming, with or without an 'e', can't be fully packed out in the downstairs parking lot. And all those pointy white pickets lined up in perfect rows would have given Freud something to mull over, I reckon."

"The thing about Big Mal is that you never could tell which way he hung. To the right or the left? One moment he's a Tory, the next a greenie. He was also one of these guys who wasn't shy about where he took off his trousers."

"Now you've gotta hand it to Julia; for a sheila she certainly had a decent set of cojones on her. That's what you need in politics, a bit of the mongrel, particularly when it comes to knifing a limp Prime Minister for the good of the country like she and I both had to."

"When I first heard the expression Kevin '07 I thought somebody was taking the mickey. Rudd the Dud is what the boys in Sussex street always called him, and for pretty good reason too, I suspect. We always used to say that even after a visit to Scores he'd be lucky to make Kevin '04."

"And speaking of banana benders, that fat bloke from Queensland hasn't got a hope in hell of ever making it to the Lodge, with or without a double dissolution. I mean, I doubt he can even see his old fella, so what hope have the rest of us? And as for that Tasmanian shrew, if she really is looking for a well-hung bloke, let me tell you, joining a party called Pup ain't a promising start."

The Keating Analytical Method is also particularly handy when it comes to assessing complex events surrounding some of the lesser known occupants of the Lodge; among them Sir 'Willy' McMahon, Black 'Jockstrap' McEwen and the mysterious disappearance of Harold Holt.

"It was freezing cold that morning off Portsea, even though it was Christmas. My guess is the bloody idiot had gone skinny-dipping to impress all the floozies on the beach. By the time he'd caught a few waves he looked down and was too embarrassed to come back out of the water."

The former prime minister saves his most revealing analysis for a humble and modest assessment of his own physical prowess, to which he devotes the final six chapters of his highly-anticipated tome:

"Of course you didn't need to be Einstein to figure out pretty early on that I was the bloke who actually won the landslide against Malcolm Fraser in '83, I was the bloke who opened up the economy, I was the bloke who beat the pilots, and I was the bloke who won the America's Cup. I reckon I was the biggest prick of them all."

❖

A Tasmanian Greens Senator decides the real problem in the world today is people who insist on using the word "terrorist".

Abu Psycopath

Financial Review
6/9/14

Moonlight filtered in through the bay window, casting a soft glow.

Senator Whisky-Washy stroked his stubble and wiped his lips as he cracked open another bottle of his award-winning chardonnay, then put his feet up in front of the dying embers of the log fire to contemplate the deeper issues of the day. After all, what point was there in being a powerful Greens senator if you couldn't affect real change in this troubled world of ours?

"I should have a go at solving this Middle East bizzo," he said to no-one in particular, for his missus had long since toddled off to bed.

He gazed long and hard at the label on the bottle, seeking within its sensitive curves and graphic understatement the inspiration that previous great minds of the eons, from Archimedes to Rousseau, had found lurking there. Yet all that came back at him was the one word: Chardonnay. A word that in itself held so many meanings — some good, some bad. A single word, the Senator mused, that once simply defined a varietal of grape, but now conjured up so much more. "Chardonnay socialists", he muttered to himself. "That's one connotation." Or "chardonnay lovers", that would be another. Even the abbreviated "chardy drinker" meant something else entirely. Three different uses of the word that described vastly different demographics and mindsets. Why, even the great winemakers of Chablis had been forced to put the tautological descriptor 'Chardonnay' onto their wines these days, whilst others sought refuge in words like 'viognier' and 'pinot gris'. "Surely, surely…" With a whoosh Senator Whish quickly poured himself a top up, sensing a big idea approaching.

And then it hit him. Eureka! Of course! The so-called "vexed" problems of the Middle East were no different to the subtle and intricate complexities of his own area of expertise, the wine market, where success or failure often came down to the choice of one simple word. The Senator slammed his fist excitedly down on his knee, accidentally spilling wine all over his Pale Green pyjamas, a gift from his constituents. But he didn't care! He was on fire! (Not literally, he thought, hastily checking that his slippers weren't too near the grate.)

"That's it! One word…" he shouted. "Terrorist!"

Grabbing a pen, Senator Whish-List quickly jotted down his thoughts, knowing that such moments of inspiration — like the last drops of a vintage Grange — were too precious to waste. "If we call people 'terrorists', we're attaching a label to them. But people aren't bottles of wine, after all. They're individuals, deserving respect and tolerance, no matter how deprived their social background or cultural circumstances, none of which is their fault. Indeed, what is clear is that by using labels such as 'terrorist' we rekindle inner feelings of racial humiliation and colonial domination."

The Senator excitedly refilled his glass. He was on a roll now!

"A person labelled 'terrorist' will be unlikely to recover from such a social stigma and will feel they've got to live up to that label, otherwise their sense of self-esteem may be permanently damaged, which explains the violent urges and extreme actions undertaken by these under-privileged individuals who need our sympathy not our condemnation… so to affect real, lasting change throughout the Middle East we need… we need to… we need to… change the labels!"

The Senator slumped back in his chair, exhausted. This was not just A Big Idea. This was The Big Idea.

"By thoughtlessly describing those folk who are fighting for what they perceive to be righteous religious beliefs as 'terrorists', we are merely reinforcing their sense of alienation. Obviously, anything that causes 'terror' can be defined as 'terrorism'. To the Iraqis, the Americans are terrorists. To the peace-loving suicide bombers of Palestine, obviously the Jews, er, I mean, the Israelis are terrorists! Which begs the question — what or who is actually a terrorist? And the answer? Nobody. Nobody is a terrorist unless we make them one by demonising them with insensitive labels that diminish their sense of self-worth." Senator Whish-Fulthinking smiled to himself, and raised a glass to toast his inspirational idea: "Abolish one word, and we bring peace to the world."

Twelve thousand miles away, sunlight streamed in through the narrow window, casting a harsh glare on the scene.

Abu Psycopath stroked his beard and wiped the blood off his knife as he cracked open another round of high-grade ammunition, then put his feet up in front of the dying man on the floor to contemplate the deeper issues of the day. After all, what point was there in being a powerful soldier of Allah if you couldn't affect real change in this troubled world of ours?

❖

The opposition leader rallies the faithful at a South Australian union meeting, warning of the mortal danger posed by the Japanese and their submarines, which once threatened Sydney Harbour. A former prime minister is questioned about her boyfriend and his slush fund activities at the Royal Commission into Trade Union Governance and Corruption, whilst in South Africa, a famous athlete is found not guilty of murdering his girlfriend, but gets sentenced for 'culpable homicide'.

Cannibals and cripples

Financial Review
13/9/14

The world was shocked this week to learn of a ragged group of soldiers who have been living on a remote island to the south of Papua New Guinea, unaware that World War II ended 69 years ago.

Led by Captain "Wee Willy" Shorten, the group were discovered living in a fantasy world of their own creation, gabbling incoherently that a Japanese submarine invasion of the mainland is imminent.

The group were discovered when they came staggering out into the open, starved of relevance and desperate for any original ideas, having been forced to eke out their existence on a diet of pure humbug and hard Greens for the last six years.

Initial reports suggest that the group had taken to barbaric acts of savagery, frequently cannibalising their own. Two severely composed reputations were discovered rotting close by, identified only by the initials K and J, and both cadavers bore the hallmarks of a killing frenzy and multiple stab wounds to the back.

All of the survivors spoke of their desperate mission to find their way "to the light on the hill", believed to possibly be a reference to a long-since abandoned semaphore distress signal, or possibly a clever decoy designed to lure gullible voters into a deadly trap. Medical experts concluded the group had been living in a state of denial for exactly twelve months, at which point they had been severely traumatised by being blasted into political oblivion.

"Wee Willy", whose diminutive stature and deformed speech patterns are indicative of extreme political malnutrition, appeared desperate to galvanise the support of a local group of South Australian trade unionists, repeatedly shouting warnings about "slanty-eyed nips" and "yellow bastards" who were coming to steal their submarine-building jobs.

Experts noted that the individuals all suffered from a bizarre form of group-think, which renders them incapable of comprehending the complexities of the modern world. Observers note they all appear to be locked into a peculiar mindset that is firmly rooted in the distant past, from a time when they were all successful undergraduate socialists at second-rate universities or wealthy union officials at now-bankrupt businesses.

One of the motley group, a loud-mouthed woman who sees herself as the natural leader and goes by the name of Tanya, was clearly in a state of immense confusion about which war she was fighting, convinced that the modern, democratic state of Israel are a bunch of war criminals. Another of the group, who identified himself only as Tony Burqa, had completely lost his mind and kept clambering up onto any podium that would have him and yelling out that the "good guys" were the suicide-bombers of Palestine.

Self-appointed "Treasurer" of the group, Chris Bowenarrow, displayed a perplexing attitude to money, which he seems convinced grows on trees. Concepts such as thrift, productivity, social responsibility and enterprise are entirely alien to the group's closeted way of thinking, in which it is assumed everything is for free and nobody ever has to pay anything back.

Anthropologists are keen to study the group in greater detail, in order to try and determine the mystery of whatever happened to the core values of the Labor party.

In other news this week, there were howls of disbelief when a judge ruled, after months of fraught testimony and courtroom dramas, that there was insufficient evidence to find Julia Priministorius guilty of making a killing out of her boyfriend's slush fund.

Julia, whose nickname is the "Blade Thruster", was the golden girl of the June 2010 Olympic sprint down the corridors of power and into the Prime Minister's chair. Her marathon effort, which made her an instant hero to millions of able-bodied left-wingers, left her reputation permanently crippled.

For hour after hour, she had sat motionless in the dock, repeatedly bursting into lengthy bouts of obfuscation such as "I can't remember", "that's not true" and her popular catch-cry "I did nothing wrong".

Much of the forensic evidence in the case came down to whether voters believed her claims that she woke up in the middle of the night and heard a noise in the bathroom. "Immediately I presumed it was a local tiler called Bill the Greek or Con the Crook or whatever — I can't handle these woggy names — and I knew he was working overtime to get extra penalty rates," she claimed in her tearful testimony. "I immediately felt that my life was in danger because he had come to try and get his hands on my money."

"I reacted instinctively and didn't even bother to check whether Bruce was in the bed next to me or not. At that time of night he was normally out in the back garden with Little Ralphie burying all our spare cash in a brown paper bag."

The leader of the Greens explains the best way to combat terrorism is by us all "coming together" and rejoicing in our "multiculturalism".

Christine's academy

Financial Review
20/9/14

Here at Christine Milne's Academy of Elegance, Diplomacy and Etiquette, we pride ourselves on teaching young ladies (and young men — it's a modern world, after all, and there's no room for sexism!) how best to engage with the challenging and culturally diverse practices often found in Islamic (and other religious denominations, too — we don't want to stereotype now, do we!) youth organisations (we prefer not to employ the derogatory term 'terrorist', as Mr. Whish-Uponastar explains in his lectures!) and to do so in the most diplomatic fashion, in order to promote peace and harmony amongst the rich, diverse peoples that make up our vibrant multicultural world.

Beheadings: The best way to prevent a beheading is to understand the frustrations and grievances felt by the person holding the knife. Often these Aggrieved Individuals have been so traumatised by our insensitive and intolerant Judeo-Christian way of life that they feel the need to cover their faces in a balaclava. Yet we are all just people under our various disguises! Reach out and find some common ground. Ask them how their day has been so far. Or whether they find the desert air a little dry for their skin at this time of year.

When chatting to an Aggrieved Individual, maintain eye contact, keep your back straight and your feet firmly planted on the ground with your ankles close together (some cultures are more sensitive to aspects of female physicality and body stance). Speak in a clear voice, and enunciate with precision (particularly culturally appropriate words such as "jihad" and "Koran", which may cause some offense if said in a light-hearted or "jokey" fashion). Above all, make sure you don't sound patronising with your request and you'll soon have him eating out of the palm of your hand! (Although he may chop it off first.)

Posting material online: Often such Aggrieved Individuals feel the need to film their activities and post them on YouTube. Could there be a more classic attention-seeking device or desperate cry for help? (Don't confuse the Aggrieved Individual's desperate cry for help with the gurgling sounds emanating from the man in an orange tee-shirt who is kneeling on the ground.) Calmly avert your eyes (particularly if things get a bit sticky while the jugular is being sliced) and point out to the Aggrieved Individual the dangers of allowing potentially embarrassing personal material to make its way onto social media, where heaven-knows-who might view it! Quietly point out the dangers of adolescent high-jinx filmed in the excitement of the moment turning up years later when you least expect it. At a job interview, for example! Explain that we all need to express ourselves but that there is little logical point in seeking instant celebrity when your face is covered up in a ski-mask and they'll soon see sense and turn the camera off.

Kidnapping schoolgirls: Should you find yourself in the delicate situation where a large man with a machine gun barges into your classroom and expresses his desire to take you and your girlfriends on a lengthy excursion to a jungle camp followed by a slave market, try to avoid any knee-jerk reactions. We girls can get a little emotional and teary at times, but this is not the moment to be fussing and drawing attention to yourself. Calmly pack up your iPad and books, making sure they fit neatly into your satchel. If you urgently need to go to the bathroom — don't. At stressful times like this self-control and personal dignity are paramount.

When you get to what is called the "base-camp", you will probably find many aggrieved men who express their frustrations with the anglo-centric view of the world through certain physical practices of dubious social worth. Try not to scream too loudly because this only encourages more of them to do the same all over again.

2014 — The Year of Living Decisively

When you reach the slave market, do not take the price attached to you as a genuine measure of your worth as an individual human being. Some girls will be priced higher than you, and others lower! Try to avoid feelings of inadequacy, or indeed superiority — we are all worth the same in our own unique ways.

Random public executions: Sydney is a big noisy city full of different people planning culturally exciting events. If a young man sidles up to you with a video camera in one hand and a machete-shaped canvas bag in the other and asks you which way to Martin Place, give your directions in a simple but precise fashion. If he insists you accompany him, explain you are deeply sympathetic to his plight but have other plans. Be firm and say 'no' — as diplomatically as you can.

❖

As war rages in the Middle East, many Australians are confused about who is the enemy. Prime Minister Tony Abbott causes outrage by suggesting the Syrian situation is one of "baddies versus baddies".

Who's fighting who?

Financial Review
27/9/14

Confused about who's fighting who in the Middle East? Here's a definitive guide to our enemies, our enemies' enemies, our enemies' friends, and, er, our friends' friends (not that they actually have any).

ISIS: Group of medieval beheaders who plundered their name from an obscure Bob Dylan song, in which a gang of grave-robbers despoil "the pyramids all embedded in ice". (Disclaimer: nothing to do with Islam.)

ISIL: Not to be confused with a popular brand of nasal spray, this group of crucifiers and rapists have been marauding across the desert looking for a brand name that makes them sound even scarier than Al Qaeda. Thus far no luck. (Disclaimer: nothing to do with Islam.)

IS: Grisly bunch of murderers keen to establish an Islamic caliphate across the entire Middle East. (Presidential disclaimer: nothing whatsoever to do with Islam, nope, no way.)

Al Nusra Front: Formerly Al Qaeda in Iraq until aligned with sworn enemy the Syrian Free Army to defeat sworn enemy Bashar Al Assad and now aligned with sworn enemy Hezbollah to defeat sworn enemy the Islamic State.

Jabbah Al Hut: Extremely fat and incredibly villainous slug-like militant leader who believes in capturing foreign princesses and enslaving them on the end of a long chain for his own peculiar lustful pleasures. (Disclaimer: nothing to do with Islam at all, as it happens.)

Al Qanda: Fanatical group of left wing panelists who broke away from the less radical *Lateline* organisation early last week in order to form their own Ultimo caliphate; subsequently denounced for being "too extreme". The group comprises an army of hysterical female warriors who spent years training in secret undergraduate locations throughout Australian universities honing their skills in perpetual victimology. The group are convinced that "Western imperialism", "strategic amnesia" and "Israeli war crimes" are responsible for their dramatic slump in the ratings around about 10pm last Monday night. Also notorious for radicalising gullible young Aussies via YouTube clips encouraging them to "join the audience" or "follow us on Twitter, using the Al-Qanda hashtag at the bottom of your screen".

Al Kemba Bookshop and DVD centre: Revered place of cultural learning specialising in ancient manuscripts and popular classics such as *The Protocols of Zion*, *Why Adolph Was a Top Bloke* and *How Come All Women Are Shameless Hussies?*

Al-Di: Popular invasion by foreign mercenaries hell bent on driving out sworn enemies Coles and Woolies with cheap German imports.

2014 — The Year of Living Decisively

You can call me Al: Traditional form of jihadist greeting.

Anti-Baathists: Violently aggressive university undergraduates in desperate need of a wash hell bent on protesting about having to pay fees. (Disclaimer: nothing to do with studying.)

Iran: Large country full of sensible, intelligent, moderate political figures many of whom are convinced a ninth-century imam hidden in the bottom of a well will come back to life and lead believers to paradise. Also madly developing nuclear warheads. (Disclaimer: nuclear weapons to be used for peaceful purposes only, obviously.)

Al Marcos Baghdatis: Firebrand tennis player who almost won the 2006 Australian Open before he completely lost his head in the final set. (Disclaimer: nothing whatsoever to do with Islam.)

Saudi Arabia: Fanatical sect of extremely wealthy sheiks who seized control of their own oil wells beck in the 1970s and have been terrorising motorists at the petrol bowser ever since. (Disclaimer: Crude currently $USD/bbl 92.74, up 1.3%.)

Sharia Hansen-Young: Fanatical law all unto herself.

Hamas: Peace-loving band of flower-waving ex-hippies committed to strumming guitars and singing Kum-bay-allah whilst cultivating the gifts of their native Gazan soil by digging tunnels into Israel so they can murder all the Jews. (Disclaimer: maybe just a teensy weensy bit to do with Islam.)

Hezbollah: Murderous group of terrorist thugs (see also all-round good guys, keepers of the peace, party of Satan etc).

Egypt: As per Bob Dylan song, except pyramids all embedded in riots. (Disclaimer: best avoided if you're a Westerner, female, journalist, or worse — all three.)

Tony Burqa: Charismatic leader of the Al Carrist sect of Hippocrites who believe it is the sacred duty of all True Believers to aggressively oppose the building of bingo halls in East

Jerusalem as they are so obviously a major threat to world peace. (Disclaimer: nothing to do with Islam but everything to do with Labor's western suburbs vote.)

❖

A security move that would see Muslim women who cover their faces sit in a separate enclosed public gallery at Parliament House is reversed by the Speaker.

Tony Burqa

Financial Review
4/10/14

Prime Minister Tony Abbott was forced to intervene on Thursday night to demand a reversal of new rules that would see Tony Burqa forced to sit in a separate area of the parliamentary gallery.

Speaker Bronwyn Bishopsgate and Senate President Stephen Parrott had earlier announced "interim arrangements" whereby Tony Burqa would have to sit in an area reserved especially for noisy, rowdy out-of-control children. The special section of the chamber, which is usually crammed full of ill-disciplined, uncouth undergraduates and belligerent ex-student leaders, is commonly referred to as "the Labor front bench".

According to Human Rights Commissioner Tim Woodrow-Wilson, the idea that Tony Burqa should be segregated purely because of his outlandish and confronting political views was an affront to democracy. "Just because Tony Burqa refuses to cover his face in shame for having been a member of the Gillard team doesn't mean he shouldn't be allowed to sit in our parliament and watch a proper government in operation," he said. "Indeed, it may do him some good."

The furore was sparked earlier in the week when the Prime Minister was asked on radio to give his opinion of Tony Burqa. "Personally, I find Tony Burqa's views fairly confronting," he admitted, "but that doesn't mean he shouldn't be allowed to appear in public."

Deputy leader and Foreign Minister Julie Archbishop went on to comment: "People are free to wear whatever opprobrium they like," she said. "Some may be offended by Tony Burqa's unsubstantiated comments about Israelis trashing Palestinian water supplies, others may be deeply affronted by his view that it is "bravery" to engage in "politics in a different way" by "putting your life on the line or at risk", particularly if they are related to victims of Hamas suicide-bombers, but in Australia we don't have a choice about who Labor choose to dress up their front bench with, no matter how disturbing they appear."

But former Labor Speaker Anna Burqa (no relation) said the plan came "out of nowhere" and was devoid of any logic or rationale. "Why should people have to identify themselves as sympathetic to a repugnant mob like Hamas just because they hope to be part of our next government?"

However, thousands of women were quick to rally together to show solidarity for Tony Burqa, including fellow frontbencher Tanya Plibershiekh. "I've been wearing a veil ever since I first entered parliament," she said, defiantly. "If you force me to remove my cloak of respectability I could be fully exposed as an angry undergraduate extreme left wing activist who believed Israel is a "rogue state" with a "war criminal" for a leader. Why shouldn't I be able to conceal whatever parts of my past I feel like in order to hang on to my cushy job as shadow foreign affairs spokeswoman?"

❖

The Attorney General introduces a bill that creates a new definition of authorised covert intelligence operations called "special intelligence operations", or SIOs, with Section 35P making it an offence to disclose information about these SIOs. Meanwhile, an ABC interview with an Islamic "hate preacher" goes off the rails.

Pythonesque

Financial Review
11/10/14

SFX: Roly poly circus music.
Voice Over: And now for something COMPLETELY different...
(Camera pans up to reveal a man entering a smart office under a hill in Canberra. The sign on the door says "Attorney-General". The office is lined with thousands of brand new books.)
Michael Palin: Good morning! I'm the journalist from the *Financial Review* and I'm here for the interview. You must be Senator George Brandis?
John Cleese: Maybe I am, maybe I'm not.
Palin: Oh, er, I see. You don't know if you're George Brandis?
Cleese: Depends.
Palin: On what?
Cleese: On what you interview me about.
Palin: Oh, that's easy. The new national security legislation, section 35P...
Cleese: Aha! You mean the new legislation whereby I can lock up any silly old duffer I feel like simply by saying that what we are talking about is a Special Intelligence Operation and therefore you'll get ten years in the slammer if you report it? That legislation?
Palin: That's the one! (Licks his pencil and scribbles in his pad.) It's a bit harsh don't you think?
Cleese: What is?
Palin: The new legislation.
Cleese: What new legislation?
Palin: Section 35P.
Cleese: What's that?
Palin: Section 35P... you just told me it meant you could lock up any silly old duffer in the slammer for ten years...
Cleese: No I didn't.
Palin: Yes you did! I've got it right here, you just said: "Section 35P means I can lock up any silly old duffer I want simply by saying it's a Special Intelligence Operation..."
Cleese: Precisely.
Palin: Precisely what?

Cleese: Precisely my point. You won't say that I said anything whatsoever about locking anyone up or indeed that I said anything about any Secret Intelligence Operation at all.
Palin: Yes I will. I'm a journalist!
Cleese: No you won't.
Palin: Will!
Cleese: Won't.
Palin: But... but you just said it.
Cleese: Maybe I did, maybe I didn't. But if you repeat what I said you'll get ten years in the slammer, so it doesn't matter what I said because you won't dare report it, which is just the same as me not having said it in the first place. Ex-post facto: I never said it!
Palin: But that only applies if it's a Secret Intelligence Operation! You said so yourself!
Cleese: There you go again! Proving my point. *You* just said: "it's a Secret Intelligence Operation". I heard you plain as day. Well, that's a very serious offence; reporting on a Secret Intelligence Operation. Ten years, I'd say. Oh, and by the way, you can never report that we've locked you up, it being a Secret Intelligence Operation and all.
Palin (blustering): But just saying "it's a Secret Intelligence Operation" doesn't make it a Secret Intelligence Operation!
Cleese: Of course it does. It says so right here in the legislation. Section 35P...
Palin: You said section 35P doesn't exist!
Cleese: No I did not!
Palin: Yes you did!
Cleese: Did not.
Palin: Did.
(Awkward silence. Cleese gets up and starts nonchalantly dusting his groaning bookshelves with a feather duster and whistling to himself.)
Palin: Look, this is absurd! What could possibly be secret about you and me sitting round discussing a Secret Intelligence Operation that is neither secret, nor intelligent, nor indeed an operation?!
Cleese (whistling and dusting): Ten years is a long time without bending over for the soap, you know.
(Palin looks horrified.)

Eric Idle bursts into the scene dressed up as a lifesaver in Speedos.
Eric Idle: How do we end this farce?
(At that moment a giant foot comes crashing down and quashes Section 35P.)

Meanwhile, over at the ABC:
SFX: Roly-poly circus music.
Voice Over: And now for something COMPLETELY different...
(A man dressed as a woman is sitting in a TV studio.)
Terry Jones (in a high pitched voice and dodgy wig): Good evening, and welcome to *Lateline*. I'm Emma Over-reachy and I'm here to interview the head of Al Qaeda in Australia, Mr His-Butt Terror. Mr Butt Terror, did you decapitate that parrot?
(Camera pans over to Eric Idle dressed in a fake beard holding a decapitated parrot's head and a large knife covered in red and green feathers.)
Idle: Well, let me explain very clearly why I find your question disconcerting. Millions of parrots have lost their lives...
Over-reachy: I'm sorry. Just answer my question. Did you kill that parrot? Yes or no?
Butt Terror: Look, let's put this in context. For thousands of years John Howard and George Bush and Tony Abbott...
Graham Chapman (rushing in): Will this farce never end?
(Iranian jackboot comes crashing down and squashes the entire Middle East.)

❖

Bill Shorten's leadership runs into trouble when he backs Tony Abbott on national security measures, much to the horror of many in his party. Meanwhile, the West struggles to contain the Ebola outbreak, and the ANU divest themselves of stocks in certain energy companies.

Pliberbola virus

Financial Review
18/10/14

Authorities within the Australian Labor Party were scrambling this week to try and contain an outbreak of the deadly Pliberbola virus, with frantic calls for the exposed leadership of Bill Shorten to be immediately quarantined.

"We cannot believe the virus has breached all our defences, which have been carefully built up over the last year, all to no avail," exclaimed one frustrated health-of-the-party worker. "This latest epidemic has taken us all by surprise. We were completely unprepared."

Up until now, Labor authorities had believed they would be able to contain any outbreak of Pliberbola and keep it restricted to the inner-city slums of Newtown and Brunswick, but the rapid spread of the virus into the mainstream is causing widespread alarm and panic.

Pliberbola is believed to be the deadliest leadership virus known to mankind, primarily because it attacks its host from within its own ranks, leaving the victim fatally wounded and almost certain to suffer a massive hemorrhaging of support from all orifices (particularly those on the left side of the body).

The Pliberbola crisis was triggered when Bill Shorten recklessly wandered into the national security debate without adequate protection against the extreme danger of being infected by a deadly dose of bi-partisanship caused by getting too close to Tony Abbott.

"Pliberbola is the most virulent strain of undergraduate socialism the world has ever seen," said a spokesman for Bill Shorten who could not be identified because he was dressed from head to toe in a white suit and a mask. "Wiv what we are now seeing I fink I'm in real, er, I mean I fink vat Mr Shorten could be in real trouble here."

The virus is believed to have mutated in the '70s in the Democratic Republic of Marrickville in a freakish contact between batty undergraduates and hardcore Marxist union enforcers, or apes, which in turn infected the gibbering idealists of the Greens. How the virus crossed the species barrier to infect normal, sane, rational human beings is not known, although the first identifiable case has long been rumoured to be a large man with a booming voice known only as Gough, who was so severely infected he had to be put down by the CIA.

The Pliberbola virus, or an early strain of it, is also rumoured to have been behind the abrupt death of a popular Labor leader whose name has long since been forgotten but is known only by his case number (Oh-Seven). This mysterious psychopath bled to death although epidemiologists point out that this was largely due to a mercy killing inflicted upon him by a caring and helpful redhead nurse who repeatedly stabbed him in the back after it had become obvious he was mentally deranged and incapable of performing the most basic bodily leadership functions.

Unfortunately, the nurse herself soon started displaying worrying symptoms and it wasn't long before she became the third documented victim of the virus; slowly bleeding to death in front of a large and adoring crowd at the Sydney Opera House, before being canonised following the release of her tragic autobiography *Moi Fantasy* (soon to be a major film starring Saint Cate Blanchett as Mother Julia).

In other news this week, a siege in a brothel came to an end after five years when a mystery man known only as Craig came out with his hands in the air. "I've been held hostage by my credit card and phone records for years now, but I still maintain I'm completely innocent and I've done nothing wrong," he complained as police carted him off. "After all, everybody inside that bordello is in it up to their armpits. Kathy, Michael, the lot of 'em."

Meanwhile, the owners of Australia's largest energy companies have decided to ditch all their shares in the ANU. "We decided that taking students from this institution and giving them lucrative careers is no longer in the interests of those who share our values," said a spokesman. "Basically, we'll only be offering jobs to people who understand that you can't run a successful economy on windmills and solar panels."

❖

Gough Whitlam dies and a nation mourns. Meanwhile his childhood home faces demolition after the Heritage Council rejects a bid for it to be listed on the state's heritage register.

Preserving Gough

Financial Review
25/10/14

Former prime minister Gough Whitlam's childhood home in Kew, Melbourne, was saved from demolition on Thursday when the state intervened with a conservation order.

Labor authorities also scrambled to have a "no demolition" order placed on Mr Whitlam's most prized asset, his political legacy, following numerous attempts by right wing shock jocks and others to bring it crashing to the ground.

"Just because Whitlam's reputation has been neglected over the past few years is no need to do away with it altogether," said one concerned local resident. "You know, a good lick of paint and a bit of sprucing up and Gough's legacy could be as good as new!"

Fans of Mr Whitlam's iconic construction believe his legacy should be preserved intact despite having been dangerously undermined by two freak landslides in 1975 and '77. "Let's face it, it was nearly destroyed but we've hardly got anything else to remind us of our once-glorious past," said a concerned Labor supporter. "We even used to have a light on top of a hill, but that vanished years ago."

However, critics of the former PM were convinced that there was little worth preserving of his so-called masterpiece. "When it was constructed in the mid-'70s Gough's legacy was a real rush job," said one concerned local. "The whole thing was thrown together in less than three years, with no concern about its long-term structural viability. Money was no object back then, but even so they blew the lot in record time. Gough meant well, but he was surrounded by a bunch of fantasists and cowboys. First they tried to borrow $4 billion from some dodgy Pakistani loan shark and next thing you know they were booted off the site altogether. If you look closely the cracks are everywhere. It's a miracle the thing has stood this long."

Experts point to numerous botched attempts over the years to patch up the original flaws in the design of Gough's legacy. "You can see over here in the prized Medibank wing that they ran out of money pretty quickly. They tried to fix it up in the Fraser years but then Hawkie came along and it was back to square one. Mathias and Joe got badly burned when they tried to plug some of those gaping holes a couple of months back and now nobody dares to touch it, even though you can see all that money still pouring down the gurgler over there."

However, others praised attempts over the years to restore Gough's basic conceptual design. "One owner of the legacy, a dysfunctional little chap called Kevin, was determined to add his own stamp to the original. See these garish bright green fibre cables over here – they come right into the living room – that sort of detail cost us an absolute bloody fortune but none of it actually works. And his pink batts in the ceiling were a friggin' waste of money, of course. Bloody deadly too."

Another admirer, who took on the project with her hairdresser boyfriend, promised to enhance the legacy by installing multiple disability ramps, until it became apparent she had lied to everybody and didn't actually have any cash set aside to do so.

Many dispute how much of the original design was actually the work of Whitlam himself. "The foundations for most of what he built had already been carefully put in place by Mr Holt before he mysteriously disappeared," said one knowledgeable local.
"All Gough did was take the credit for it."

But the keepers of Gough's flame are more concerned about preserving its sentimental value rather than worrying about historical accuracy. "Basically, before Gough came along this place was an absolute dump. Now we can see there are free schools and free universities and free hospitals and wonderful art galleries and Blue Poles and a vibrant multicultural neighbourhood and loads of Thai restaurants and Greek delis and no soldiers in Vietnam and women can vote and Aborigines can live happily ever after in their own dreamlands and there's no White Australia policy and peace and harmony fill the land and…"

Others were less optimistic. "The whole shambolic construction is built on the flimsiest foundations and propped up by endless spin and re-writing of history. To be honest, we'd be best to bulldoze the lot and start again."

❖

Man Haron Monis takes eighteen people hostage in the Lindt café siege and makes them hold up an Islamic State flag. Two innocent people die. But it wasn't terrorism, we are assured.

Terrorist or nutjob?

Financial Review
20/12/14

In this day and age, it is increasingly difficult to ascertain whether you are a bona fide terrorist or simply an insane lunatic murderous deviant psychopath whack job. Such identity questions can be extremely vexing, often leading to inappropriate labelling that can result in permanent psychological scarring and even irreversible damage to self-esteem.

In order to help you avoid such insensitive cultural stereotyping, simply fill in the following Personal Psychoanalytical Profile Questionnaire to find out for once and for all whether you may indeed class yourself as a genuine terrorist or simply a Class A fruitloop. This will help when you are next applying for a

Way Beyond Satire

permanent visa, the dole, disability allowances, bail, a fire arms license, legal aid or perhaps even a UN aid program or two in accordance with your basic human and democratic rights. Remember — answer the questions as truthfully as you can.

You have recently converted to a particular strain of Islam when you find yourself in the middle of the desert surrounded by a pathetic group of bleeding and wounded soldiers who are screaming and begging for you to spare their lives. Do you feel an unstoppable urge to a) calmly tighten the hessian sacks over their heads to help muffle the noise? b) calmly remove the hessian sacks from their heads so you can get a better swing with your machete?

You have recently converted to a particular strain of Islam when you are walking down a busy New York street minding your own business and chance upon a group of off-duty policemen having their photo taken. Do you a) offer to take the shot for them and carefully line it up so as not to chop off their heads? b) pull out your axe and try and chop off their heads?

You have recently converted to a particular strain of Islam when you and your brother learn that there is a marathon planned for the following week. Do you a) run around the block to get fit? b) kill and maim as many people as you can with a bomb and when the police come for you run around the block until they shoot you?

You have recently converted to a particular strain of Islam when you find yourself and your young child holding up the decapitated head of a Syrian soldier. Do you feel an overwhelming compulsion to a) take a selfie? (Yes, you're a terrorist!) b) take a selfie and brag about it on Facebook? (Yes, you're also a nutjob!)

You have recently converted to a particular strain of Islam when you learn that the Melbourne police are looking for you to ask you some questions. Do you feel an irresistible urge to a) go and meet them at the police station and attempt to explain yourself? b) go and meet them at the police station and attempt to stab them to death?

2014 — The Year of Living Decisively

You are sympathetic to a particular strain of Islam when you are strolling down the street and chance upon your local hot chocolate shop. Do you feel an irrepressible urge to a) wander in and take everybody hostage? (Yep, terrorist.) b) organise a boycott of the insidious Zionist purveyor of hot chocolate to protest against the "apartheid" Israeli government? (Nope, just a sad nutjob.)

You happen to control a country that has a vast stockpile of chemical weapons when you learn that a group of villagers up in the mountains have refused to vote 99% in favour of your continuing democratic right to be their supreme ruler. Do you feel an instantaneous urge to a) declare the ballot invalid and start all over again? b) gas them all?

You happen to control a large country with a vast nuclear arsenal when you discover that your currency is down by nearly 60% in the last few months due to the collapse of world energy prices and US and European sanctions against you. Do you feel an irresistible desire to a) jack up interest rates overnight and then if that doesn't work prop up the currency by selling left over reserves on the foreign markets to help stabilise the situation? b) invade Ukraine?

You happen to control a country that is armed to the teeth with nuclear warheads and learn that a couple of unfunny comedians in Hollywood have made a film that would normally sink without a trace that takes the mickey out of you. Do you a) hack into the computers of one of the world's largest entertainment networks and thereby give the film unimaginable free worldwide publicity? b) organise a private screening for friends and family and then if anyone laughs at the wrong moment have them executed on the spot? c) nuke the planet?

2015 — The Year of Betrayal

The rumours began over the summer Christmas break. Or that's when I first heard them, at a swish lunch party. Rumours that some in the Liberal party were so unhappy with Tony Abbott that they were contemplating the unthinkable — to dump him à la Rudd-Gillard-Rudd.

Weirdly, much of the discontent appeared to focus on the Prime Minister's Chief-of-Staff, the striking but largely unknown Peta Credlin. Ms Credlin was said to be bossy, pushy, thick-skinned, too close to the Prime Minister, didn't suffer fools, too demanding etc. All of which struck me as exactly the qualities anyone in the private sector would kill for in a right hand man, or woman.

Joe Hockey was the other bone of contention. The job of Treasurer demands the ability to "sell" the ideas as much as make the numbers add up. Having been spoiled by Treasurers with the communications skills of Peter Costello and Paul Keating, it was assumed Hockey would easily slide back into that style after the hilarity and chaos of his predecessor Wayne Swan. (I used to joke at the time that whenever I was stuck for a political gag during the R-G-R years, all I had to do was say or write three words: World's Greatest Treasurer.)

Hockey struggled, but mainly because of the intractable Senate, who blocked nearly all the savings measures that were critical to returning the budget to surplus at any point in the future. But, unfortunately, the thing about incessant destabilisation is — as Kevin Rudd had shown — that it works. And Australians, instead of being traumatised by leadership turmoil, had found their new intoxicating drug. By the end of the year, Tony Abbott had been replaced by Malcolm Turnbull.

And Australia had its fix.

❖

2015 — The Year of Betrayal

Hard on the heels of the Lindt café siege, 2015 dawns and sees Islamist terrorists murder sixteen people and wound another 22 at Charlie Hebdo's Parisian offices and at a Jewish supermarket.

Abu Har-don

Financial Review
17/1/15

Abu Har-don adjusted himself under his robes and slammed his sweaty fist hard on the table. "Please! Can we just get on with the friggin' WIP. I haven't got all day," he snarled. He hated these boring Work-In-Progress meetings. A bloody waste of time. Besides, he wanted to get back to his room ASAP and reacquaint himself with his 9-year-old Yazidi slave girl who he thanked God was eagerly waiting to perform the Dance of the 72 Virgins just for the delight of him and his four jihadist mates. She was looking particularly pretty now that those chunks of hair he'd ripped out of her scalp in Raqqa were starting to grow back.

Mustafa Wankh stared up at Abu from the other end of the table. Mustafa was the cell's internet whizz kid, in charge of PowerPoint pressos, YouTube clips and the like. He was an irritating little oik with a high-pitched voice and a horrible accent which owed its nasal twang — apparently — to his upbringing in the western suburbs of some infidel city in Dawa Al Australi.

"Oi've assembled a whole bunch of cool Google stats for youse guys about the Charlie Hebdo Op," Mustafa said, unable to contain his excitement.

"Yeah, yeah, I know," snapped Abu impatiently. "Twitter and all that social media shite is all well and good but can somebody here give me a proper decent bloody debrief for once? You know. Stats. Results. Data. Something I can put in the annual report to show our shareholders? They're demanding quantifiable results now you know."

Abu's colleague Ali Grubb stared menacingly down at his notepad, shifting awkwardly in his seat so he could focus through his one good eye. "We killed seventeen non-believers in Paris. Four of them Jews," he said, blinking with pride.

"Four Jews." Abu nodded thoughtfully, jotting the numbers carefully down on his pad. "And what were the others?"

"Khartoumists," said Ali, adjusting his glass eye with his grubby fingers. "From, er, Khartoum I guess."

Mustafa frowned, then scratched his head through his black IS headscarf. "I think he means cartoonists, sir. We killed a whole bunch of Parisian cartoonists."

Abu stared at him blankly. "Why?"

Mustafa smiled awkwardly. "Well, you know, they, er, they insulted, ah... you know... they insulted, the, er... bloke upstairs..." He nervously pointed his index finger skywards, as he'd been taught to. "I mean, not Him, I mean, the other, er... the Profit dude..."

"It's 'Prophet'," said Abu, irritably. These Westernised teenagers were supposed to be useful idiots, he thought to himself, but in his experience they tended to be more 'idiot' than 'useful'. "And how many people did we terrorise, so I can put that in my report too?"

Ali Grubb blinked, the shrapnel in his one good eye still making it weep yellow pus. "A million people marched in the streets of Paris against..."

"Against Islamophobia! Excellent!" said Abu, rubbing his hands with glee. "That's more like it. Were they chanting 'death to the Jews', 'free Palestine' and 'death to these, er, Cartoonists'?"

Mustafa stared closely at his iPad. "No, sir, quite the opposite! They were marching *in favour* of the cartoonists and free speech and democracy and all that. Everybody's wearing badges saying 'Je Suis Charlie'. Even the Egyptian President Sisi now says true Islamic imams must fight against radical..." Mustafa felt a sharp kick under the table, and immediately snapped his mouth shut. Opposite, Ali was glowering at him furiously (as much as a jihadist can glower through one slightly gungy weeping glass eye).

"I, er... but at least we taught these dogs a lesson they won't forget," said Abu triumphantly. "I don't expect we'll be seeing any more of these blasphemous infidel cartoons..."

"Oh no, sir, quite the opposite!" said Mustafa, his fingers wiping excitedly across the screen of his iPad. "The latest edition of *Charlie Hebdo* has gone global — it's got the Profit on the cover and everything! It's incredible! Even Keyser Trad grabbed a copy! They reckon five million at the very... ouch!" Mustafa snapped his mouth shut, grimacing at the sharp pain in his shin. Across the table, Ali Grubb was staring at him, drawing his finger across his throat.

"Well, anyway, what about our Australian Op? The glorious martyr of Martin Place. Surely the infidels of Australi are now cringing in terror at the thought of our own noble holy warrior, Man, er, what's his name, blessed be he in Paradise..."

"Not quite, sir," said Mustafa. "They actually think he was a total whackjob. And it's got them all talking about 18C again. My Mum says... ow!"

Abu Har-don shifted awkwardly in his seat. Then he sighed. "We are winning this bloody thing, aren't we?" he said, glancing around the room. There was a deathly silence.

❖

Over the Christmas holiday period, rumours of plans to topple Tony Abbott swirl around the media.

Loda Waffle

Financial Review
24/1/15

More rumours of increased rumblings within the Coalition backbench reached fever pitch when an anonymous backbencher was overheard grumbling to another anonymous backbencher in the lounge at Canberra airport about "never getting to spend enough time with my family", sparking frenzied speculation of a possible leadership spill as early as whenever we've got a blank space in this newspaper to fill over the weekend.

Speaking exclusively to this column on strict condition of anonymity, seasoned Canberra insider and veteran political reporter Maken Itallup had this to say:

> "Mate, it's not like any one particular thing you can point your finger at, but you know ... like, it's out there. You can sniff it in the air. I'm not saying it's going to happen tomorrow, or the next day, or next year, or ever... but hey, there's a vibe. You can feel it. It's like one of them tsunamis building up miles and miles out under the ocean, mate — one minute you're just floating along on your lilo and then there's this weird rumbling sound that you can't ignore and the next moment it's like — wooosh! It hits you like a tornado, I mean, er, like a tidal wave or a, er, whatever... It's like... how much are you paying me for this again mate?"

The panic surrounding his teetering leadership is believed to have prompted a rattled Prime Minister to issue an urgent message to his entire backbench containing a coded plea for unity. The suspected 'unity' email, possibly written by the hand of the controversial and deeply unpopular Peta Kremlin herself, was issued late on Friday evening just as MPs were departing for their constituencies, prompting speculation about both its timing and content, and is believed to contain the words "Have a nice Australia Day weekend everybody. See you all next week". Veteran reporter and anonymous Canberra blogger Loda Waffle offered to exclusively decipher its meaning for this column:

> "Mate, I think it's pretty significant that the PMO sent one email out to everybody as a group, like, you know, rather than to each individual as a person in their own right. This could spell real danger for the PM over the long weekend, I mean, we're all individuals you know, I'm not sure how I'd feel if my boss couldn't even be bothered to hand-address each email, I mean, like it goes to that whole thing of not listening to your colleagues and thinking you're above them and, er... and then when he says 'see you all next week', that's pretty damning too, like, maybe he's worried some of them won't bother coming back because he's like... er, how much did you say you were paying me for this again mate?"

However, other commentators were quick to point to the false bravado and desperation of the opening salvo 'Have a nice Australia Day weekend'. Renowned social media commentator and feminist psychologist Ima Twitt spoke exclusively to this column: "Here we clearly see a man struggling to overcome his inability to express himself in a more female-friendly manner, a man who has huge problems appreciating the role I, er, I mean, we women play in the community, and a man whose leadership is clearly lacking any kind of caring, compassionate, sustainable, er, leadership."

As the Prime Ministership of Tony Abbott teeters on the brink and enters the final phase of a potentially irreversible spiralling death-roll this column also spoke exclusively to renowned political analyst Iva Storytosell to predict the likely outcome:

> "Like, mate, this is clearly the beginning of the beginning of the end, or indeed, possibly, the end of the beginning of the beginning, depending on where you stand on this whole issue. I mean, here we go again, and if what they're saying on Twitter is correct, and I mean, like I'm agnostic one way or the other on the value of social media but, hey, if you gaze long enough into any tea leaves you can see that er, ah... who are we talking about again mate?"

❖

Following the knighthood for Prince Philip, events move quickly in what is described as an "orchestrated ambush", and Tony Abbott is forced to call a spill motion to defend his leadership. He will survive, 61 for and 39 against, in what he calls his "near-death experience". Despite Turnbull failing to win the leadership (this time), many pundits worked themselves up into a frenzy about the possibility of a Prime Minister Malcolm Turnbull. With the spill scheduled for the following Monday morning, I speculated on what Q&A might be like that evening...

Q&A

Financial Review
7/2/15

"Good evening, welcome to a very special edition of *Q&A*. I'm Tony Jones, and joining me this evening to answer your questions is the Prime Minister, Malcolm Turnbull, who..."
Cue wild applause from audience, screams of delights, whoops and cheers.
"We'll get to Malcolm in a..."
More wild applause, stomping of feet, and loud wolf whistles.
"If I could just have... quiet please... if..."

A title comes up on the screen: Audience ALP 33% Coalition 45% Greens 9% Others 2% Unspecified 11%.

Manic applause continues, camera pans across ecstatic crowd squealing with delight, pounding their feet and clapping hysterically. Malcolm Turnbull, dressed in a smart black leather jacket, is sitting by himself on the panel alongside Tony Jones. He waves and smiles back at the ecstatic crowd.

Tony attempts to quiet things down. "If... yes, well, thank you... quiet now please... we..."

Slowly the noise starts to subside, then suddenly a lone woman's voice yells out "I looooooove you Malcolm!" Audience erupts into laughter and applause, as the camera pans to a middle aged woman clutching a poster of the member for Wentworth cut in the shape of a heart. Grinning, Tony Jones holds up his hand again for quiet. "Thank you, madam, and I'll take that as a comment." Audience erupts into more laughter.

A young man with pierced nose and dreadlocks who is sitting at the back leaps to his feet and yells out "I love you too Malcolm!"

Audience erupts into wild applause and re-invigorated stomping of feet. Tony Jones and Malcolm both grin at each other.

There is a sudden commotion from behind the panel. Tony Jones sharply turns his head. The camera pans up to the balcony, as a group of rowdy UTS students start to unfurl a banner. Tony Jones looks momentarily flustered. Then he grins. The banner reads 'We HEART Malcolm'.

Malcolm Turnbull leans forward, his face breaking into his trademark Cheshire cat grin. "Thank you, thank you!" He pauses, then announces: "And I love you all too!" The audience erupts into more squeals of delight and laughter and applause.

Tony Jones gestures with both hands for the crowd to calm down. He turns to the camera. "Thank you, and you too can join in tonight's historic edition of *Q&A* simply by following our special qanda hashtag at the bottom of your screen." Up on the screen pops: #qandaweloveMalcolmtoo.

"Now, I think I'm safe in saying it's a long time since any Prime Minister of this country got such a warm welcome. Firstly, Prime Minister, allow me to congratulate you on your stunning victory earlier this morning in the party room ballot. I'm led to believe that it was an absolute landslide result for you and a crushingly humiliating defeat for former Prime Minister Tony Abb..."

As one, the audience leap to their feet and start booing, jeering, hissing and cat-calling. The sound is deafening, drowning out both men. Malcolm and Tony hold up their hands for silence, but to no avail.

Tony Jones grins. "Clearly our audience agree too!" Malcolm

Turnbull smirks, and shrugs with false modesty. "If I could just say... if I could just say..."

The audience quickly go quiet.

Malcolm puts on his serious face. "I understand emotions run high at a time like this, but I think, well, I would personally like to, well, so to speak, despite all our manifest differences, and despite his, well, quite frankly, disastrous performance, well, nonetheless, if I may just take this opportunity to say, as it were, to say, humbly, and with the deepest sincerity, how much Tony Abb..." Audience erupts into hysterical screeching, booing, swearing, hissing and foot stomping, drowning Malcolm out. Tony Jones calls for calm, then turns to the camera.

"And our first question tonight comes from Taneka Green of Newtown. Taneka is a philosophy and environmental economics student at Sydney University."

Grainy footage of a young woman in a room full of Al Gore's *An Inconvenient Truth* posters comes up on the screen. She has tears in her eyes.

"Oh Mr Turnbull, my friends and I are all so excited that finally — finally! — after all these years we have somebody running this country who feels compassion for his fellow human beings and cares about saving the planet. Please, please just tell us how quickly you'll put a price on carbon, release the asylum seekers from Nauru, close the detention centres, scrap university fees, restore free healthcare for all, stop demonising refugees, stop demonising the unemployed, stop demonising Muslims, jail the Islamophobes, bring in the Gonski reforms, stop all coal mining, ban CSG and legalise same sex marriage?"

Malcolm Turnbull stares back at the audience with a fixed grin on his face. The audience is deathly quiet.

❖

Eager to capitalise on the turmoil within the government, the opposition leader declares it to be his "Year of Ideas" and begins by outlining his economic plans.

Wiv Compassion

Financial Review
14/2/15

My Sustainable Plan for Economic Growth Wiv Compassion:

1. Wiv my plan for a compassionate Labor guvviment we will make sure that lots of people have jobs and stuff so if they go to TAFE and get a Diploma in Plumbing or Patio Design wiv a Masters in Tile Laying then wiv that degree they can go and join a union and pay their membership fees and then go and get a job. Wiv a job you earn lots of money and a really good wage too coz that's why Labor introduced the Minimum Wage.

2. The main problem wiv the Minimum Wage is that it's too Minimum coz it's not the Maximum Wage which is what is only fair so under my guvviment we will raise the Minimum Wage so that people who are earning money make loads more of it and have a fair quality of life wiv proper Labor values.

3. It's an absolute disgrace wiv the banks and big business and everybody taking billions of dollars of profits and dividends and stuff out of the economy every year so we've got to put it back in a fair and compassionate way in line wiv Labor values so my guvviment will put a Compassionate Big Business Levy in place to make sure that everyfink is fair and everybody is getting their fair share of the banks' profits.

4. As my good friend Ged said on radio there is nuffink wrong wiv borrowing as much money as you want if you're going to put it to good economic use which is a no-brainer and she should know all about that and besides which wiv interest rates down really low then now is the time to take out a loan from the bank so under a Labor guvviment we

will borrow loads of money from all the different banks and that way we can build critical infrastructure and that means more people getting jobs which is good for the economy because they will all pay more taxes.

5. Savings are really important for a guvviment. For instance, my good friend Daniel in Victoria has saved over a billion dollars by not building that East West tunnel thing, so now I can put that billion dollars on my bottom line plus at the same time we've helped save the planet by not digging a hole right through it.

6. As I told my good friend Leigh Sales on the ABC that wiv my new economic policies we will soon be back in surplus coz as they say if you don't know where you're going any road will get you there.

7. Wiv my good friend Chris as my Federal Treasurer he will take all the tough decisions and tough measures to bring the budget back under control like he said on Sky News and that means he won't be rolling up into a little ball like Tony Abbott instead he'll be rolling up into a Big Ball like Clive Palmer and that means the days of Santa Claus are well and truly behind us so Chris can be the Easter Bunny instead.

8. Unlike the guvviment of Tony Abbott I believe climate change is real and I don't believe it is crap because the one thing you can't argue about is the science and the science clearly shows that wiv climate change you need a carbon tax which is pretty lucky coz the whole point of a carbon tax is to raise as much money as possible in a fair and compassionate way wivout it actually doing anyfink.

9. Wiv more money for schools under Gonski there will be lots more kids learning stuff like Indigenous Maffematics and Sustainable Social Improvement Studies and that means they will grow the economy wiv all their new skills.

10. Wiv our new Compassionate Border Control and Immigration policies there will be way more jobs created coz there will be loads of Community Liaison Assistants whose job it will be to help Compassionate Migrants and Sustainable Asylum Seekers find suitable public

accommodation close to critical amenities such as Centrelink and the local mosque.

11. Wiv my new Compassionate Jobs Promotion Scheme I will appoint Professor Truggs to set up a special Commission of Humane Employment Services employing over two hundred staff members to humanely assist Oppressed Prisoners seeking compensation for having being unfairly imprisoned for murder, wife-beating, rape and so on.

12. In order to return as rapidly as possible to surplus I will instruct Treasury to establish a Special Commission to Urgently But Responsibly and Compassionately Return To Surplus under the auspices of the Hon. Wayne Swan (retd) to report back with an interim report outlining a Plan for Action to be implemented midway through 2051-52 (or as soon as possible thereafter).

❖

Repeatedly pressed by talkback host Alan Jones to outline current tax levels, shadow treasurer Chris Bowen is embarrassed when he is clearly unable to name Australia's tax-free threshold.

Fool on the Hill

Financial Review
21/2/15

Me: And joining me for this week's Pollies Pop Quiz is shadow federal treasurer Chris Bowen. Good evening Chris.
Him: Pleasure to be with you Rowan. I love a good Pop Quiz.
Me: Excellent. Well my first question is — to which well-known Canberra senior parliamentarian could the title of the Beatles song 'The Fool on The Hill' accurately refer?
Him: Well, that's an easy one. Obviously the 'Hill' which features prominently in the title of the song is, in this instance, none other than Capital Hill, which is where Parliament House is of course situated, at a symbolic axis connecting the site to the parliamentary apex. Now, specifically, this is the new modern,

environmentally-friendly Bob Hawke-era Parliament House to which I am referring, and shouldn't be confused with the old stale, stagnant, musty Menzies-era Parl...
Me: I'm sorry but my question was to whom could the song title refer — who is the 'Fool'? —not the whereabouts of the 'Hill'...
Him: Well, if you'd just let me finish, it does depend how far back you want to go, and as I was saying, the new Parliament House on Capital Hill was opened in 1988 by Bob Hawke, possibly our greatest ever Prime Minister, a true Labor hero of course, in fact the very embodiment of...
Me: Yes, yes, but if you would just answer the question. Who could the 'Fool' be?
Him: Well, I am attempting to answer you Rowan if you would stop talking over me. Bob Hawke was a visionary Labor leader, like I said, and indeed, his economic reforms, which of course were instigated by Paul Keating, who we all know is one of the great...
Me: The 'Fool'? Who is the 'Fool' in the song title? Who could it be? Any idea?
Him: If you'd just let me finish. The 'Hill' is situated to the south...
Me: I'm not interested in the 'Hill'. I'm only interested in the 'Fool'.
Him: Hmm?
Me: The 'Fool'.
Him: Well hang on...
Me: Who is the biggest fool in Canberra? The 'Fool on the Hill'?
Him: Well, that of course is highly subjective, depending upon a complex set of criteria, which require serious development and analys...
Me: This is a Pop Quiz. Shall I give you a clue?
Him: Well, obviously I would need to evaluate all the relevant...
Me: How about a former Treasurer who doesn't even know what the lowest tax threshold is? Does that help?
Him: As I was saying, these are complicated questions that need to be looked at in context.
Me: Alright — how about in the context of someone who wants to run the nation's finances who once told Parliament that — to quote — "China has not floated the Yen" — when of course the Chinese currency is the Yuan. Could that be an apt description of a 'Fool'? After all, the Yen is the currency of China's sworn enemy, the Japanese...

Him: Well, obviously that's an extreme example, I'm not sure...
Me: Or perhaps someone might be considered a 'Fool' if, for example, they're in the Treasury portfolio but they repeatedly appear not to grasp the difference between gross and net debt. Would that qualify?
Him: Well there's no need to get all technical, Rowan. That's hardly fair.
Me: Or here's another clue: how about someone who dismisses the billions of dollars that this country has to borrow each month just to meet its interest payments on the horrific debt he and the government he was a part of accumulated — and again I quote — he dismisses it as "just rhetoric"?
Him: Well...
Me: Or what about a former Immigration Minister responsible for border protection who not only had a $5.2 billion dollar blowout in his portfolio but managed to let 24,886 people on 395 boats sneak in at the same time? Perhaps that might indicate a degree of fool...
Him: Well I hardly see how...
Me: Or how about a former Minister for Financial Services who once confidently claimed their government was in surplus when in fact they were smack bang in the middle of running up the biggest deficit in our nation's history? Perhaps that might qualify as...
Him: I'm not entirely sure what you are driving at here...
Me: Or how about a bloke who wants to run our nation's finances but his credentials in government include Grocery Watch, Fuel Watch, and the Petrol Cop... all of which had to be dumped because they were completely useless...
Him: I'm sorry, Rowan, but this is supposed to be a Pop Quiz, not a third degree interrogation. What was the question again?
Me: Which parliamentarian could best be described as 'The Fool on the Hill'?
Him: Well it's obvious.
Me: Yes?
Him: Tony Abbott.

❖

Way Beyond Satire

An Indian spiritual leader called the Guru of Bling is accused of convincing his followers to remove their testicles in order to prove their loyalty to him and to get closer to God.

Smarmy of Wentworth

Financial Review
28/2/15

The world was shocked last week to learn of a mysterious Indian sect whose followers were persuaded by their charismatic guru — the so-called "guru-in-bling" — that in order to find enlightenment, they must first of all castrate themselves. Apparently, up to 400 devotees have self-castrated over the past few years.

But latest reports seeping out of Australia suggest the practice is far more widespread than authorities initially feared. Rumours are circulating of an obscure cult in Canberra who fervently believe that only through mass castration can they attain electoral nirvana.

"We were taken into a dark room two weeks ago, and had to decide in secret whether or not to castrate ourselves. Thirty-nine of us did exactly as we were asked and lopped off our balls, but the other 61 have refused — so far," admitted one member of the sect, speaking in a high squeaky voice on strict condition of anonymity. Those familiar with the arcane practices of the sect believe that bitter jealousies and rivalries between several swamis within the cult will see an attempt made to repeat the mass castration later in the year.

"We are making every effort to make the others see the light and hopefully, any day now, the rest will join us in ritual self-castration for all the world to see," said one of the 39 disciples of one of the gurus, with tears streaming down his face.

"We were led to believe that only those who get castrated will be able to meet God at the ballot booth," said another, squatting awkwardly on a fluffy pillow.

Devotees of the practice believe that only through self-castration can the cult purify themselves of the earthly sins of the last budget and rid themselves of the stain of poor opinion polls. Some also believe it is the only way they will ever be accepted into the lavish temple of Qanda in Ultimo, where the charismatic "guru-in-waiting" Mahareshi Mal regularly supplicates himself before a large circular audience, bowing down before the goddess Gaia and paying homage to the high priests of political correctness, begging forgiveness for the many sins of his colleagues. In particular, the guru was heard repeating over and over his favourite mantra that it was "just a captain's pick" as well as "deploring all the shocking stories about the Prime Minister that I, er, I mean some deplorable individual has leaked out of cabinet". The guru, also known as the Smarmy of Wentworth, was also heard pleading with his disciples to "remember it's all about the children".

However, others disagree that the path to salvation requires the removal of testicular fortitude. "There is virtue in having balls. In fact, it takes balls to have balls. We all took a solemn vow to pursue the path of fiscal responsibility and austerity and to support our leader. The days of profligacy and self-indulgences must end. We are fast approaching the end of the age of entitlements."

There were some concerns that the current unpopular leader of the cult, who ritually bathes once a year in the purifying waters of Manly wearing nothing but a slim red loincloth, would look pretty silly in his Speedos if he joined in the mass castration.

"We think he still has his balls," said one devotee. "Last week he said he'd invade Iraq all by himself, cracked down on the homegrown terrorists, told the towelheads that 'Religion of Peace' stuff is a load of tosh, gave the dole bludgers their marching orders, refused to sack Joe and Peta from their jobs just because the hand-wringers are baying for their blood, and finally told that annoying Triggs woman to rack off. All of that takes some balls."

Meanwhile, in other spectacular news this week, one of Australia's leading journalists, John Lyin, exposed the hitherto unknown and explosive story about the inner workings of the Abbott government in a series of earth-shattering exclusives:

> "There was a fearful hush in the room, as the entire cabinet of men cowered in fear, trembling in dread, at the fiercesome female who stood before them. A telling chink of crystal upon crystal and ice swirling in the glass broke the eerie silence, as the most powerful woman in the land rose to her full imposing six foot six height before taking a deep breath and with one sweep of her auburn hair declared her intention to single-handedly invade the Middle East and restore peace and harmony to the globe. Never in the annals of history has one woman held such might and power in the palm of her hand, never has one woman so debased the democratic process, never before has..."
> (Cont'd every day for the next two weeks until Abbott is gone.)

❖

A Senator suggests Australians should keep feral native animals as their household pets in order to save them from extinction. Meanwhile, rumours of another leadership challenge swirl around Malcolm Turnbull when he is spotted dining at the Wild Duck with Clive Palmer, whose PUP senators continue to desert him.

The Well-hung Lambie

Financial Review
21/3/15

Senator David Leyonhjelm has suggested Australians should keep feral native animals as their household pets in order to save them from extinction. He won't have to look very far.

The Shortened quoll: Often mocked as the Dr Gerbils of the animal world, the Shortened quoll was first discovered in 2006 by a group of miners trapped deep under the ground in a Tasmanian rat-hole in desperate need of help. Much to everybody's surprise, the first creature to emerge safely from the aptly named grub shaft into the full glare of the TV spotlights was in fact this nimble, light-footed little creature (originally from Victoria) who scurried off to become leader of his party. The Shortened quoll looks cute and cuddly but owners should beware — when you least expect it, it will sink its razor-like teeth into your back causing instant loss of caucus support and certain death.

The Well-hung Lambie: Often found swinging upside-down high in the canopies of the Tasmanian wilderness from its unusually long appendage, the Well-hung Lambie is a ferocious creature believed to be distantly related to Queensland's famous red-haired Ipswich dingbat. Both creatures emit a loud, coarse shriek that grates upon the ear, and owners of these pets should be wary of their sharp tongue and long claws.

The Low Bellied Pliber Snake: Looks can be deceptive. Pretty to the eye, this inner-city reptile quickly turns a deadly shade of dark green as it slithers through the undergraduate, sorry, the undergrowth around Newtown spitting its poisonous venom at any perceived threat to its status in the feral kingdom. Owners beware: it will devour its young when the time is right (i.e. soon after the next election).

The Prickly Xenophobe: Originally of Greek extraction, and believed to have hopped on a boat that berthed by mistake in Adelaide, this furry little critter makes the ideal pet for those who value their sense of independence. However, most owners soon become intensely frustrated at this animal's flighty, skittish, unpredictable nature and its insatiable desire to hog the limelight. Loves being photographed and having its tummy tickled.

The Shrill Necked Pyne: Also known by its nickname "the Fixer", this loud, warbling bird — also from South Australia — emits a fruity, high-pitched cackling sound before repeatedly fouling its own nest. Owners should note that it will keep on doing this until it eventually gets its own way.

Way Beyond Satire

The Wentworth White Ant (or termitus spillus): Deceptively charming and extremely popular in Sydney's eastern harbour foreshores where it is a popular pet among wealthy lovers of fine chardonnays and latte, potential owners should nonetheless beware: left to its own devices it will quickly undermine the foundations of your house, and in all likelihood, bring the whole edifice crashing down around you.

The Mathias Cormorant: Immediately recognisable due to its foreign-sounding, guttural song, this is in fact a rather dull and boring animal, known to many bird spotters as the Belgian Plodder.

The Yellow-breasted Penny Currawong: With its distinctive floppy jet black crest, piercing brown eyes and strident warbles, this defiantly aggressive bird (the females of the species have been known to mate with each other) is often mistaken for its distant cousin, the South Australian cuckoo.

The Fat-bellied Coolum Foul: A particularly malodorous creature, this over-sized mammal likes to gorge itself on wild duck as well as feeding on self-promotion and endless publicity which makes for a singularly unpleasant pet — or even dinner companion. Often mistaken for a dinosaur, due to its heavy footprint, the Coolum Foul will aggressively move into and then destroy its natural habitat, whether it be in the desert, near tropical reefs, or even the grounds of a luxury golf resort.

The Sloth with Eyes: Large, heavy, solid slug-like creature that begins life coupling with a Coolum Foul before breaking away and pursuing its own path towards oblivion. Difficult to house train.

The Victorian Motoring Galah: Often regarded as the Ringo Starr of the animal kingdom because of its extraordinary habit of landing on its feet in a golden nest egg, this particular galah (distantly related to the Bogan moth) has the unusual habit of flinging kangaroo droppings around the place, but will invariably fall instantly silent if confronted by a camera or someone actually asking what it thinks.

The Western Sydney Pelican: Coming in a variety of plumages from bright pink to bland beige, the Western Sydney Pelicans are best known by their individual variety names (the Nodding Liar Burke, the Spangled Bowen Drongo, the Anthony Albatross etc). These pelicans have been fighting over the dismembered scraps of the once-proud Labor party for years. Western Sydney Pelicans can also be served up as an extremely tasty and popular halal dish.

❖

Former PUP senator Lambie announces the formation of the Jacqui Lambie Network (JLN) and details its 12 core principles; including that her party is opposed to Sharia Law being imposed in Australia either formally or informally. Meanwhile, calls by Labor elders to reform the party are rejected, whilst a deal is negotiated between the US and Iran over nuclear proliferation.

Sharia in Tassie

Financial Review
2/4/15

In shock news today, and despite the newly-formed Jacqui Lambie Party having vowed to oppose it ever happening, the federal government announced its plan to introduce Sharia Law into Tasmania.

Said a spokesperson for the government: "Obviously we are keen to get Sharia Law up and running throughout the whole of Australia, and indeed we've already made great strides towards this in western Sydney and via successful schemes such as halal Vegemite and lamingtons, but we thought it best to start with Sharia in Tassie first. After all, thanks to the Greens, Tasmania is the closest thing we have to a traditional stone age society in Australia."

The spokesperson noted that the government had agreed to tweak Sharia laws to give them a distinctly Tasmanian flavour:

Way Beyond Satire

"We've decided to update the main tool of legal enforcement. In classic Sharia, the machete is favoured for beheadings, lopping off limbs and that sort of important post-judicial work. However, most Tasmanians feel far more comfortable with a chainsaw. We think the typical handyman 4.4kW cordless can do a really nifty job for those smaller infringements, such as petty theft or parking fines, but we're recommending something with a decent bit of grunt, such as the standard High Powered 30 tonne Wood Splitter, for your adulterers and the like."

Experts predict that the introduction of "Tasharia" (as it has become known) will lead to a dramatic lowering of the divorce rate among Tasmanians, many of whom in the past have been known to engage in pagan-style extra-marital, infidel-style infidelities, known locally as "New Years Eve in Hobart" or "Office Christmas Parties".

There was some confusion amongst locals, however, when informed that under the new Sharia laws such debauchery would now see them getting stoned in public. "And...?" was the most common reply.

It is also expected that the introduction of Tasharia will encourage an uptake in traditional marriage. "In the past, rural Tasmanians often felt embarrassed about marrying their 9-year-old cousin, but under these new laws that's no longer even a crime," said one delighted old-timer from the slopes of Cradle-Snatcher Mountain.

Critics have long complained that Sharia has serious shortcomings as a suitable legal system for a modern society because it was designed exclusively to suit the pre-industrial communities from the seventh century and thereabouts. "Again, we found little evidence of any advanced industrial activity in Tasmania that would be at odds with these new, I mean these old, laws," said the spokesperson. "In fact, those handful of factories and businesses that we did occasionally stumble on were for the most part in the middle of shutting down."

In other news this week, Labor Senator Sam Dastardly declared that from now on anybody who told the truth about anything whatsoever to do with Labor's policies would immediately be expelled from the party. "It's a bloody disgrace," he exploded in front of a Sky News TV crew. "As a party we have spent the last seven years perfecting the delicate skills of lying, dissembling, spinning and telling-the-biggest-whoppers-of-all-with-a-straight-face into a sophisticated art form. The last thing we need is Martin Ferguson, Paul Keating, Bob Carr, Michael Costa, John Faulkner and other nobody's wandering around telling the truth." Meanwhile overseas, tense negotiations over Iran's nuclear capabilities have continued in Lausanne between The Islamic Republic of Iran and the six major world powers: the US, UK, France, China and Russia plus Germany (known as the P+1ssweak).

Delegates have announced the successful securing of a preliminary deal of a positive framework to allow the future extension to the deadline for further talks to be implemented to allow them to pretend they aren't being taken for a ride by a bunch of mad mullahs. A spokesperson for Barack Obama emphasised the President is very keen to keep the talks going for as long as it takes to get some kind of piece of paper he can stick in his memoirs and label his "legacy".

The Iranians expressed their satisfaction with the decision. "The negotiations will end when solutions have been found that see these crippling sanctions lifted for all time and in a manner that gives us exactly what we want," said Iranian negotiator Hamid Al-Centrifuge.

A diplomat close to the negotiations explained that the only slight hiccup in the current provisional agreement was a tiny, insignificant technical detail to do with the fact that Iran was still insisting on its universal human right to nuke Israel into oblivion at the earliest opportunity, swiftly followed by Saudi Arabia and Egypt.

"Other than that, they've 100% agreed to only using their nuclear arsenal for doomsday purposes," he explained.

❖

Publicity-seeking senators start agitating about multinationals.

Google tax

Financial Review
11/4/15

There were explosive scenes today at a Canberra Senate inquiry into multi-nationals rorting the tax system by using the laws of the land to work out how much tax they can get away with not paying. Aggressively taking the corporate leaders of Google, Microsoft and Apple to task, renowned tax warrior Senator Sam Dastardly and his fellow publicity seeker Senator Nick Xenophobe repeatedly used their iPads and iPhones to google how quickly their remarks were being quoted on Twitter and how soon their words and images were being spread for free across the internet. "Any inquiry that results in people getting to see a Double Iranian Greek sandwich inside a Canberra black hole is a good day for my self-promotion cam... er, I mean for public policy. It's important to shine a light on Nick and me, er, I mean to shine a light on the dark corners of corporate tax minimisation," said Senator Dastardly, posing for a selfie.

❖

Enlivening the ongoing Recognition debate, a prominent Indigenous leader suggests, among other things, that a poetic preamble be especially crafted to the Constitution, rather than amending the legal document itself.

We the undersigned

Financial Review
18/4/15

Dear Noel,

Here's the first draft of the Declaration. Get back to me with any changes. Cheers.

2015 — The Year of Betrayal

We, the proud people of this wide, brown land (is brown OK?), *insomuch as it be the Oldest Continent on God's Earth* (is God OK? I get to the Snake-Rainbow thing later) *and insomuch as it be Home-of-Sorts to those Whitefellas who have repeatedly sought refuge on these our ancient and vulnerable shores* (I think "invaded, raped and pillaged" is a bit strong, but up to you) *which stretch from the teensiest grain of million-year-old sand nestling beneath the sun in Our Great Deserts to the flash of a silvery fin in the tropical waters that embrace Our Bountiful Shores* (is that poetic enough?) *do hereby in the Spirit of Compassionate Humanity* (the luvvies'll luv that bit) *declare in this Historical Declaration of the Rights of All Ye Divergent Yet United, Proud Yet Put Upon, Aggrieved Yet Aspirational, Ancient Yet Modern Tribes And Cultures of Indigenous Australia* (too clunky?) *that, er, We Were Here First* (may as well get to the point). *So rack off!* (I think a bit of Aussie colloquialism gives a suitable post-modern flavour, don't you?)

We hold this Truth to be self-evident (I nicked that from Jefferson — he's dead so no copyright) *and wheresofor as it may have once been deemed Terra Nullius insomuch as pertaining to so-called Constitutional Documents of the Discredited Colonialist Imperialist Era that was in fact a Straightforward Land Grab by a bunch of Marauding Convict Murderers and Other Such Felons* (that takes care of the legalities quite nicely, with a bit of historical context thrown in). *Bloody Bastards! Should've whipped yer bloody butts when we had the chance!* (more post-modern phraseology, I think, helps hang it all together).

We also hold these Truths (Jefferson again), *insomuch as the Passage of Time heals all Wounds, much as the Streams of the Land purify the Soil upon which they pass* (I really like this bit so please no changes!) *and through which The Rainbow Serpent Creator Peace Be Upon Him* (I nicked that last bit from the towelheads — keep the multiculti mob happy!) *has delivered to us throughout the Eighty Thousand Years* (I bumped the numbers up a bit just to be on the safe side) *whereupon our Peoples have Trod this Land armed with*

nothing more than the Spirit of the Ancestors (I like that!)
and some sticks and spears and wotnot (I couldn't remember
the name of the stick/rope rocket launcher thing but anyway
putting in words like Boomerang and Didgeridoo all sounds
a bit Rolf Harris don't you think?) *and whereas we weren't
actually all that Technologically Advanced so we're pretty darn
lucky we didn't get colonised by the Spanish or the Belgians or
the Turks* (I mean, hello? Aztecs anyone? Incas? Armenians?)
*but instead we got the Pommy Bastards who at least didn't
Wipe us off the Face of the Earth* (I nicked that phrase from
the ayatollahs, don't think it's copyright) *and insomuch as
we have Retained Many of Our Cultural practices such as
Storytelling and Painting with Dots and Catching Fish* (I think
we should stay well clear of the spearings and wifebeating
and incest stuff) *and insofar as we Took Care of the Land
for a Hundred Thousand Years* (I bumped it up a bit more,
I mean who really knows?) *with these Massive Bushfires
which allowed us to Kill All The Animals* (I know that's a bit
un-PC what with climate change and animal rights, but I
couldn't find anything else) *and whereas within the Sands
of Time we suffered Many Grievances, in particular with
the Stolen Generation which was finally Put to Rights by
Our Kindred Kevin Rudd Who Should Be Next UN General
Secretary* (do we really need this bit?) *who delivered unto us
the Greatest Symbolic Gesture of the Modern Indigenous Era
when he said Sorry insomuch as Sorry always seems to be the
hardest word* (I nicked that from Elton John — his agent says
it's fine but can we put in some gay marriage blurb?).

*In every stage of these Oppressions which included being
forced into the Welfare Trap wherein we were Obliged through
happenstance to take vast sums of taxpayers money and blow
it all on Grog which some Insensitive Souls deem Lifestyle
Choices we have sought to accommodate the Invaders, Rapists
and Pillagers* (there, I got it in finally) *through letting them
live on Our Lands but not for much Longer unless they pay us
Massive Compensation in the form of Wads of Cash.*

We The Undersigned etc

(Did I leave anything out?)

2015 — The Year of Betrayal

❖

The foreign minister visits Iran to negotiate intelligence sharing and the return of refugees.

Hummus vs Hamas

Financial Review
24/4/15

Department of Foreign Affairs and Trade (DAFT) Ministerial Diplomatic Briefing Notes. Section 666: Negotiating with Iranians.

Wardrobe: In order to avoid looking like a "plate of meat" (see *Appendix A: Sheik Dim Halali's hot Islamic fashion tips*) and thereby encourage uncontrollable lustful urges amongst your hosts, we recommend the Minister cover her head with either a scarf (which can double as an attractive fashion statement) or a smart black hat. If in doubt, wear both.

Greetings: Being the first to reach out to shake hands is not advisable in this part of the world, as many of those you meet may not actually still be in possession of theirs (see *Appendix C: Local judicial system*).

Food: At some stage your hosts will express their pride in hummus, an agreeable dip the Iranians make out of chickpeas and olive oil. At some point your hosts will also express their pride in Hamas, a disagreeable terrorist organisation the Iranians make out of bloodthirsty Islamists and murderous Palestinians.

Dialect: The locals are an extremely passionate and vocal community who like to shriek at the top of their voices whilst spitting in your face. Do not be alarmed, for these are just charming harmless ancient cultural poetic phrases of endearment that roughly translate as "Death to the Great Satan", "Kill all the Jews" and "You are a brazen wanton hussy who deserves what's coming to you".

Cultural activities: In many countries in this part of the world, where water is scarce, it is common to come across ancient wells. Although it is our custom to drop coins or pebbles down such wells to listen to the splash, this practice is best avoided in Iran as you may accidentally hit a 9th century Imam who is patiently sitting down at the bottom. Waking him up may have unpleasant consequences (see *Appendix Z: Armageddon and the nuclear holocaust at the end of the world*).

Shared interests: Many Iranians clearly share a deep affection for Australia's famous Grand Slam tennis player John Newcombe, whom they like to refer to as "Our Newq's". You will hear his name pop up in all sorts of odd conversations, but just smile and nod politely.

Bazaars: A visit to the local bazaar is a highlight of any trip to Tehran. Have a decent wander around, because here you can buy pretty much anything you want, such as herbs, spices, breads, flowers, Kalashnikovs, Qassam rockets, Yassin anti-tank missiles, Al Quds multiple grenade launchers, Sariya 240mm mortars, Pakistani nuclear warheads, Yemeni slave girls, Persian rugs, saffron, fresh turmeric, koofteh meatballs etc.

Sightseeing: There's plenty to look at as you wander around the ancient villages admiring the rotting corpses of stoned adulteresses, but of course don't forget to look up and keep your eyes peeled for homosexuals being tossed off those sloping rooftops.

Topography: There are plenty of beautiful villages and towns dotted around the mountainous regions of Iran, and plenty of large impregnable cities dotted deep beneath them.

Literature: Do not be surprised to find a book in the bedside table of your hotel room; this is a quaint local custom allowing you to enjoy popular best-sellers as you drift off to sleep. Common titles are likely to include "The Protocols of Zion", "Mein Kampf", "Holocaust? What Holocaust?", "Auschwitz revisited" etc.

Bargaining tactics: Iranians love to haggle (must be all those bazaars!). However, here are several well-worn strategies that have been carefully honed over many years to give you the best possible advantage in negotiations:

The Saddam: Yell and scream all sorts of threats across the desert then sit back and watch as your army gets annihilated by suicidal 10-year-olds.

The Assad: Insist to the Iranians that they can use your country to base their Hezbollah troops in so they can invade Lebanon and attack Israel whenever they feel like it and in exchange ask them to give you enough chemical weapons to massacre your own people with.

The Barack: Start off by telling the Iranians how they have to mend their wicked ways or you will punish them severely. Then gradually wear them down by agreeing to every single demand they make, plus a little extra for good measure, whilst simultaneously abandoning every precept you went in with. Never fails.

The Aussie: Ask them to take back 9,000 of their own citizens who fled the joint because it's such a hellhole (or because they're gay, female, Christian, or quite fancy the idea of living in a country that isn't terrorised by religious police) and when they say "no" offer to give them your military intelligence so they can go and massacre Syrian rebels, sunni Iraqis and Kurds instead.

❖

Participants in an SBS doco express outrage at the way they have been portrayed as a bunch of no-hopers living on the margins of society. Meanwhile, Joe Hockey and Tony Abbott prepare their second, and what will be their final, budget.

Struggle Street

Financial Review
9/5/15

Participants in a taxpayer-funded documentary have expressed shock and outrage at the way they have been portrayed as losers and no-hopers living on the fringes of the political world. Entitled *Struggle Street*, the series has caused a furore among the downtrodden residents on the depressed outskirts of Australia's most affluent city, Canberra.

The opening scenes portray beautiful shots of a sparkling Lake Burley Griffin, and delightful scenes of coffee shops in Kingston, before the camera races over the hill, and we see shocking scenes of violence, alcohol use, swearing and moral depravity that occur daily only a short distance away, in a dingy underground enclave dubbed by the locals "Parliament House".

The producers are unapologetic about the dysfunctional individuals on display. "It's warts and all. We just turned up and filmed what was really going on. The intense tribal hatreds, the abusive behaviour, the endless lies, the bitter enemies and the shallow friendships. All fuelled by this pathetic and insatiable addiction to opinion polls."

"It's disgusting," said one viewer. "I've never seen scenes of such barbaric depravity. To think this goes on in a supposedly civilised society! Every afternoon around 2pm the lot of them turn completely feral! And we the taxpayers are funding it!"

Yet many of those who participated in the series claim they have been duped and betrayed. "Vat camera crew lived wiv us for years on end," complained one disgruntled star of the show, known only as Bill. "Vey tried to make out like I'm a complete idiot wiv nuffink between my ears but vat's not true coz vis is my Year of Ideas and I've had lots of vem — it's just vat I can't remember where I put vem. I feel like I've been stabbed in the back — and vat's usually my job!"

The series follows the lives of those who almost succeed but never quite make it, identified in the series only by their first names, such as Tanya, Malcolm, Adam and Albo. "These are the stories of those struggling to hang on," says the deep, menacing male voice over. "When you're dealt a lousy hand, who says you can't win? And when life sticks the boot in, who says you can't

fight back? That's the way it goes when you live on the fringe."
In one scene that has drawn a lot of criticism for its savagery
and lack of humanity, the ruthless tomboy Tanya decides to beat
up Bill because he isn't gay enough. She invites him to meet
her in July under a railway bridge to sort out their differences
but when he turns up he is mugged by reality and nearly
loses his leadership.

In another disturbing scene, a podgy girl with dark rings under
her eyes, who is identified only as Sarah, passionately believes
she is going to be the next leader of the street gang known by
their colour, Green, but she is suddenly ambushed and betrayed
by the charming but ruthless migrant kid Richard, a self-deluded
fantasist who hallucinates that he is living in the "mainstream".
In the final scene Sarah is seen wandering off into the dense bush
shrieking about boat people and taking potshots at Richard with
her slingshot and living on a diet of nuts and completely nuts.

Mysteriously, one scene featuring the ambitious narcissist
Malcolm had to be cut when the producers turned up in February
as planned but nothing actually happened, although they expect
some action to take place later in the year.

Dysfunctional families feature regularly throughout the series,
with one scene depicting an overweight slob called Clive (scenes
of him eating junk food and farting repeatedly at the camera had
to be cut from the promo after viewers complained they "felt
sick"). Clive is chronically depressed because most of his equally
dysfunctional offspring, including the halfwit Glenn and wild
child Jacqui, decided to abandon him and run away from home.
Critics questioned whether taxpayers should be forking out
over a million dollars just to witness the antics of such immoral
layabouts. In one scene, described as "repulsive", Jacqui decides
to stop the entire country from repairing its budget while she
heads off on her pointless quest to find a man who is "hung
like a donkey".

Described by one critic as "political porn", the series has so
outraged one local resident, identified only as Joe the Garbo,
that he intends to protest by driving up to Parliament House this

coming Tuesday morning and dumping a load of rubbish all over the front lawn. "Most of it will be recycled handouts, minimal tax cuts and child-friendly policies," he explained, "and other such trash. Tony asked me to make sure it's all very dull and boring."

❖

Eager to make up for his disastrous (i.e. poorly sold) 2014 Budget, Joe Hockey starts afresh.

Budget night

Financial Review
13/5/15

Joe eased himself onto his plump, leather office sofa and let out a gentle sigh of relief. It was over. He glanced up at the cigar box tucked between his bust of Margaret Thatcher and his well-thumbed biography of Milton Friedman, but then thought better of it. With a weary shake of the head, he pulled out a stick of mint-flavoured Nicabate and popped it in his mouth. Outside he could still hear the camera crew packing up, as the sounds of laughter and distant raised voices echoed down the corridors of Parliament House. He closed his eyes for a brief second, allowing himself a small smile. He'd done it. He breathed slowly, savouring the exquisite pleasure of the moment. The serenity. The sense of satisfaction. Nine long months he had agonised over this Budget, the numbers and politics gestating in his brain. What would it be like, he often found himself wondering, to be a woman giving birth to a second child when the first one had been so, well... so despised? He'd been so proud of that first baby of his, so pleased with how it had come into this world full of so much promise. Yes, they'd had cigars that night. And rightly, too! It was a great Budget! But the way the press had turned on it, then the public, too! Savaging it like some medieval lynch mob. So unfair, so cruel. Joe shook his head. Must snap out of it! That was a year ago. The past is the past. It was over. He grinned to himself. Outside in the corridor laughter and applause echoed up and down the labyrinthian corridors. The cheers from the gallery still rang in his ears. Budget No 2 was nothing short of a triumph! The press had loved it. Emerging from the lock up, they'd slapped him on the back and shaken his hand. Even Mark Kenny! And Phil Coorey too! He raised his fingers and stroked the side of his cheek where Laura had leaned over and given him a great, big sloppy kiss! Speersy reckoned the Budget was a game-changer and Paul Murray and Peter Van Onselen had both agreed — live on air! — that this was the moment the Coalition's fortunes had turned around! Joe cocked his head to one side. From next door he could hear Laurie Oaks singing the Budget's praises to Emma Alberici on *Lateline*. Naturally, they were all saying it was Scott Morrison's "genius" that had made all the difference. Joe sighed good-naturedly. So what? Teamwork. The point was, of course, that it had all come together under his own expert guidance. History would — in fact, already was — citing this as the moment the Abbott government's fortunes turned around. No wonder... Thump! Thump! Thump! Joe almost jumped out of his skin. The Nicabate flew out of his mouth and hit Margaret Thatcher square in the eye. "Mr Hockey, wake up!" someone was yelling outside the door. "It's 7.27. You've got to deliver the Budget in three minutes!"

❖

A train from Washington, DC bound for New York City derails and crashes near Philadelphia, with eight passengers killed and over 200 injured. Meanwhile, Bill Shorten delivers his Budget In Reply speech.

Gravy train wreck

Financial Review
16/5/15

The world was shocked on Thursday night when a gravy train carrying the hopes and dreams of the Australian Labor Party came crashing off the rails around 7.30pm on the outskirts of Billadelphia. Labor party officials and other fellow travellers claim to have witnessed several fatalities in the upper echelons of the first-class carriage, describing horrific scenes of mangled rhetoric and broken syntax.

Amongst the unbelievable devastation, the credibility of the entire opposition was crushed beyond recognition, fiscal responsibility was tossed out the window, and numerous reputations were spotted littering the freezing foreshores of Lake Burley Griffin. One terrified victim was almost unrecognisable, apart from his unique pronunciation of the words "nuffink" and "wiv", as he lay on the ground in a mass of overblown promises, ludicrous tax-cuts and laughable concessions.

"It is an absolute disastrous mess," local mayor Anthony 'Albo' Nutter told reporters. "I have never seen anything like this in my entire life."

Many more were injured when the gravy train, hurtling from Lower Surplus to Greater Deficit, derailed at Budget Junction in the working-class suburb of Tradies Right-Offs exactly eighteen months into the three-year trip.

"That was the moment disaster struck. We came completely unstuck when we hit the Coalition's small business package on Tuesday night which everyone was raving about, even the ABC. We suddenly felt the ground shake and our entire world flipped over."

Passengers spoke of the chaos when Labor's entire "unfairness" strategy abruptly careered off the tracks, with mobile phones and laptop computers flying off the shelves.

The damage from the derailment is expected to run into billions of dollars, as small business people rush to take advantage of the unexpected windfall. Rorting and looting of paid parental leave schemes is also believed to be widespread.

Officials declined to speculate on the precise cause of Thursday night's train wreck, though some experts suggest it may have been caused by an unexpected sharp turn to the left which occurred in exactly the same location only 48 hours earlier. According to witnesses, cracks were clearly visible in the age of entitlement when the Hockey Express, with 123 members of the Coalition clinging on for dear life, shook violently as it went into an abrupt U-turn the previous Tuesday evening in the same place at the same time, yet somehow narrowly survived. "This sent out all the wrong signals," said Mr Nutter. "After the Coalition's Budget, Bill was all over the place. He panicked and went completely off the rails. Five per cent tax cuts! Hundreds of thousands of free university places! Free 'digital coding' lessons for kiddies! Tax breaks for maths teachers! Half a billion dollar innovation fund! The nightmare just went on and on. We thought it would never end. It was like time had stopped and we were back in 2008."

One expert warned casualty estimates were only preliminary, hinting at a higher toll to the Labor leader's likelihood of survival.

"We thought this Budget In Reply speech would be the light at the end of the hill, er, I mean tunnel," said one victim. "But it was just another oncoming Labor train wreck."

Mr Nutter couldn't confirm whether all those on board had been accounted for, though spin doctors insisted the scene was safely under the control of Nurse Pliber-tracks and Mr Train-whistle-Bowen-up-around-the-bend.

Some of the injured — many of whom already had blood on their hands from previous leadership spills in 2010 and 2013 — were unable to shift from under the weight of increasingly negative opinion polls. A large metal dagger was seen protruding from the back of one of the passengers, though it was unclear whether this was a result of the accident or was in preparation for the ALP's national rail conference in July. Dazed members of caucus were seen wandering around, wobbling in their support for Mr Shorten.

Others pointed out that if Mr Shorten hadn't landed on such a soft interview with Leigh Sales the damage could have been far worse.

Another fellow traveller, Mr Palmer, who was gorging himself in the dining car at the time of the crash (and the rest of the time as well), said the gravy train seemed to be going along quite smoothly until one by one people started jumping ship and leaving him stranded all alone with his Oriental Express companion. Passengers also described seeing a brash, uncouth Tasmanian woman and a well-hung "brick with eyes" kicking out the windows trying to escape and set up their own party.

The crash was the latest in a series of accidents that have plagued federal politicians from both sides of the tracks over the last couple of years. Experts say that the damage to taxpayers' wallets will take decades to repair.

❖

Thieves in London break into the Hatton Garden Safe Deposit Company, an underground safe deposit facility, and steal up to £200 million; supposedly the largest burglary in English legal history. Meanwhile, the Shadow Treasurer comes unstuck at the National Press Club, whilst the opposition leader flounders badly.

Heist

Financial Review
23/5/15

The world heaved a sigh of relief this week following the arrest of a notorious gang of jewel thieves responsible for what is widely regarded as one of the richest hauls in criminal history. The audacious heist, which is believed to have netted the villains several billions of dollars worth of precious savings stolen from the deposit boxes of little old ladies and widowed pensioners, originally had police completely baffled — but not for long.

The break-in took place only a few weeks ago at the Shorten Gardens Safety Deposit Company, when the gang — rumoured to number among nine of the country's most highly experienced swindlers — snuck into the vaults under cover of the Budget and raided a trove of retirees' superannuation savings. Said one expert criminologist: "This mob has form. They knew exactly what they were after. They've done it before and they'll do it again. Nobody's safe is safe anymore."

Cunningly, the gang used a decoy method to disguise their actual intentions, with police believing the gang leader himself was responsible for delivering a "dummy" Budget In Reply speech that confused the pundits while the hardcore villains got on with the real job. Once inside the public's trust, the thieves were able to help themselves at their leisure, as they smashed their way into long-held tax concessions, hard earned savings, pathetically low interest rate term deposits, dwindling shares, assets, family homes, children's inheritances and other irreplaceable precious items.

"We probably would hav got away wiv it," said the man many believe to be the gang's notorious leader, Bill 'Pie-face' Shorty, speaking from under a blanket as he was led away from Bowen Street Magistrates Court, "if it wozzn't for vat idiot Chris. Now we've got nuffink."

Forensic experts believe he was referring to the foolhardy appearance of a shadowy figure — presumed to be the shadowy gang's shadowy Treasurer — at the so-called National Crime Club lunch on Wednesday, a regular gathering of drunken gangsters, left wing anarchists and other members of the Canberra Press Gang. Unable to control his excitement, Chris Bowen-straight-to-jail-do-not-pass-go boasted about the genius of his plans and the unprecedented size of his haul.

"It's the breath-taking arrogance that always gets them in the end," said one seasoned crime reporter. "All you have to do is sit back quietly and wait. Before you know it, one of them will crack and start flashing the cash around. They just can't help themselves; they try and show some restraint but it's not in their DNA. Next thing they're handing out the loot to all their mates — to the unions, to minority groups, to public servants, to the unemployed and anyone else they want to bribe or impress. Last time around, one bloke got so carried away we caught him red-handed handing out $900 cheques to dead people."

The tell-tale sign came when hidden microphones captured Chris Blowen'-the-Lot making sly, underhand references to his plans to organise another lucrative carbon tax heist. "That's when we knew we had him. This is the same gang that pulled that whole climate change swindle a few years back and everybody got badly burned. Particularly little old ladies with electricity bills, small business people, tradies and so on. We weren't going to sit around and let these crooks get away with that kind of scam again."

Meanwhile, in other news this week federal opposition leader Bill Shorten explained to reporters why it is necessary for compassionate Australians to allow Australian jihadists who have been busy beheading people in Syria for the last couple of years to now return home to Australia in order to lead productive, fulfilling lives and become proud, rehabilitated members of our vibrant multicultural community.

"Basically, wot we hav seen wiv these poor boys — and let's face it, wiv these poor girls too coz I believe in equality of the sexes and we shouldn't discriminate against anyone just because they wear a hiccup, I mean a kneecap, er, I mean a jihad, um, I mean wiv a scarf on their head although I fink we need a conscience vote for marriage equality coz I believe climate change is real and so I fink we need to cut taxes by 5% which is wot I said wiv my superb speech the uvver night and that is why Chris needs to raise taxes as much as poss... er, so vat, um, so vat we continue to hold Tony Abbott to account and bring our boys home from the trenches of Syria and Iraq where they have been doing nuffink except helpink innocent people whose heads they chopped off get a proper chance at a caring and compassionate and, er, sustainable, and, ah, um... where's Tanya?"

❖

The Treasurer is ambushed by a young lady and a giant tampon on live TV, the Leader of the Opposition comes out of the closet on same sex marriage, and the first inquest into the Lindt café siege puts awkward questions to the Attorney General about a letter he received.

The Tampon affair

Financial Review
30/5/15

The world of politics erupted in a furore this week when a large Norwegian freight vessel, the MV Tampon, appeared on the horizon and sailed directly into Australia's stormy political waters. The vessel's captain, Tony 'Qanda' Jones, refused to turn around and instead insisted on delivering his cargo of major distractions and political gaffes directly to the 24/7 news cycle. Horrified witnesses reported seeing the re-structuring of the GST struggling to survive, whereas others claimed the Age of Entitlement had been successfully resuscitated thanks to the timely appearance of the Tampon.

Speaking from Canberra, a defiant Prime Minister Tony Howard refused to offer any help, maintaining: "I will decide what populist measures get put to the Australian people and the circumstances in which they are put there."

Many critics were quick to accuse the government of deliberately taking advantage of the so-called "Tampon affair" in order to stoke fears of PMT in the community prior to calling a snap election. "We should broaden the base of the PMT so it applies to everyone, not just women," a spokesman explained.

The MV Tampon was initially spotted on Monday night lurking in the Ultimo darkness some thirty feet north-north-west of the Treasurer on the *Q&A* panel, before it abruptly changed course and took centre stage. Eager to flee from awkward questions about his rental arrangements, Mr Hockey, a public servant suffering from extreme fiscal fatigue, was quick to clamber on board the Tampon. A distress call was relayed to Canberra within minutes:

"SOS! Mayday! Policies overboard! This evening at 22.13.45 a group of unruly federal Treasurers, numbering just one, grabbed hold of a large number of awkward GST exemptions involving women's hygiene products and started to throw them overboard one by one. They are still floating out there on social media and all over the news cycle."

An unrepentant Mr Hockey remained defiant. "I was drowning out there. And Tony Jones refused to throw me a lifeline. I had no choice other than to grab hold of the first thing that floated by. Unfortunately it just happened to be a giant tampon, but at least it was still in the wrapper."

Meanwhile, in other major distractions this week, opposition leader Bill 'Willy' Shorten stunned the commentariat with his sudden announcement that he plans to introduce a 'Marriage of Convenience' Bill into parliament at the earliest opportunity, possibly even Monday.

"Nuffink in the world today is as important as people being able to hop into bed wiv each uvver no matter wot side they bat for," he told a stunned media conference. "Wiv my Marriage of Convenience Bill I can snuggle up to whoever I want to, even a person I loathe of the opposite sex, such as my good friend Tanya here."

Supporters of Bill's Bill have long agitated for the right of members of the right faction of Labor's far left to be officially allowed to join together with members of the soft left faction of the moderate hard left in order to partake of any available support for the most popular left-wing issues of the day, such as gay marriage and Palestine.

Explaining the details of his proposed Bill, Mr Shorten maintained that it was only fair that he had the same legal rights as Tanya Pliber-samesek to steal the issue of marriage equality for his own political ends. Speaking to reporters from his local pie-in-the-sky shop, a forthright and determined Mr Short-of-ideas said: "I hav no idea wot Tanya said about carpet-munchers and shirt-lifters shagging each uvver senseless and, er, I mean, about the sanctity of marriage equality, but I agree wiv every word she said."

In other news this week, a defiant federal attorney-general Senator George Bandaid denied that he had been irresponsible in not passing on the contents of a bizarre letter he received late last year to the appropriate authorities. "It was obvious that the letter was written by a complete fruit-cake who was trying to extort $350,000 out of the taxpayer and hand it over to some asylum-seeking wife-murderer. I simply tossed it in the bin and forgot about it," he explained. "And that wasn't the first time Professor Triggs had written to me either."

Meanwhile, Sheik Taj Halal bin Bankstown stunned Australia this week with his shock admission that he had tried to warn successive governments about the dangers of Islamic radicalisation many years ago. "I said at the time that if we wanted a secure, peaceful and successful multicultural Australia then the last thing we should do is let any of those scumbag Shia bastards in and if we did we'd have no choice other than to chop their heads off," he explained.

❖

An irate Prime Minister Abbott confronts his colleagues over an explosion of leaks detailing a cabinet split on national security and proposals to strip Australians with proven links to terrorism of their citizenship. Meanwhile, at the Royal Commission into the unions, the Leader of the Opposition fails to answer questions over allegations raised about false membership drives at his former union — and the ABC have a new political thriller.

Cabinet leaks

Financial Review
6/6/15

The world of politics was rocked to its core this week following an explosive number of leaks from an unprecedented number of cabinet ministers, all of whom leaked that they had nothing whatsoever to do with the unprecedented number of recent cabinet leaks.

Speaking exclusively on strict condition of anonymity, a senior communications cabinet minister emphatically denied that he had anything to do with ever leaking anything ever under any circumstances from any cabinet whatsoever.

"Seeing as you ask, allow me to emphatically deny ever having leaked the fact that if the public had even the slightest inkling of what really goes on behind cabinet doors they would come to precisely the same conclusion that Lucy and, er, I mean that my good wife who shall remain anonymous and I have repeatedly come to; namely, that Tony is a war-mongering right wing nut job who wants to strip innocent terrorists of their underwear, er, I mean of their citizenship and parade them naked through Martin Place on Australia Day and the only way to stop him is by making me prime minister."

However, other senior cabinet ministers have also denied being behind the recent cabinet leaks, leading to intense speculation among commentators as to who is really not behind the unprecedented number of leaks that haven't ever occurred.

Speaking exclusively via my answerphone message service, a senior cabinet minister who spoke to this paper on the strict condition that I never reveal her name, said she is horrified by the recent number of leaks and categorically denies having anything whatsoever to do with any of them. "One of the advantages of being the only woman in cabinet is that I learned shorthand at secretary school in Perth before I joined that law firm so I've got the ability to jot down exactly who said what to whom and when they said it," the anonymous cabinet minister whom I refuse to identify in any way whatsoever said via email from wherever she's gadding around the globe at the moment. "What is abundantly clear from a close study of my detailed notes which I have just sent you is that Tony is about as popular as herpes on a honeymoon and it's high time we made Malcolm or me prime minister."

However, reports leaked to a popular Sydney talkback radio show from another anonymous cabinet minister who appears on it every week have led to feverish speculation that the real

2015 — The Year of Betrayal

purpose of the unprecedented number of leaks coming out of cabinet is a smokescreen designed to discredit those who have never leaked anything out of cabinet ever before. "What we're seeing here, Ray," the senior cabinet minister said live on air on condition of strict anonymity, "is a mad frenzy of lunatics like my close colleagues and good friends Julie and Malcolm sticking the boot into me just in case there's another leadership spill when of course everyone knows, Ray, that the job's already mine by a country mile. See you at the footy mate."

"Yeah see ya Scotty mate. Oops. I wasn't supposed to mention yer name. I'll cut that bit out later."

Meanwhile, speaking on strict condition that somebody attaches his name to any leadership speculation whatsoever, the Treasurer sent a group email to anybody who would take it denying that he had any leadership ambitions. "This isn't about me. It's about how well Tony and I have rebounded, er, I mean how well the economy has rebounded since my massive spending splurge, er, I mean since my brilliant Budget. Any talk of me succeeding Tony is pure speculation at this stage... or at least I desperately hope it is."

In other news this week, former union leader Bill Backstab denied that he had ever had anything to do with rigging any elections in any way or at any time and that there was no truth whatsoever in the smears that he had signed up an entire netball team and half the workforce of Victoria in order to artificially inflate his numbers. "Wiv these allegations there is nuffink anyone can pin on me and anyfink I say will be used in evid... er, in a, er, no hang on, vat was about sumfink else. Anyway, just coz Albo won the popular vote hands down doesn't mean I don't agree wiv every word he says," he said, standing on a milk-crate at an artificially inflated union picket line.

Meanwhile, fans of the cult TV show *The Killing* were delighted to see it return to the ABC. "The plots are unbelievable," said one delighted fan. "There's this red-head man-hating liar who knits her own jumpers and this psychopathic bully and they both go around stabbing each other in the back. There's nothing like it on telly anymore. I've really missed it!"

The Treasurer gets in trouble for pointing out that in order to buy a good home in a major city you need a good job. Meanwhile, the Royal Commission into union corruption grinds on.

Get a job

Financial Review
13/6/15

In order to buy a home in Sydney or Melbourne, the Treasurer has advised that you need a "good job" with "good money". But what is a good job and what sort of home can you buy? This week, Australia's top financial paper looks at the most lucrative jobs available and where they can take you.

1. *Cleaning industry union official:* One of the quickest and easiest ways to get good money is to take it off somebody else. In this exciting and fulfilling role you get to go out to lunch with the boss and strike a deal on behalf of the workers that gives them far less pay than they would otherwise have got under the normal awards if you hadn't interfered! The boss makes squillions and then rewards you by signing up loads of union members without telling them so not only do you get the membership fees but you also get to boost your power base and leap into politics!

2. *Building industry union official*: If it's a new home in some trendy inner-city Melbourne suburb that you're after, this is a very good job that'll get you there quicker than almost any other. But first, grab yourself a girlfriend who's a lawyer, get her to set up a company using the name of your union, go to a large construction company and get them to give you loads of cash, go with your girlfriend to an auction and buy the house of your dreams, with a nice backyard handy for burying any leftover cash. And if the house needs any renos, why not give Bill the Greek a buzz?

2015 — The Year of Betrayal

3. *Construction union boss*: This is a very good job with very good pay even if you're told you have to step aside in which case you can take annual leave instead. Don't worry, nobody will complain. Not if they know what's good for them.

4. *Health services union official (1)*: people are always getting sick so there's never a shortage of people going to hospital needing their bedpans cleaned, bottoms wiped, urine-soaked sheets changed and so on. But don't worry — they're the bad jobs. The good job is the one that means you don't ever have to get your hands dirty. And it comes with very, very good money. Simply take all the union membership fees, pop them onto a black credit card, and start getting used to the high life! Best of all, you'll now be able to afford a roof over your head and a comfy bed for the night in the swankiest inner-city Sydney suburb, complete with your very own choice of our most luscious Ukrainian, Thai or Parisian escort girls ready and eager to service your mortgage in any way you choose. (Why not try all three at once? Money's no object, after all!)

5. *Health services union official (2)*: if a beach house up on the ritzy northern beaches is more your scene, this is the job for you. A good job that pays good money to not only you but your extended family as well! First, get a close family friend to set up a printing firm to make business cards and personal stationery and the like. Then get them to invoice your health union for whatever figure pops into your head for printing costs! While they're at it, get the printer to print up some anonymous brown paper bags capable of holding wads and wads of hundred dollar bills. You'll need them! The only catch is that if you forget to destroy all the records before it's too late you might find yourself having to settle for a small windowless room in a Goulburn same-sex sharing accommodation facility for a number of years.

6. *Union official national conference delegate*: This is a very good job and the money is also very good if you play your cards right. Remember, this is a numbers game so the trick is to make sure you have as many union members as you possibly can. The more the merrier! The Labor party values

innovation and creativity, so don't be afraid to be a bit imaginative about it. For example, why not sign up your local netball team or tiddlywinks club? You don't even need to tell them! The best bit is once you've got the numbers right, you're well on your way to that beautiful harbourside mansion in Kirribilli or the freshly painted Lodge. No-one can stop you! (Not even Albo.)

7. *Human Rights Guru*: Great job, great pay. And the best bit is nobody can sack you — even if they think you're as crazy as Sydney house prices!

❖

As the Cannes Film Festival gets underway, the ABC releases the second part of their popular political thriller.

Cannes-berra

Financial Review
19/6/15

David: So here we are, Margaret, back again at Cannes-berra for the annual Film Festival. Unusually this year all the talk is about just one film...
Margaret: Oh absolutely David. And I'm so excited, because in a moment we get to chat to two of the stars...
David: We're talking of course about *The Killing Season*, cult director Sarah Ferguson's latest action-packed blockbuster, also known as "Kill Bill 3". Blood, gore, betrayal, comedy, tragedy and farce. It's got the lot. It's even based on a true story! You spoke to two of the lead actors earlier... let's take a look...
Margaret: And joining me now is Tony Smurke. Tony, you play a fascinating character in this film, tell us all about it. How did you approach the character?
Smurke: Well, yes, thank you Margaret. I play a slippery, unscrupulous, devious and totally untrustworthy Labor frontbencher known as "The Snake in the Grass". When Sarah first approached me I thought, oh well, this is just your average caucus thriller and I didn't pay much attention...
Margaret: So what drew you to the role in particular?

2015 — The Year of Betrayal

Smurke: Well, when Sarah explained that my character was even more perverse than your normal Labor backstabber, in that I actually relish the act of betraying and killing my leader, I thought, well, this is really interesting... this is me! I can do this!

Margaret: So how did you prepare for the role?

Smurke: Well I practiced my most supercilious smirk, which I do every day in front of Question Time, just so that whenever the camera's on me I have this lopsided grin on my face. It can be quite unnerving, particularly when I pore over every gory detail of the plotting and scheming and pick at the entrails of the killing...

Margaret: Yes, it made my flesh crawl!

Smurke: Thank you! I rely on that sense of revulsion to convey to the audience how futile and pointless and without justification the actual slaying was, and to express my, I mean my character's, complete lack of morals and principles.

Margaret: Yes, that certainly comes across. It's almost as if you want to build your part in the whole killing process, like some kind of psychopathic narcissist. Is that fair?

Smurke: Oh absolutely! I agonised over whether to appear at all in the film, but in the end my vanity got the better of me.

Margaret: And your favourite scene?

Smurke: Well, we had to do several takes, but I'm particularly proud of the bit where I walk along the corridor and down a staircase on my way to stab Kevin in the back without actually saying anything. I did it all with my facial expressions! As a method actor I've always felt that what you don't say is more important than what you do say. That way you can deny it if the "merde" hits the...

Margaret: Which it did. Thank you Tony, a totally convincing performance. And joining me now is legendary ham actor Sam Dastardly, or "Dasher" as your character is called...

Sam: Hi Margaret!

Margaret: Now, Sam, your role is absolutely pivotal to the plot — and indeed to the plotters. In the past you've always been typecast as a sort of Mr Bean lookalike. Does this film make you a serious player now?

Sam: Absolutely! I even do all my own stunts, like the scene where I sit on a bench and make a phone call that will destroy the electability of the Labor party for decades to come. That took a lot out of me. My credibility in particular.

Margaret: It sure did! But what I enjoy most about this film is that nobody ever bothers to question what gives you, a nerdy little oik from the back office, the right to bring down a popular first-term prime minister? Is it your sense of entitlement, your absolute power...?
Sam: You're spot on, Margaret, that's what drives the whole narrative. Howsie and I work-shopped it for ages...
Margaret: Well, that clearly shows. Thank you. And now, David, as for the real villain...
David: You mean Kevin... or Julia?
Margaret: No, no, they're just a couple of comedians. The real mastermind... well, I won't spoil it for you but you only ever catch glimpses of him lurking in the shadows on his mobile. Whenever the killings are happening, there he is again, saying mysterious things like "I hav nuffink at all to do wiv it even though I don't know wot it is I didn't do".
David: Sounds terrific! Will there be a sequel? Will the killer get killed?
Margaret: Of course. Albo's been tipped to play the lead.

❖

As the Pope lectures the world about climate change, Labor prepare for their upcoming 47th National Conference.

Torture museum

Financial Review
26/5/15

Looking for something more daring for your next Canberra trip? Bored of seeing the same old faces at the Portrait Gallery? Can't cope with another visit to Questacon? Have we got the thing for you! Twinned with Amsterdam's famous Museum of Torture, the latest must-see spot on the crowded Canberra tourist circuit is the macabre Museum of Labor, opened last week by avid knife-collector and curator Bill "Switchblade" Shorten.

Strictly for the strong of stomach, this unique museum displays some of the most gruesome methods used to torment innocent

victims of the Australian public throughout the ages.
The Museum layout is a maze of small, dark smoke-filled backrooms accessible only by joining a union, but don't worry, Bill will sign you up for one even if he doesn't tell you about it. Each room houses one or two wax dummies of union officials (not to be mistaken with the actual wax dummies) as well as famous implements of torture which are usually locked behind glass but can be brought out for special celebrations such as the National Conference in July. The dark lighting and theatrical design of the museum adds to the scary mood. You never know who'll pop up out of the shadows wielding a bloodstained knife or which direction they'll come at you from!

Highlights of the Museum include:

The Rack: (Also known as The Kevin Chair.) This is a complicated set of medieval rules and regulations based on an arcane algorithm which the Labor Leader is forcefully strapped into, giving him or her a false sense of security, whilst the plotters get on with sharpening their implements behind him in the darkness.

Emily's List: A sadistic ritual whereby women of extremely limited talent and ability are placed on a pedestal well above their natural position and forced to stand for parliament. The results are too scary to reproduce here.

Scold's Bridle: Particularly popular with female members of the party, most of whom have been drawn from the sinister Emily's List (see above), the Scold's Bridle gives the wearer a sense of virtuous moral superiority as they scold the public about imaginary issues such as misogyny, feminism, looking at your watch and "causing offence".

Heretic's Fork: This cruel and unusual punishment was devised specifically to weed out heretics and those who have yet to toe the party line. Local MPs must go into the *Q&A* torture chamber (see next page) and swear that they "believe" in climate change and have "changed their mind" and now passionately support gay marriage.

The Mangler: A bizarre form of torture guaranteed to reduce even the most hardened listener to tears within minutes, the Mangler takes perfectly usable words from the English language and mangles them beyond recognition. Make sure Curator Bill gives you his own personal demonstration! We guarantee you'll be "screamink" for mercy long before the final "wiv" and the umpteenth "nuffink".

The Brain Fryer: Cunningly used to fry even the most intelligent brain, these meaningless utterances will literally do your head in; such as "I don't know what she said but I agree wiv every word she said", "Everybody is somebody" and "If you don't know where you're going any road will get you there".

Mass dunkings: A vicious trick in which an entire generation were drowned in Labor debt with no escape.

The Q&A torture chamber: Your heart will literally be pounding as you enter this scary chamber, which attempts to replicate the Spanish Inquisition of the middle ages. As you take your place at the large round table, keep an eye out for where the real danger lurks — in the audience! Who knows what convicted criminals or terrorism supporters are waiting to pounce!

The Julia Cradle: Closely related to impalement, this gruesome punishment entails having the victim sit in his office, after which he is tied down by lies onto a "wedge of false hope" with the intent of stretching the victim's leadership over the shortest period of time, slowly impaling them on their own programmatic specificity and psychopathic dysfunctionality. To add to the overall chaos and ritual humiliation, the victim was usually flown to Copenhagen a few months earlier and stripped of all political and moral credibility. Unfortunately, the device was rarely washed clean, and often re-employed three years later on the person who originally used it!

Iron maiden: (Also known as The Pliber Stocks.) This torture device consisted of a shadow cabinet with an unhinged front and blood-splattered interior, sufficient enough to enclose at least a dozen undergraduates. Once inside its vice-like grip, the ministers would be unable to move without exposing their hard left, socialist, anti-capitalist, pro-Palestinian leanings and extreme Green sympathies.

Papal bull: This unique form of psychological torture was eagerly adopted by the Labor party after they realised with astonishment that the Pope was spouting exactly the same eco-claptrap as they were.

❖

The ABC are, yet again, accused of political bias following the inclusion of a man charged with terrorism offences being included in the studio audience to ask a question.

Bias? What bias?

Financial Review
4/7/15

"And you can join the conversation by following the twitter hashtag at the bottom of your screen. But our first question tonight relates to the vexed and controversial issue of whether or not Israel is a proto-fascist, racist, totalitarian state that should never have been allowed to exist in the first place. With us in the audience we have Otto Adolf Eichmann, a reformed and rehabilitated Obersturmbannführer. Otto, you spent your retirement years being mercilessly hounded by the Israeli government until you were illegally kidnapped from Brazil by sinister agents acting, I believe, on behalf of the Zionist entity, and on top of which you were twice deprived of your basic human rights, firstly by being flown illegally to Tel Aviv where you had to suffer the ignominy of a so-called fair trial and then of course by being hung. Otto, what is your perspective on Israel? Should a Jewish state even be allowed to exist? Or did the entire world make a huge mistake, in your opinion, by creating a phony and entirely illegitimate state out of what was clearly the once proud, historic and noble State of Palestine?"

"Ja."

"Thank you Otto, and now moving on, because I think we've given that topic more than enough time for tonight, I'd like to discuss the vexed and controversial issue of climate change and the way the Abbott government is threatening the entire eco-system of the Great Barrier Reef and indeed the survival of the entire human race due to its disgraceful slandering of the lucrative renewable energy industry courtesy of Tony Abbott's extraordinarily defamatory attack on the visual appeal of windmills. And I'll take a question from the audience on this topic. Um, the gentleman with the grey beard and the dark glasses, I believe you have a question for the panel?"

"Thank you, yes. Several years ago the highly respected and incredibly visionary Australian of the Year Professor Flannery warned that global warming would lead to catastrophic climate change which of course we are seeing now all around us just as I predicted. Is it not the case that I, er, I mean Professor Flannery was completely correct in every single one of his predictions and that he should immediately be reinstated as National Climate Change Commissioner on three days a week with my full salary plus compensation plus inflation plus super?"

"Thank you, Tim. I'll take that as a very astute and pertinent comment because we're running out of time and we've more than covered that topic tonight. But I'd just like to address another issue in which we are seeing the Abbott government floundering to the point of chaotic dysfunction with reports of cabinet ministers literally gouging out each others eyeballs and that of course is the vexed and highly controversial issue of marriage equality, or gay marriage as some people prefer to offensively label this hugely popular and emotional cause. I'll take a question from a random member of the audience. The woman at the back in the blue dress with the, er, neatly trimmed black eard. Yes, you sir, er, I mean ma'am, er..."

ank you sweetie. I think we should all be able to marry
ver we want to so long as we love each other and I think
bott is actually suppressing his true feelings because of his
ve upbringing, I mean, he used to wear a frock didn't he?"

2015 — The Year of Betrayal

"Well, I'll take that as a comment but I'm afraid we won't have time to go to the panel on that one because we've got a lot more to cover tonight particularly the vexed and controversial issues currently arising out of the so-called Royal Commission into Trade Union Corruption which is, of course, nothing more than a vicious Abbott government attack upon the basic human right to join whichever trade union Bill Shorten wants you to whether you agree to it or not. I'll go to the audience on this one. The gentleman there in the yellow vest with the knuckle-dusters and the large wrench. You have a question for the panel, I believe?"

"Get nicked."

"OK, well, I'll take that as a comment, but before we go I'd like to take a question on the vexed and controversial issue of impartiality at the ABC and whether or not the panel agrees that the Abbott government is engaged in a vicious political attack not only on the national broadcaster but on all progressive and fair-minded Australians that can only be described as cultural genocide and our question tonight comes from a random member of the audience who is a well-respected public servant who has devoted her entire career to compassionately improving the basic human rights of the entire nation. Gillian?"

❖

In the run up to the Labor party National Conference, delegate's scramble to declare their conversion to same sex marriage, debate a new policy on turning boats around, and the punters wonder whether the Leader of the Opposition can survive.

Delegates' guide

Financial Review
24/7/15

Dear Delegate,
Welcome to the 47th Labor Party National conference.

This Conference promises to be one of the most memorable and inspirational in recent times.

But before we get started, here are a few simple and safe housekeeping tips to ensure we all get along together just fine and dandy with no ghastly PR stuff-ups.

Security: Sharp objects, such as knives, switchblades, daggers and other body-piercing implements capable of causing severe spinal damage or back pain must be handed in at the front desk, where our security officer Ms Pliberstab will ensure they are kept safely out of harm's way until she can put them to good use later on.

Dress code: Union officials and other key delegates are invited to dress in a smart yet casual fashion, preferably in a cheap-looking shiny suit with appropriately baggy pockets for the comfortable yet discreet storage of thick wads of bank-notes, IOUs, knuckle-dusters and large brown, anonymously-labelled envelopes.

Press and media seating arrangements: For those paid-up members of the Labor Party who also coincidentally might just happen to be editors, announcers, writers, news anchors, camera operators, script-writers, researchers, journalists, production members, sub-editors, cartoonists, typesetters, graphic designers, dispatch riders, tea-ladies, or in any other way vaguely associated with full-time employment at the ABC please make your way directly to the Platinum Pass seats at the front of the hall.

Finding your way around: National conferences are vibrant, exciting places full of the great diversity of compassionate individuals and keen minds you would expect of today's progressive and enlightened Labor Party. Make sure you mingle and make the most of this exciting opportunity to meet new like-minded friends and faces. (Note: a comprehensive list of who you wouldn't be seen dead with can be obtained from your friendly factional adviser.)

Language: It is understandable that some minority communities within the broader harmonious Labor family take offence at the use of certain insensitive phrases, which have consequently been banned from being uttered within the Conference area itself. These include the words: Rudd, Gillard, Swan, Kevin, '07, surplus, carbon, tax, mining, tax (again!), building, education, revolution, batts, pink, killing, season.

Burkes: There are many Burkes within today's sophisticated, inclusive Labor Party, and it is wise to know one Burke from the other in order to avoid any unpleasantness or confusion. For former Speakers, follow the loud whining sound coming from the Emily's List Stand. For leadership contenders, check out the Burke Support Group at the Friends of Hamas and Hezbollah Stand in the Palestinian Free Love, Peace and Harmony Pavilion.

Burqas: These may be worn within the Conference area at all times in order for delegates to express their solidarity with the enlightened and compassionate feminist policies of the modern multicultural movement within Labor's western suburbs branches.

Carrs: There are many Carrs within today's economically-inclusive Labor Party, but it is wise to know one Carr from the other if you wish to avoid a) getting bored to death with a tedious speech about government subsidies or b) being bored to death with a tedious speech about the health properties of organically-processed yak's yoghurt.

Inclusive economics: This is a popular, modern, progressive Labor phrase that must be used at all times within the Conference area as a mandatory replacement for the following words: Marxism, Socialism, Communism, Trotskyism, Stalinism, Maoism, Castroism, nationalisation, forced, collectivism, redistribution, wealth, anti-capitalism, economic, vandalism, theft.

Climate change: At the moment the climate is broadly in favour of Mr Shorten but Ms Plibersek expects this to change rapidly and dramatically over the course of the weekend.

Boat tow-backs: Boats may be turned around only when it is safe to say so within earshot of a News Corp journalist.

Marriage Equality: If you haven't already announced your genuine, heartfelt and dramatic conversion in favour of Gay Marriage, this is your last chance to do so before pre-selection.

Fergusons: This is a common name once associated with the proud heritage of the great history of the legendary and noble Labor Party, but it is prudent not to mix your Fergusons up if you wish to survive the weekend intact. Here's a quick and easy way to remember one Ferguson from the other: Laurie, God. Martin, Devil. Sarah, traitorous presenter from hell.

Fringe activities: Why not hone your acting skills in one of our Slimebuckets' Re-enactment Master Classes with renowned thespians Sam Dastardly and Tony Burqa demonstrating how to make a complete goose of yourself on national TV?

Canteen: The Conference canteen is open to all delegates for the entire duration of the Conference. Plastic cutlery is freely available, sharper implements can be found located in Mr Shorten's spinal column.

❖

A piece of debris and a suitcase wash up on the beaches of the island of Reunion, and are deemed to almost certainly be from the missing Malaysian airline MH370.

Flotsam and jetsam

Financial Review
1/8/15

The world was stunned and thrilled to learn the news this week that a fragment of Labor's economic credibility has been washed up on a remote Indian Ocean island. Natives of an isolated palm-fringed tropical tax haven called Reunion Corruption were spotted carrying a battered object that they had found lying discarded on the beach, which, according to experts, could actually be the remnants of Labor's missing economic credentials.

ALP015's fiscal credibility vanished into thin air several years ago and not a single trace of it has been seen since. Indeed, many regard the ability of the ALP to remain aloft and up in the polls whilst running for years on empty as one of the great aviation mysteries of all time.

"First the wheels came off, then the wings came off, and then they panicked and just jettisoned every economically responsible platform that they had ever had," said one forensic expert. "So it comes as a real shock to find a tiny piece still intact and bobbing around in the ocean after all these years."

Other experts were quick to query the veracity of the discovery, expressing doubt that the ALP's missing economic credibility could ever be located again. "The tides of history have moved on. Labor's socialist fantasies and "compassionate" spending have been swirling around and around in circles for years now and will ultimately drag the economy down to unimaginable depths from which there is probably no return."

However, other commentators pointed out that Labor's fuselage design, based on an old Hawker-Keating model from the last century, had drifted so far from its original economic moorings and taken such a battering over the years that it would be impossible to salvage it. "First the rudd came completely unstuck, then it went into a redheaded nose-dive which of course they had no hope of surviving."

Experts unanimously agree that the disaster of Labor's economic management couldn't have happened without deliberate human involvement. "Left to itself a modern economy will run along perfectly smoothly. What's clear is that this economy was deliberately tampered with. Whoever had their hands on the wheel was trying not to alert the voters as to what they were really up to. Economies just don't dump their surpluses and turn their wealth-generation systems off and then introduce a carbon tax all at the same time without someone being at the controls," a source explained. "Somebody made this disaster happen."

A major search for the stricken economic credentials culminated in a bizarre national conference last week, in which a variety of conspiracy theories were put forward by distraught delegates, most of whom refuse to believe that the party is finished until they see the wreckage for themselves at the next federal poll. Many cling desperately to the forlorn hope that the party can survive by scrambling onto floating fads such as gay marriage, climate change, Indigenous recognition and the republic.

"There's so much flotsam and jetsam out there, just waiting for us to grab onto. If we cling on long enough, there's still hope" said one tearful woman, Tanya Plibersunk, who lost her entire credibility over the course of the weekend and had to be comforted by a "proxy" vote.

To add to the excitement, early yesterday a mysterious piece of baggage also washed up on the island. Although it will take experts many years to determine if the item is authentic, there is speculation that the floating object is in fact part of Labor's new border protection policy. "Labor's credibility on stopping boats sunk without a trace very quickly, much like many of the boats themselves. Now we have a policy 'option' that is clearly designed to look like a boat being turned around when it is safe to do so, when of course any expert will tell you it is nothing other than a piece of useless junk that wouldn't survive five minutes under a Labor government."

An anonymous spokesman for the troubled airline has denied that the washed-up item in any way resembles "a short man wiv a dodgy union background".

Meanwhile, in other news this week, the Speaker of the House Bronwyn Bishop announced that the constant booing from the opposition benches was finally getting to her. "It's got completely out of hand," explained a spokesperson for the embattled LNP player. "It used to just be when she was in the House but now they start booing wherever she goes, even to a friend's wedding or at a local fundraiser. The booing's got to stop."

Others denied that the booing had anything whatsoever to do with race. "Bronwyn was attending a secret committee meeting that day that just happened to be at the races."

2015 — The Year of Betrayal

❖

A senior Labor figure who has been leading the attack against government MPs' expenses finds his own use of taxpayer-funded expenses and entitlements comes under the spotlight, including family trips to resorts.

In-flight entertainment

Financial Review
8/8/16

Here at Entitle-had Airways, we pride ourselves on offering our First and Business Class guests the finest taxpayer-funded entertainment. Just sit back, put your feet up, and let our highly trained staff serve you (and the kids, and the girlfriend!) a slap-up gourmet meal while you enjoy our world class in-flight entertainment. Choose from the following selection of great movies!

Catch Me If You Can: The true story of a real-life con man (played by Leonardo Di Caprio!) who passes himself off as a trustworthy politician. The laughs come thick and fast as he rushes from junket to junket with his family in tow and a supercilious smirk on his face, always one step ahead of the Man from the Finance Department. Watch out for the brilliant COMCAR chase at the end!

The Untalented Mr Berk: Working as a young man in the labour movement during the 1990s, an uninspiring, smirking fantasist (played by Matt Damon!) is seduced into joining the Labor party. Soon he's hobnobbing with all sorts of shady characters for free at the fanciest ski-lodges, where he is tricked into thinking he has a modicum of talent by a deceitful female Prime Minister (played by Cate Blanchett!). When he is promoted to the front bench he develops an even bigger smirk along with a taste for the good life, travelling by limo to all the best rock concerts with his kids, before coming badly unstuck in the end.

Way Beyond Satire

North by Northwest by South by Southeast by North Northeast: In this lightning paced, action-packed Hitchcock thriller, the hero (played by Cary Grant!) is a suave and successful executive who gets mistaken for a sanctimonious, self-righteous western suburbs politician who's been living the high life at taxpayers' expense. From New York to Monaco, from Cairns to Uluru, he gets chased by a desperate gang of journalists, politicians and a cool blonde from the Finance Department eager to pin him down on his extravagant entitlements.

Walkabout: This classic Nic Roeg psycho-thriller from the '80s helped redefine Aussie cinema, as a smug, smirking Sydney politician and his entire family get lost in the outback wandering for days on end around a five star resort at Uluru looking for the spa and champagne bar.

To Catch a Thief: Set in the luxurious all-expenses-paid principality of Monaco, this classic romantic comedy stars Cary Grant (again!) as a hypocritical front bench attack dog known as "the Berk" who is given the task of catching The Speaker out on her helicopter expenses. The plot backfires when it becomes apparent the slipperiest character is in fact "the Berk" himself.

Roman Holiday: Gregory Peck stars as a sleazy politician who takes his girlfriend, sorry, his "chief-of-staff", on a whirlwind romantic tour of Italy and Spain, all first class travel paid for by the taxpayer, before marrying her.

Four weddings, two rock concerts, a climate change conference and a funeral: Rushing from one lavish event to the next courtesy of the bankrupt taxpayer, a shifty young western suburbs politician with a distinctive smirk and preening sense of entitlement (played by Hugh Grant!) swears a lot when he gets questioned about his expenses. The final scene is a career funeral (his own?).

Plaza Suite: Hilarious Neil Simon slapstick comedy where a smirking politician rushes from one opulent hotel suite to the next hoping to order a silver service dinner for his kids without bumping into his mistress.

The Cook, the Thief, the Wife and the Kiddies: In this dark romantic comedy a smirking politician takes his wife and family to some of the best restaurants in the world courtesy of the taxpayer before finding himself almost being eaten alive by his own expenses scandal!

The Terminal: In which a hypocritical Labor frontbencher and his entire family spend months on end trapped inside some of the poshest first class lounges in dozens of airports across the globe attempting to "save the planet". (The film's title refers to the hero's leadership prospects.)

In other news this week, former prime minister Julia Gillard ran a series of ads in Australia's major newspapers in which she apologised for a major error in her recently released autobiography, *Moi Story*. "When Oi said that moi time as the first fe-moil proim minister of Austroilia had been an historic resounding success Oi obviously meant to say it had been an unmitigated disastrous foilure that nearly bankrupt the whole noition. I apologoise for any embarrassment or misunderstanding Oi moi have caused."

❖

The politics surrounding the same sex marriage debate heat up, as, after a heated party room meeting, Tony Abbott offers a plebiscite on the issue.

Same-Sex Kama Sutra

Financial Review
15/8/15

Confused about your Same-Sexuality? Worried you don't know the safest position to adopt to get the most out of the gay marriage debate? Don't be afraid any longer! Join in the fun with our Gay Lover's Guide to the Same-Sex Kama Sutra!

Fifty Shades of Non-Grey: Nowadays, with the gay marriage debate well and truly out of the closet, every ambitious politician worth their weight in rainbow badges needs flexible, versatile, ever-changing positions they can try out for size. But don't worry — you might be a grey-haired conservative from the sticks or some boring old fuddy-duddy union official but there are still dozens of ways you can get in on the act and thrust yourself into the Same-Sex Debate! Just follow our clear and simple Kama Sutra directions to the French letter.

The Penny Dreadful: Two women lie face to face, by which we mean they both tell bare-faced lies at the same time! To enhance the enjoyment, one of the women should pretend to be a prime minister while the other pretends to be her finance minister. The first woman lies face down to the electorate and says that she doesn't support gay marriage because she hates all forms of marriage and doesn't want gay people to have to suffer this dreadful institution. The other woman whispers with a straight face that although she herself is gay she believes marriage should be exclusively between a man and a woman. The fun part is trying to maintain your twin positions during six long years in power! Then when the other side gets elected, do a complete about-face and get hot and bothered trying to wriggle out of what you said before!

The Western Suburbs Contortion: First, place your feet firmly in an electorate full of recent immigrants and other religious minorities that back in their homelands would rather throw gays from the rooftops or stone lesbians alive than countenance embracing any form of Same-Sex Marriage. Then slowly twist yourself around so that you are facing the other way. Use your imagination to see how long you can maintain your support!

The Padlock (also known as the Shorten Sweet): This is all about maintaining control and prolonging your leadership. First, make sure you stimulate your caucus by teasing them and encouraging them to follow their own conscience and do and say whatever they please. Encourage them to speak up loudly! Even shout it from the rooftops! Then when they are at their most electorally aroused in eighteen months time padlock them into a binding vote.

The Rolling Plebiscite (also known as The Monk's Delight):
First, look your loved ones in the eyes and say there will never be Same-Sex Marriage on your watch. (Warning: Don't actually look AT your watch — that's misogyny!) Then, over several months, move back and forth in circular motions looking for an easy way to safely shift position. Finally, assemble a room full of sweaty farmers and nervous Nellies and tell them they can have a Plebiscite. When they get all excited, mention it won't be until after your next election. Brace yourself for a massive backlash!

The Ascent to Desire (also known as the Wentworth Member):
An extremely popular position, and one you can perform regularly and successfully in any cramped inner-city suburb. Why not try it out riding on a tram from St. Kilda to Geelong? Move as far to the left of your partners as you possibly can whilst always pretending you are firmly still on the right. Don't be afraid to use twitter or Q&A to increase the friction. It's a delicate balancing act, but at all times keep one eye on the main prize!

The Splitting Brandis: At first glance this appears to be the classic missionary position, but a closer examination reveals it to involve the legal practice of splitting hairs on constitutional affairs before you go down on all fours and kneel before the decisions of the High Court.

The Dyson (also known as the Royal Emission): An inappropriately named position, this is believed to refer to a well-known brand of vacuum cleaner. Sit in front of a room full of naked union corruption, and insist they all expose themselves. Then accept an invitation to a slap-up Liberal dinner. Make sure you suck all the political oxygen out of the air!

❖

There are calls for Commissioner Dyson Heydon to stand down from the Royal Commission into Trade Union Governance and Corruption because he accepted, and then declined, an invitation to speak at a Liberal party dinner.

Royal Commissioner

Financial Review
22/8/15

If the Royal Commissioner decides to step down, who should replace him? In the spirit of healthy bi-partisan co-operation, Labor's Parliamentary Dyson Heydon Urgent Replacement Committee have prepared a comprehensive (union-approved) shortlist of highly qualified candidates for this controversial post:

Bob 'Concrete Boots' Spanner QC: Open, fair-minded and scrupulously unbiased, Mr Spanner rose to prominence during the turbulent 1970s as a junior assistant attached to the Rooty Hill branch of the CFMEU responsible for the incorporation of non-unionised members of the local workforce into their respective chapters of affiliated branches using the most efficient appropriately persuasive recruitment methodology. Upon his release from Long Bay in 1990, Spanner opened his own private practice specialising in big business-to-union Financial Compliance Techniques.

Deirdre Drear SC: A towering intellect of the modern feminist movement, Ms Drear came to prominence during the mid-'80s when she graduated with full honours from her local inner-west TAFE under their highly-praised Feminist Intellectuals Full Honours Quota Program before successfully earning a coveted position as an intern at her local law firm under their greatly-acclaimed Feminist Intern Assistant Quota Scheme before being awarded a Senior Councillor's Assistant Deputy Position at her local Council under their globally-awarded Council's Mandatory Feminist Quota Allotment System.

Mustafa In Qu'iry QC: A pillar of western Sydney's vibrant middle-eastern community, this self-styled Sheik specialises in Labor party politics and multicultural branch recruitment strategies. Mustafa arrived in Australia in the late 2000s under the extremely popular and highly successful Rudd-Bowen Nautical Immigration Assistance Program under which he was given an iPad, an iPod, a mobile phone and a law degree. His influential paper ("Why

Sharia Law is Good For You If You Want to Keep Your Head On") has been widely circulated in Arabic* and is extensively quoted throughout western Sydney's vibrant ethnic communities where it is particularly popular as a guide on how to adapt to confusing anglo-saxon concepts such as how to vote freely in a federal election (*English translation unavailable).

Sebastian Greene SC: A veteran of the environmental movement, Mr Greene spent most of the '90s living in the upper branches of a spotted gum tree in the Nimbin State Forest studying the hallucinatory properties of the Stoned Skank. He is a globally acknowledged expert in Critical Coal Seam Gas Project Disruption Techniques and Expert-in-Residence on Catastrophic Climate Change and the Viability of Increased Renewable Energy Targets at ABC Radio National.

Professor Anne T. Semite (Syd Uni BA-S): A graduate of Sydney University's highly acclaimed and UN-approved Institute for the Unbiased Study of Peaceful Resolutions to the Genocidal Israeli Illegal Occupation of the Oppressed Palestinian Peoples (including Balcony Extension Violations and Other Morally Repugnant Jewish Settlement Atrocities Perpetrated Against Mankind), Professor Semite brings to every task a nuanced and balanced approach that allows her to fully appreciate all sides of the complex historic arguments about why Israel should be wiped off the map.

Sam Dastardly: A highly-acclaimed actor and former stunt double in the televisual reconstruction industry, Mr Dastardly came to prominence in his own mind following his successful employment of a mobile phone on a Melbourne street in 2010 in which he confirmed that the "fix was in" — as was the knife. Nowadays "the Senator" as he is fondly known to nobody specialises in grandstanding in front of globally-recognised multinational corporations with his highly-acclaimed solo performance of "Take Your Zillions And Invest Them Where The Sun Don't Shine".
Gay Wrights QC: Former truck driver and Surry Hills Bachelor of the Year, Ms Wrights is a leading lesbian holistic songwriter/experiential artist whose sustainable climate-friendly air-water sculpture "My Rainbow" won a $400,000 grant for Eco-Indigenous Transgender Equality Recognition.

Zanthia Twit SC: Highly-acclaimed international author, mummy blogger and media personality, Ms Twit came to prominence on September 7, 2013 when her highly topical feminist tweet "Tony Abbott is a f—kwit" went viral throughout the known twitterverse. Ms Twit specialises in appearances on *The Drum*, *The Project* and any other chat show that will have her where she is lauded for her forthright views and unintelligible comments.

Zappy Moolah QC: Highly controversial former terrorist suspect, prison inmate and chat show audience member, Mr Moolah specialises in drawing attention to himself by being as outrageous and offensive as he possibly can.

Tony Smurke SC: Only recently appointed an Honorary Temporary SC (Stand-in Commissioner) Mr Smurke has a long and distinguished parliamentary career where he rapidly became a world-renowned authority on world-renowned authorities, requiring extensive first class travel (accompanied by relevant staff members/family/girlfriend etc) to attend critical world-renowned summits at various world-renowned destinations throughout the, er, world.

❖

The spill approaches.

Canning

Financial Review
5/9/15

The expenses scandal has led to further leadership speculation, with leadership aspirant Malcolm Turncoat immediately leaving his harbourside mansion by limo and private jet and hopping onto a tram from St Kilda to Geelong so he could express his loyalty to his leader, Tony Abbott, and to the rest of his cabinet colleagues. "Happy to be on this tram," he tweeted, "having never been one for helicopters."

Meanwhile, in the upcoming Canning by-election, opinion polls show an unprecedented surge of support for the Liberal's surprise candidate, who was out and about in the shopping centres over the weekend. Said one excited punter: "What a sensational candidate! He's a straight-shooter and he has a fantastic service of record for this country. Yes, I'll definitely be voting for John Howard."

❖

The government decides to accept an extra 12,000 refugees from Syria.

Assimilation kit

Financial Review
12/9/15

Welcome to the wonderful land of Australia, your new Compassionate Home. In order to help you assimi... oops, sorry, we mean "integrate", here is your own personal "Lexicon to Life in Oz". Although there is no pressure on you whatsoever to learn any English, these are some popular words and phrases you may choose (or not! It's up to you!) to learn.

Christianity: In your land, this refers to a once-proud religion based on the teachings of Jesus whose followers are now routinely decapitated, raped, burnt alive or driven from their ancestral homes for adhering to their beliefs. In this country, Christianity refers to an entirely different religion whose followers are embarrassed at even the merest mention of Jesus and believe that God is actually called Gaia and digging coal out of the ground is the Original Sin.

Torture: Don't be alarmed. Although this word may bring back horrible memories of having your toenails ripped out because of your beliefs, in this country "torture" is more frequently used to describe the act of listening to members of the Labor party attempt to explain their "beliefs" on free trade, turning round boats, growing the economy and so on.

Wiv: This means "with".

Work: In your old country "work" usually meant doing some sweat-inducing labour in exchange for a handful of Syrian pounds; the precise number depending on how productive you managed to be on the day (average monthly salary $208.72). Bugger that! Here in Australia work involves traipsing from one government department to another filling in forms so you can receive as many welfare benefits are as up for grabs depending on how many sprogs you have (potential annual salary $50,000).

Marriage: In many lands you may be familiar with, marriage is usually a forced relationship between a man and a woman, a man and pre-pubescent young girl, or a man and as many women as he wants. Or all of the above! In this country, however, marriage is only legal between a man and a woman but that's all about to change because that is medieval and barbaric thinking that has no rightful place in a modern, progressive society such as ours (now yours!) and very soon marriage equality will allow you to marry your boyfriend rather than have him thrown off a rooftop.

Cultural warfare: In your country, this usually involves dynamiting ancient ruins and beheading any archeologists you find sniffing about the place. In this country, we've found it far more effective to win our culture wars simply by stopping kindergarten children from learning how to read and write and instead focusing on learning about indigenous Australians, same sex parenting, and catastrophic climate change.

Jews: In your land, Jews, Yehudi, Israelis etc (the terms are interchangeable) are cursed as unbelievers and despised as infidels who should be butchered because that's what it says in a bunch of rambling verses in the region's most popular religious book. In our land, Jews and Israelis (the terms are interchangeable) are cursed and despised because they dared to stick a couple of extra balconies on retirement villas in East Jerusalem and build a concrete wall to stop Palestinians blowing themselves up at children's birthday parties in Tel Aviv pizza parlours.

Doomsday/Armageddon/End of days/Apocalypse etc:
In your part of the world, these phrases usually refer to the return of the non-cartoonable guy and/or the bloke at the bottom of the well and the subsequent annihilation of the entire planet courtesy of the ayatollahs' Obama-funded nuclear weapons program to be built within the next decade in order to usher in heaven on earth in 2030 or thereabouts. In this part of the world similar apocalyptic warnings uniquely refer to the imminent destruction of the entire Byron Bay beachfront courtesy of the evil Abbott government's refusal to set an emissions reduction target higher than 26% (or thereabouts) by 2030.

Free trade: This is not a term you will be familiar with from your previous life in socialist totalitarian Syria. It means Australians can buy and sell stuff to anybody who isn't Chinese.

Free speech: Here in your new home we pride ourselves on our unswerving commitment to the concept of freedom of expression, whereby you may freely speak your mind and hold your own opinions of any topic whatsoever so long as you first proclaim your profound and heartfelt beliefs in multiculturalism, climate change, same sex marriage, the republic, recognising Indigenous Australians, the ABC, the perfidy of Israel, and a total and unequivocal hatred of anything and everything to do with Tony Abbott.

❖

In a lengthy speech, Malcolm Turnbull challenges Tony Abbott for the prime ministership.

Waffle, not slogans

Financial Review
19/9/15

A little while ago I met with old onion breath and advised him that I would be challenging him for the leadership of the Liberal Party, and I asked him to arrange or facilitate a backstabbing in the Party Room to formalise my coup d'etat. Of course I've also resigned as Communications Minister, because, let's face it, the job is a pathetic insult to what can only be described as my astonishing skills, talents, gifts and abilities as a Master Communicator.

Now this is not a decision that anyone could take lightly except me. I have consulted with many colleagues, particularly Wyatt Twerp and some other bloke and all my supporters in every walk of life from the humble harbourside villas of Vaucluse to the everyday wellness spas and wine boutiques of Woollahra. This course of action has been urged on me since I first met my adorable Lucy at the Potts Point Yacht Club Young Millionaire Bankers Dance and cheekily introduced myself in my typically modest yet flamboyant, colourful yet erudite, casual yet profound, intellectual yet witty manner such as it is I am blessed with that she was standing in the humble presence of not only the greatest orator but also the greatest prime minister this nation would ever have. But this is not about me. It's about all of us, including me. As my adorable Lucy has reminded me every morning since then, it is clear that the Abbott Government is an unmitigated disaster incapable of providing even a skerrick of the exhilarating yet energising, inspiring yet incisive, firm yet compassionate leadership that has always been my hallmark. This savage but necessary, cruel but kind, benign but brutal betrayal of a hopelessly flawed leader whom I have generously supported through thick and thin, up hill and down dale, in good times and in bad, is not the fault of anyone other than old budgie smugglers himself and his unfortunate habit of winking during radio interviews.

Now we are living, as Australians, in the most exciting time imaginable, known indubitably to future historians as the Era of Malcolm. The big economic changes around the world offer enormous challenges and opportunities, so we need a different style of leadership. We need a style of leadership that focuses less on everybody else and more on me. A style of leadership that respects people's intelligence by allowing them to listen to me whenever possible as I explain all the complex issues of the day to them. A style of leadership that values style as well as substance in order for me to stylishly and with enormous substance and great oratory flourishes such as I am bestowing upon you now set out the course of action I believe we must take in the interests and indeed the spirit of a great, fair and equal society. We need waffle, not slogans.

Now if we continue with Mr Abbott as Prime Minister, it is clear enough what will happen. He will learn from his mistakes and grow into the role just as every other Prime Minister before him has done, and, er... hang on, that's not it... I mean he will lose government because I will keep undermining him until he does and then that's curtains for him but also for me and that is not something I or the ABC or future historians could tolerate.

Now, what we must remember is that our Party, the Lab... sorry, I mean the Liberal Party, has the right values. What Mr Abbott has not succeeded in doing is translating those values into ideas that will excite the Australian people, values like "loyalty" and "commitment". Not for us the savage, shocking, barbaric and utterly cruel casting aside of a first term prime minister and tossing him onto the lazy Susan at the local Vietnamese such as we witnessed under, er, ah, might drop that bit — um, I mean, what I bring to this role is a firm but compassionate, equal but aspirational, calm but urgent approach to turning back the rising oceans and tackling the dire threat of imminent catastrophic climate... er, might save that for Paris... I mean, what I have is the unbridled passion to fight for the inalienable rights of every precious human being whether they be straight, gay, bisexual, transgender, skoliosex... or... hang on, must've got these pages mixed up... sorry, I mean, er, why indeed should the snotty-nosed offspring of some dotty foreign monarch be our future Head of State when of course, as Lucy always says, it should be me? That is what I am committed to deliver to this great nation if the Party Room honours me with their support. Plus you get bloody Morrison as Treasurer. Thank you.

❖

In a lengthy TV interview, the new Prime Minister Malcolm Turnbull lays out his more innovative approach to communicating with the public in order to advocate for his economic plan.

On the table

Financial Review
26/9/15

One night in a Point Piper restaurant:
"Good evening, sir, may I take your order?"
"Well, of course you may, and may I just say what an absolute delight it is to be here under such, well, obviously these are difficult circumstances for us all, and by that I mean — clearly — not just for me — well — it's not just about me per se, but what I've learnt from my previous meals here, I think I've learnt — I don't think, I know I've learned — to be more respectful of other diners and to — there is so much I recognise on the menu, and that is — that is, you know, other people may want something different..."
"Will you be having a starter?"
"Well, that's not actually something I have considered in isolation, by the way — I am more focused on what the entire table are having tonight, and obviously I intend to consult widely on..."
"Beetroot soup or mushroom tartlet, sir?"
"Well, like I say, I've always been very circumspect about starters, or entrees, or antipasto, or nibbles or whatever you in the galley prefer to call the first course, but — the important thing is to be open-minded, consult, engage intelligently, explain the various dishes to the guests in a manner that respects their intelligence and then make a decision, and having made a decision, then argue, and advocate..."
"Avocado's off tonight, sir."
"Sorry?"
"... chef says we could do roast tomato instead."
"Well, look, there are — you probably can't really — you can't really rank them 'cause they are very different. I mean, the... the... clearly the roast tomato is, and this is not a revelation, by the way — the roast tomato is, if you like, sweeter, whereas, in terms of a more balanced dining experience..."
"So no roast tomato?"
"Well, I'm... I'm not going to rule things in or rule things out at this stage. This is one of those... this is one of those restaurant games you people play. One of the things I'm trying to do is to

change the dining paradigm so it's more rational. You know, 'cause you get into this crazy situation where waitresses — or indeed waiters — are encouraged by chefs to say, 'Order this, order that' or they're asked to say, 'How would you like it, rare or..'"

"So just mains?"

"No, no hang on! Hang on! You're not listening to me. I was about to explain that the object of dinner — the sole object — is to reduce your hunger. There are many different ways you can do that. You can do that by having a starter and a main; you can do that by sharing a variety of smaller, tapas style dishes if you prefer; you can do it by selecting at random from the lazy Susan; but in truth, what I am keen on is some kind of fixed price or set menu. It's capped. It will reduce — it has cut our bills in the past two years to less than $14 a head. So, we're not looking for gastronomic theoretical purity here; we're looking for practical innovation, agility, a nimble…"

"I'm sorry, sir, but you have 44 people in your party who are feeling pretty hungry now…"

"Well, there is — look, these leadership tussles always do — you know, there is always some leftover…"

"You may take any leftovers home, sir. It's entirely up to you."

"Well, you know, I'm not great at analysing myself, to be honest. I'll leave that to others. I don't find myself particularly interesting — even though everybody else does — but I feel I am very — confident and centered in myself. I feel — but not in a sort of ebullient way… I'm far more agile, engaging…"

"I need to get your order in, sir…"

"Of course you do, but I don't believe in rushing these things in a sort of hasty way, but equally I believe you can make decisions very quickly. So I won't put a timeframe on it. Our plans will change, all plans change. But when we do make changes we will do so in a considered yet swift, measured yet innovative way in tandem with the guests, the adorable Lucy, myself, and, er, me. And then I'll tell you what we've decided. And if necessary, I will argue, and persuade, and cajole and engage with you and the kitchen…"

"Kitchen's closed now, Mr Turnbull."

In other news this week, Malcolm Turnbull is backing an unprecedented crackdown on domestic violence against prime ministers. "Four prime ministers have been slain in the last five years alone," said Mr Turnbull, "It's a national disgrace."

❖

The agile new Prime Minister quickly organises a summit of stakeholders to chart an exciting and innovative new economic direction for the nation. Meanwhile, the United Nations releases its updated list of new committee members.

Summit

Financial Review
3/10/15

Sabra Salespitch: Tonight on the ABC we look at the astonishing economic summit — described by many as "outstanding" — that took place in Canberra today under the inspirational and innovative guidance of Australia's exciting — and dare I say it, outstanding (giggles at own joke) — new Prime Minister Malcolm Turnmeon. (Insert shot of PM walking through floating blossom along Canberra foreshores — add Vivaldi strings.) Joining me to discuss this historic summit are three of the key figures whose job it is to reform our decrepit economy after the torpor and misery of the Abbott-Hockey years. (Insert shot of ex-PM eating onion — add horror music.) Good evening. First to you, Judy. How lucky are you! Sitting opposite Malcolm all day! (laughs) Sucks to be you!

Judy Wafflalot: Look, yes it was an outstanding meeting. Truly outstanding. It was a very constructive outstanding meeting. It was a discussion where people were really listening to one another, even when the other one was talking. And we all agreed with each other, too...

Salespitch: About what, specifically?

2015 — The Year of Betrayal

Wafflalot: That it was outstanding.

Salespitch: Yes, of course. Now Mr Copperfield, you're a highly respected union official who's spent most of your life down the mines and in the dark satanic mills of our evil capitalist system fighting for the rights of oppressed construction workers. What is the takeaway for you?

David Copperfield: I'll have a Pad Thai thanks.

Salspitch: No, no, I mean — what did you take away from today's historic summit?

Copperfield: Well, I grabbed a couple of pens on the way out. But yeah, I agree with everything what Jude said. It's good to do reform and stuff. It's like doing rehab instead of going inside for a stretch. But the main topic we done was, you know, how can we grow a bigger pie? Me and the boys, we're all up for big pies. Speaking of which, is that Pad Thai here yet?

Salespitch: Er... And of course, Sandra, how about from your perspective? Why was today's summit such a roaring success?

Sandra Goldilocks: Oh, look, I think today's meeting was — it was like opening up the doors at the end of a long cold, dark winter and crying out, Yes! Yes! YES! Let's let the sunshine in! (re-insert PM in backlit blossom, don't forget Vivaldi) It was like a new flowering, as the virginal buds of... of a young, pretty rose open themselves... to... to the pollination of... of innovation... of flexibility... of brave new ideas! As the petals fluttered away and Malcolm walked in, I found myself catching my breath and...

Salespitch: Woo! (giggles) Must say I'm feeling a little flushed myself! But allow me to play devil's advocate here for a moment. Say, Judy, can you give me an example, under the umbrella of tax reform, if we drill down under the microscope without taking anything off the table to the low-hanging fruit, of a specific policy that you could all agree to?

Wafflalot: Well, yes, of course, we looked at all sorts of areas, but not in a way that was divisive, or that in any way alienated the collaborative spirit... basically we focused on what we could all agree on, rather than what divided us... on consensus rather than...

Goldilocks: We all came together...

Copperfield: It was like a smorgasbord of ideas, speaking of which...

Salespitch: We're almost out of time, so just quickly, what was the one thing you all agreed on?

All together: Tax the crap out of self-funded retirees' super!

Salespitch: Sounds innovative! And I'm afraid that's all we've got time for. Tomorrow, I'll be looking at foreign affairs, and the way in which this exciting, innovative, flexible new Prime Minister has overcome years of... (cont'd on ABC24)

In other news this week, the United Nations released its updated list of new committee members:
UN Committee for the Protection of Schoolgirls and Teenage Hitchhikers: J. Saville (UK), I. Milat (Aust) T. Bundy (USA) Dr. B'oko Har'em (East Congo).
UN Committee for the Abolition of Illicit Narcotics: Prof. P. Escobar (Columb), Abu Poppy (Afghanistan), Ms Krystal Me'th (USA).
UN Committee for Peace with Israel: Mustafa Nuke (Iran) A. Eichmann (Ger) Yasir Bloodba'ath (Pal).

Meanwhile, further evidence that Australia's new Prime Minister Malcolm Turnturnturn is introducing a kinder, gentler discourse to the national conversation emerged this week when, in another stunning departure from the practices of his reviled predecessor, the new PM indicated he would be modifying his language in order to "reach out" to members of the multicultural community.

Said an ethnic spokesperson: "To describe those who go around beheading, crucifying, raping, torturing and burning people alive in cages as a 'death cult' is deeply offensive to members of our community."

2015 — The Year of Betrayal

❖

Prime Minister Malcolm Turnbull defends his use of a non-government email service.

Secret emails revealed

Financial Review
10/10/15

Explosive and shocking revelations rocked the world of politics this week when it was revealed that Australia's new Prime Minister, Malcolm Ozemail, has been operating a secret email account to conduct his own personal and political affairs.

Details of the account, which operates under the obscure name of Abbottsaprik@malcolm.com, have been leaked to this column:

Hey Luce, What's for dinner?
Tony LOL. Where are you now, babe?
Sitting in a pram.
Huh???
Sorry, autospell. A tram. In Geelong.
A what???
It's like a train thingy, you know.
No I don't. Sounds dreadful. What are you doing?
Undermining Abbott just like you told me to.
How exactly???
Tweeting.
Well you'd better get a bloody move on. Time's running out. He's going to win the stupid Canning thing and then we're, I mean you're, cactus. And then there's the TPP, Chafta, the Syrian refugees stuff. All of it popular. Then he'll go and reshuffle in November and kick out Hockey and stick in that smirking bloke who stopped the boats as Treasurer. With all that before Chrissy he's bound to bounce back in the polls! Timing is everything, remember hun.
OK, OK, OK, I'm hearing you doll. I'll email Arthur and see where we're at.

Hey Arthur matey, L reckons we've gotta get our skates on — how are the numbers looking?
I can't recall.
Huh?
I have no recollection of that matter.
No you idiot I'm talking about my bloody spill! How are my numbers looking?
Oh, that! Yeah, I reckon we're looking pretty darn good. I've got, er, Mal Broughtrade and um, what's his name, that twelve-year-old? Wyatt Twerp. Yeah. They're both in.
AND…?!? Those two clowns have been in for bloody months! A two-bit sleazebag and the Milky Bar Kid? Is that it?? That's my entire funky new dynamic team?? You promised me you'd be Frank Underwood meets Cesare Borgia if I made you my numbers man!!
Did I? I can't remember. But, ah, anyway, the good news is Julie's hot to trot so long as she gets to keep flying around the world at the pointy end and Scotty's up for it so long as we make it look like it's all nothing to do with him — that's the deal.
You promised.
Did I?? Bloody hell. How do we do that then?
Well, here's my cunning plan — he goes into the spill and then — he votes for Abbott! And he makes sure everybody sees his ballot paper!
WHAT'S THE FRIGGIN POINT IN THAT!!! YOU'RE SUPPOSED TO BE THE MACHIEVALLIAN BRAINS IN THIS BLOODY COUP!!! HOW DOES MORRISON VOTING FOR THAT PRICK HELP ME TOPPLE HIM?!?!?
Well it shows Scotty's got clean hands for next time around.
You mean it shows he's having a two bob bloody bet each way, that's what it shows!
Well, surely that's what you want in a Treasurer, isn't it? — The cautious approach. Anyway, my new plan is maybe we don't wait 'til Christmas — this Canning by-election will be a total disaster for Abbott and then whammo! In we go for the kill!
But he's going to WIN Canning! Luce says so!
Is he? Even with all those stories about that religious nutjob candidate? Dammit. That sure puts a spanner in the works. The last thing we want is TO WIN in Canning!! Coz what with all those free trade deals and Syria stuff even friggin Abbott will get a

2015 — The Year of Betrayal

bounce in the polls and then knowing our luck some towelhead loony'll go and decapitate a cop in Bankstown and Abbott'll go all hairy-chested over every bloody news program and start banging on about Team bloody Australia and death cults and the shock jocks'll be singing his praises and he'll rocket up in the polls and then we're... I mean you're... bloody cactus!!
OK, OK. So we gotta go before Canning. What's the excuse?
How about "a good government has lost its way"?
Nup. Been done. What about "we won't change any policies but we need a better salesman"?
I like it.
"In order to restore confidence in the economy."
Love it. But we need a lot of new exciting digital-sounding touchy-feely stuff to distract everybody with.
How about "innovation"?
What's that mean?
Er, new stuff.
Perfect.
And maybe "flexibility".
What's that mean?
Whatever you want it to.
Even better.
And I thought we could "build consensus" and be a "kinder, gentler" government.
That's genius. Coz all my focus groups keep telling us that people are sick to death of all this political infighting and backstabbing and stuff. "Kinder and gentler" is perfect.
So when do we go in for the kill and stab the bastard? Monday?
Sounds good to me.

❖

The Prime Minister and his Foreign Minister urge Australians to take a more "holistic" approach to tackling youth radicalisation by "reaching out" to members of their local communities and showing "mutual respect". But how?

Radicalised party tricks

Financial Review
17/10/15

After close consultation with the relevant authorities such as the police, education, immigration, child welfare, social welfare, social engineering, social inclusion, religious tolerance and multicultural affairs government agencies, this column has prepared a comprehensive *Guide to Mutually Respecting Radicalised Youth*.

Birthday parties: In order to take a more holistic approach to the traditional birthday party, with a little bit of imagination and multicultural flair you can adapt everyday party games so that your child's radicalised classmates feel more at home. Here are some easy suggestions.

Pin the tail on the donkey: Why not chop the tail off the donkey instead? With a machete preferably, but any old kitchen knife will do. Then you can lop off the front right hoof and the back left hoof too if the donkey's been caught doing anything naughty like stealing the birthday cake!

Hide and seek: Always a party favourite, but try to make sure the game is fair for all the local neighbourhood kiddies by first removing those pesky GPS tracking bracelets from any alienated or radicalised 14-year-olds.

Bean bag throw: Use rocks instead.

Eleven fingers trick: Kids will squeal will delight at this one, as you hold up your hands and prove you can count eleven fingers (one of which belongs — or used to belong — to the kid next door).

Funny mummy wrap game: Kids love stories of ancient Egypt and the mummies of old kings and dead pharoahs. Why not make it more culturally inclusive by getting the kids to smash a few old vases or other ancient Greek or Assyrian antiquities? Millennia of fun for everyone.

2015 — The Year of Betrayal

Heads up, seven up: Get all the 7-year-old kiddies to stand at the front of a room or in a flat, dry, dusty outdoor space. The remaining children lay their heads on the chopping block (or on a table) with their eyes closed (no peeking!). The 7-year-olds walk around the room and each one chooses a person to decapitate before yelling "Allahu akbar!" at the top of their voices. Repeat until everyone is dead.

Pass the parcel: Enhance the holistic multicultural flavour of this popular game by stacking the parcel full of old bits of shrapnel (household nails will do) and an explosive timing device. Seconds of fun for the entire family!

One legged race: Much more challenging when all of the contestants really do only have one leg left.

What's in the bag?: Ok, this one's way too easy for most radicalised kiddies — so make it harder by asking what sort of head is in the bag? Shia or Christian?

Teen games: Teenagers can be so hard to please these days, what with spending hours and hours locked in their bedrooms watching ISIS propaganda clips, so why not reach out to them with these excitingly inclusive multicultural games designed to drag them away from their laptops!

Capture the Flag: Another classic party game that's tons of fun. Again you'll need a large, flat, dusty space to play in. Divide the players into as many teams as you like and give each a flag. Flags can be made of anything, like a black cloth with white squiggly writing or even an old tea towel on a stick will do the trick. Each team must hide their flag somewhere on their side. The object is to sneak — in an agile way! — onto the other team's side and steal their flag. But if you get tagged in their space you lose and get put in a cage and burned alive. (Make sure you capture the fun on your iPhone so you can post it on YouTube at the after party!)

Spin the bottle: All the boys and girls sit in a circle and spin the bottle. Whoever it stops at, she's your Yazidi sex slave!

Truth or Dare: Already popular among the under-16s in certain parts of western Sydney, the latest — more holistic! — version of this game involves truthfully answering the question "would you like to shag 72 virgins?" before being handed a pistol and dared to go and shoot a cop.

Meanwhile, in other news this week, Australia's new Prime Minister Malcolm Croesus declared in parliament that it was no news to anybody that he is "richer than Turnbull".

❖

It is the anniversary of a popular 1980s movie franchise.

Back to the Future

Financial Review
23/10/15

The world of entertainment was thrown into a frenzy this week with news that *Back to the Future IV* — the long awaited fourth installment in the popular '80s movie franchise — is currently being filmed on location in Canberra, Australia.

Spoiler alert: copies of the script have been leaked to this column. In the new film, a boyish looking man/child — played by 12-year-old Wyatt McTwerp, an unknown MP from Queensland — teams up with a mad professor — to be played by Australia's most popular stand-up comic and ham actor Mal 'Doc' Turnbull — and together they travel thirty years into the future. Their bold plan is to fix up all the bad mistakes of the miserable Abbott era by bringing in an emissions trading scheme, legalising gay marriage, introducing a republic (with 'Doc' as President) and then, if they still have time before the clock chimes at midnight, see if they can get the country back into surplus.

The 'Doc', an eccentric multimillionaire and communications genius, has invented a unique method of time travel. In order to get to whatever future he desires for himself, he's discovered all he needs to do is sit on a Geelong tram tweeting selfies and making snide comments about his colleagues and in a flash he becomes Prime Minister.

However, things go awry when the tram gets hit by lightning and the hapless duo find themselves catapulted into the future where they become stranded in Canberra on the night of a leadership coup on October 21, 2045. Not only is Wyatt still only twelve, but he is — unbelievably! — now a hopelessly inefficient and unpopular Prime Minister himself who is constantly being bullied by "Biff" Shorten and his thuggish union mates and the entire country is mired in chaos, debt and disorder. Worse, his girlfriend, played by Antonia Abbott, is an up and coming MP in Cory's Conservative Party, who is extremely popular in the opinion polls thanks to her telegenic looks, and is obsessed about avenging her grandfather's tragic downfall thirty years earlier and plans to stab Wyatt in the back and seize the prime ministership for herself.

"Obviously, it's a bit of sci-fi fantasy," said the film's director, Arthur Zameckodinos, "but we wanted to make it feel as authentic as possible."

Film buffs are in raptures looking forward to the gadgets and gimmicks that the film's imaginative scriptwriters have conjured up to portray the future.

"The most amazing idea we had is Doc's 'fibre to the node' National Broadband Network," says the films special effects guru, "but we couldn't get it to work on time or on budget."

The *mise-en-scène* proved equally challenging. "Rather than still being a sleepy town with a couple of roundabouts, a brown lake and lots of open parkland, we've re-imagined the Canberra of the future as a dynamic sleepy metropolis with a couple of roundabouts, a brown lake, lots of open parkland and a multi-billion dollar light railway to Gungahlin," said the film's art directors. "To give a truly futuristic feel we've worked predominantly with a colour palette of deep green."

Way Beyond Satire

The film reprises many of the themes of the previous blockbusters, with added twists when it is revealed that the secret to Doc's phenomenal wealth is that back in 1987 somebody gave him a book from the future that he keeps locked away labelled "Internet 1999 Share Price". In one of the opening scenes, Doc accidentally crashes his time machine into a large ugly building on the Cayman Islands scattering millions of dollars over nobody except himself but he emerges from the disaster largely unscathed, despite being hounded by Biff's gang of shadow ministers.

In one of the film's more controversial scenes, Wyatt goes to his old church to look up his birth records, only to find it is now the local Hiz Butt Terror mosque. In another hilarious scene, Wyatt sprains his ankle and goes to visit a doctor, only to be hit with a $2,347.00 co-payment bill. "Ah," says the nurse wistfully, "if only they'd done this thirty years ago, it would only have needed to be around five bucks." Another scene sees Wyatt attempting to find Israel on the map but it's now called Greater Iran.

The climax occurs when Wyatt accidentally sets the wrong date on his time machine and lands back in the dim distant past, standing in an unfamiliar location where people are handed leaflets before going into a strange booth and ticking boxes on large pieces of paper.

"Who's that?" he says, pointing at an unfamiliar face on a Liberal party poster.

"Not you, that's for sure!" replies the angry voter.

❖

The week before the Melbourne Cup, it is revealed a Victorian primary school allowed Muslim children to walk out of assembly while the national anthem was sung. And a father and his son, both fugitives, were finally captured.

Form guide

Financial Review
31/10/15

It's the race that stops the nation (from actually getting on with reforming the economy and paying off our debt) but who are the frontrunners for this year's Canberra's Cup?
Here's the form guide:

Who Shot The PM: A thoroughbred from the eastern suburbs, this extremely popular horse was making little progress on the leaders until it stabbed one of them in the back six weeks ago and is now looking like a dead cert for next year. "He's a lay down misère" said trainer and popular socialite Lucy 'Gai' Waterfront, "although he does have a tendency to pull too hard to the left."

Red Speedeaux: Currently running well in Britain's Thatcher Memorial Trophy, this is the horse that stopped the boats. Never very popular with the crowds, this warhorse nonetheless bolted home in 2013 but stumbled badly during the Credlin Leadership Stakes and had to be swiftly and forcefully put down by his colleagues so he wouldn't have a chance at the Canning Cup, despite the fact he was bound to win it.

Gust of Wind: According to trainer "ScoMo" Morrison, this cunning horse can change riders midstream and still run hard depending on which way the wind is blowing. Its owner likes to have a bob each way.

De Little Engine: A lightweight apprentice ridden by 12-year-old midget Wyatt Twerp from Queensland, this youngster has yet to prove its straps, but was shoved up to the front of the field after helping to win the Turnbull Coup.

Secret Number: Unbelievably, only a few months ago this union-owned hairy goat was a sure thing but despite lots of shady backroom deals its odds don't continue to, er, shorten. Recently has struggled to find any form whatsoever despite being popular with the bagmen.

Trip to Paris: According to stylish Perth-based owner "Pearly Queen" Bishop, this part Iranian-owned showpony has performed admirably on the international circuit but the real test will come in Paris later this month where she is expected to bring a duffel bag of taxpayers' cash and blow the lot on "catastrophic" climate change.

The Offer: According to rider "Hoe" Jockey, who prematurely lit up the cigars after being donkey-licked in 2014's Budget Derby, this duffer has been scratched from the Canberra Cup and put out to pasture in the Washington Ambassador Millions.

Quest for More: Owned by a syndicate of self-funded super retirees, this one-time winner used to be the one to put your money on for the long run. Not any more!

Meanwhile, in other exciting and inclusive news this week, the Victorian Department of Multicultural Affairs and Progressive Education in co-operation with the Friends of the Global Caliphate have released a new non-discriminatory version of the lyrics of our national anthem so that those oppressed and harassed minority groups who feel alienated by the existing divisive, xenophobic, Islamophobic (and racist!) anglocentric imperialist colonial Judeo-Christian lyrics can feel more comfortable in morning assemblies should they feel the urge to sing along.

(To be sung to the tune of the existing anthem):

Australians let us not rejoice — for we are mujahadeen,
We're not allowed to sing or dance — it's somehow quite obscene;
Our mosques abound in Islam's gifts, of beauty — don't be scared;
In history's page let every stage, Advance Sharia Fair.
In joyless strains then let us sing, Advance Sharia Fair.

(Trigger warning: the second verse may not be everyone's cup of mint tea)

Beneath our radiant crescent moon — we'll toil with guns or knives;
To make this unbelievers land — fear for all their lives;
For those who've come across the seas — we've boundless lives to spare;
With jihad let us all combine, to Advance Sharia Fair.
In joyless strains then let us sing Advance Sharia Fair.

Also this week, the notorious ScoMo fugitives, father and son shysters Malcie and Scotty, who have been on the run for the past six weeks since hijacking the government and running off with the entire cabinet, were finally entrapped in a remote house of representatives deep beneath the wild hills of Canberra. Police have confirmed that the battered corpse of a 57-year-old man in red Speedos was found buried nearby. Foul play is suspected.

❖

Struggling in vain to outline a clear economic narrative in his Mid-Year Economic and Fiscal Outlook, the new Treasurer finds himself disappointing those who had held such high hopes for him.

The Wreck of the F. Scott Morrison, a hit ballad by Malcolm "Gordon" Lightfoot

Financial Review
7/11/15

The legend lives on from Canberra on down
Of the big lake they call the economy
The lake, it is said, always gives up her dead
When the skies of November turn gloomy
With a load of iron ore, twenty-six thousand tonnes more
Than the terms of trade, she was empty
That good ship and true led by Mal's pirate crew
Saw a fat GST and was tempted

The ship was the pride of the Liberal side
Coming back from some spill in September
Her sails were trim, yet she had bags full of wind
She was adaptable, flexible, innovative
Captain Turnbull they knew had plenty to do
When he landed in Marvellous Melbourne
Then later that day with his speech underway
A certain unease they were feelin'

Way Beyond Satire

The promise of reform hit like a storm
The GST broke over the railing
And every man knew, as the audience did too
'Twas the Waffler of Wentworth come preachin'
"I know where to steer, my destiny's clear"
He yelled as they rounded Point Piper
"There's globalisation! Technology too!
My opportunity's never been greater!"

Does anyone know where the love of God goes
When the waffle turns minutes to hours?
The Cutty Spending never came in a speech that was lame
"If it ain't fair then it ain't in the budget
The object of taxation is through innovation,
We must be agile as we reach in your pocket,
We need a new idea, there's nothing to fear,
Wyatt's the key to our future, he'll unlock it"

The crowd started to snore at his dull metaphor
Of a girl in a boat with a sail
One day she goes fast, one day she goes slow
It depends on the force of the gale
"I'll do what I must to restore public trust
In our economic credentials
But which way I go depends where the polls blow
I'm afraid I can't give you the essentials"

The waffle blew them off course, with a hurricane force
Obfuscation and evasion unending
Lots of single-word slogans and PowerPoint phrases
But no mention of how to cut spending
"If a policy doesn't work", Mal said with a smirk
"I'll chuck it overboard and into the water"
"Just like you did to Tony and Joe"
The deckhands muttered amid dark laughter

Way across town bobbing up and bobbing down
Treasurer Scotty was also dissembling
"I once stopped the boats but I must think of the votes
I'll keep my powder dry 'til after the election

2015 — The Year of Betrayal

Our problem is spending, it's never ending
It's not about revenue raising",
Scotty muttered aloud, but was drowned out by the crowd
Of journos; Turnbull's skills they were praising

In the Arnhem Land sun, Josh had some fun
But Kelly was drowning, the dollar was sinking
To Paris they came, hoping the climate might change
Where Julie gave away squillions
Bill danced in the sand with Tanya in hand
But they sunk under a tsunami of union corruption
And all that remains is the faces and the names
Of an economic policy called "disruption"

In a radio station on the wrong side of town
They whispered of rumours of Tony
The said he was on track to make his comeback
Malcolm said the story was phony
But the warnings of doom soon filled up the room
The speaker was first mate John Fraser
Our birthrate is lower and growth will be slower
We're heading straight for the rocks of disaster

When MYEFO struck, poor old Scotty had the luck
Of sayin' "Fellas, I've nothing to feed ya"
Polls started to sag, the PM ran up the flag
He said, "Quick, let's just raise more taxes"
The Reserve Bank wired in, they had water comin' in
Recession was on the horizon
And later that night when his lights went outta sight
Came the Wreck of The F. Scott Morrison

In a musty old booth in a thousand school halls,
They still vote for Malcolm to lead them
But the hopes and the dreams have faded away
As the economy carries on bleedin'
The age of entitlement rings loud in their ears
The welfare system is rotten,
But the good polls will go as the punters all know
The spill of September is ne'er forgotten.

***

More details of the late night plotting that led to the coup against Tony Abbott are revealed, including the surprise presence of the Foreign Minister's Chief of Staff.

Plotters

Financial Review
14/11/15

The Chief of Staff glanced up at the single light on in the upstairs window. This must be it. Carefully he knocked on the ordinary, suburban door. Three taps, then a pause, then two more taps, just like he'd been briefed... he started sweating — or was it the other way round? Damn! He quickly re-read his hastily scribbled instructions, then tore the paper up into tiny pieces and shovelled them into his mouth, just like Julie had told him to.

The door creaked open. A young 12-year-old boy with teenage pimples wearing a silly fake nose and glasses stared out at him. "Mmmff...murpghhh..." the Chief of Staff said, desperately trying to swallow the scratchy pieces of Department of Foreign Affairs and Trade notepaper. He caught his breath. "Errgh, I'm sorry, ah... is your Mum at home? I must be at the wrong...."

"It's me... Twerp!" hissed the schoolboy, beckoning the senior political staffer swiftly out of the chilly Canberra night air and into the over-heated room. "Come on in! We've been waiting! Did anybody see you coming?"

"No, of course not," the Chief of Staff blurted out, sounding just a little too confident, even to himself. After all, who was that person alongside him at the traffic lights in Fyshwick? Hadn't they stared at him just a little too suspiciously?

"Not a soul, nobody knows I'm here," he re-affirmed, putting on his most pompous Chief of Staff's voice. "I took all the necessary precautions. I didn't even use my own ComCar."

"Excellent!" said the schoolboy, rubbing his young hands together and beaming at him excitedly. "Very creative of you! And very innovative, too! We like that sort of agility around here! Innovative, agile, creative! Just like Mal... I mean just like You-Know-Who told me..."

The Chief of Staff glanced into the lounge room. Five men in a variety of odd headgear were sitting around the dining room table, a sheaf of papers with lists and names of people spread out in front of them. "This is Mr Blue, Mr White, Mr Green and, er, Mr... which one are you again, Arthur?" said the schoolboy.

"I'm Mr Pink," growled an irritable short tubby man, although it was hard to make out what he said through his rubber Ronald Reagan mask.

Next to him, the host, wearing a Venetian harlequin mask, turned and beamed at them with a sickly smile. "There's 52 of us! Pants down!" he said breathlessly.

"Oh, er, I'd rather keep mine on, if that's alright," said the Chief of Staff, sweating nervously. He'd heard about these Canberra suburban shindigs before...

"No, no," gloated the man, "I mean we've got 52 votes for You-Know-Who even if he turns up to the ballot wearing no pants!"

"Oh, I see," he said. "You mean he'll be wearing what... a pair of Speedos? Is that really necessary? I mean, I know we aren't changing any of Abbott's policies, but..."

"No, no... we're just telling people we're not changing any policies," snarled Mr Pink.

"Why's that?"

"So we can buy time," said Mr White.

"To do what?"

"To change all his policies," said Mr Green.

"And we've got a master plan? For the economy, I mean?" the Chief of Staff asked, nervously.

"That's ScoMo's, er, I mean that's Mr Purple's job," said Twerp excitedly. "I keep forgetting what colour he is."

"Whatever bloody colour you want him to be. Depends which way the wind's blowing today," snickered Mr White, as the others all joined in laughing.

"And what about the new cabinet?"

"Julie stays where she is, Scotty gets what he would have got anyway, and Marise gets Defense," said Mr Pink.

"Who?"

"Precisely."

"And I'm being made Assistant Minister for Innovation," said Twerp, proudly pulling out his taxpayer-funded iPhone. "We've all got to download this fantastic new app. It means that whatever we say disappears as soon as we've said it!"

In awkward silence the young boy fiddled with his mobile. "Well?" said Mr Pink.

"Dammit!" said Twerp finally. "I had it here a moment ago but now it's disappeared."

The Chief of Staff frowned. "So when's it happen? Straight after the Canning by-election disaster?"

The men shifted uneasily in their seats. "I don't tughhrgrg..." said Mr Pink, before abruptly pulling off his rubber mask in a shower of expletives. His bald head glistened with sweat. "Bloody hot in that stupid thing. Look, I know we've got the numbers, but there's been this real hiccup. It looks as if we're going to WIN bloody

Canning. By a country mile."

"It's a real bugger," said Mr Blue, sighing. "In fact, it's a disaster. We need to lose Canning, and preferably lose it big."

"Why's that?" said the Chief of Staff, frowning.

"So then we can say that Tony's so unpopular he could never win a bloody election! And that's why we had to get rid of him."

❖

Visiting Germany, Prime Minister Malcolm Turnbull explains to Angela Merkel that more attention on reaching a negotiated settlement of the Syrian conflict is needed, including the prospect of dialogue with Islamic State. In what is widely seen as a swipe against Tony Abbott, both leaders agree that only a "political solution" to the Syrian crisis can resolve issues like terrorism. Only a few hours later more than 120 people are murdered by Islamists in a series of coordinated attacks across Paris, including a massacre of young people at a rock concert.

I have here the letter

Financial Review
21/11/15

It's the Hollywood blockbuster of the summer! Based on a true story! A thriller that will have you on the edge of your seat as Australia's heartthrob Prime Minister launches a daring peace raid on the Islamic State to rescue the entire world from being held hostage to a psychopathic bunch of Islamic terrorists in... Victory at Wentworthebbe!

Starring matinee idol Captain Malcolm "Spycatcher" Chamberlain and screen sweetheart Julie "Iranian bombshell" Bishop as the fearless leaders of a secret mission who risk their entire reputations and conservative credentials by parachuting deep behind enemy lines under cover of the G20 to make peace with

ISIS, the film is an explosive re-enactment of the actual events that saw the Islamic State brought to its knees through sheer innovation, compassion, persuasion, consultation, advocacy, flexibility, and agile thinking.

Spoiler alert: it ends very badly.

Scene 1: A press conference somewhere in the world.

Captain "Malcolm" Chamberlain: Well, of course, I've been giving my good friend President Idi Obama the benefit of my advice, which is both pertinent yet prescient, intuitive yet calibrated in terms of nuance and proportionality to ensure that what this coalition — that is to say this collaborative of principal determinants — what we are planning on doing, or rather, what we are planning on planning on doing, which is to say, the plan that is currently on the table, not that, of course there aren't other plans that could be on the table, it's just that...

Bomb Squadron Leader Jul-Al-Bishop: Everything's on the table, including these nifty little devices my good friends in Teheran knocked up that fit neatly under your turban and are known by the codename Thermo Nukes Death to America (delivers ferocious death stare straight at the camera. Lens cracks).

Captain Chamberlain (carries on talking): ...and, er, anyway, you can sense in this room, well, you can sense in any room where I have been with my fellow elected heads of state, and, er, I mean, when I say elected I clearly mean, in my own case, unelected, but regardless, you could sense the urgency, the passion, the commitment, the solidarity, the spirit of determination... (camera pans over to room full of unconscious journalists, some of whom may actually still be alive — just). Fade to black.

CAPTION: 24 hours later.

Scene 2: On board Aussie Air Force 1 (aka Qantas First Class). *Captain Chamberlain (is still talking):* ...but if the question is when, or how, or rather, in which manner will I be able to bring about peace in our time with ISIS, or ISIL if you prefer, or Dash...

2015 — The Year of Betrayal

Al-Bishop: It's Da'esh, not Dash. (Gives death stare out window of airplane. Window shatters. Plane goes into a death spiral nose dive — as do Coalition's poll numbers the moment Malcolm actually makes a decision.)

Captain Chamberlain (still talking): ...or indeed the fundamental entity involved in what is clearly a grotesque blasphemy upon this great religion of peace, and by the way, when I say Islam is a religion of peace I actually mean it — unlike my warmongering predecessor Mr Tony Churchill — and I have here the letter from the Mufti to prove it... (stands at the top of the plane's steps and holds aloft a crumpled sheet of paper for the cheering crowds). "Dear Infidel from Wentworth, we promise never to invade this blighted land of disbelievers, apostates, poofters and prostitutes known as the Caliphate of Al Australi which by the grace of Allah will soon be ours, yours the Grand Mufti El Caliphate bin Liner." Fade to black.

Scene 3: Somewhere in the Syrian desert. A group of terrorists are sitting in a circle holding hands with the Captain and Al-Bishop. (Soundtrack: Joan Baez's 'Kumbaya')

CAPTION: Many, many, many hours later.

Chamberlain (still talking): ...so clearly, I'm not ruling anything in or ruling anything out at this stage, but I believe, in an idealistic yet pragmatic way, with all bets both on and off the table...

The terrorists all look exhausted from sheer boredom. Some are rolling their eyes towards paradise. Others are slumped forward with heads in their hands (not their own heads, obviously), whilst others are toppling over into the sand unconscious.

Chamberlain (still talking): ...so what we need to look at is the desired outcome that achieves its purposes for all parties, after all, we all agree, both intrinsically yet exponentially, both objectively yet subjectively that — as it says in my Koran here — let us do unto others as we would...

The last terrorist groans and reaches under his robes.

Terrorist: "Think I'll pull the pin on this dude, Allahu Akbar."

Massive explosion. Fade to black.

CAPTION: The End (of the world).

❖

Australian Federal Police (AFP) officers search the home of Special Minister of State Mal Brough over his alleged (since dismissed) role in the Peter Slipper affair, whilst Labor attempt to censure the Prime Minister. Meanwhile, Tony Abbott is criticised for having lunch with fellow conservatives, whilst Anthony Albanese appears on The Bolt Report sounding more conservative than the rest of them all put together. And Prince Charles blames terrorism on climate change.

Prison flicks

Financial Review
28/11/15

This week, the Fin looks at the top prison movies of all time:

The Turnbull Redemption: All hell breaks loose when a prison inmate known as The Mad Monk attempts to smuggle a chocolate cake into a solitary confinement area known as 'the Monkey Pod', where the worst of the worst conservative inmates gather every Tuesday lunchtime to plot their insurgency and the overthrow of the grinning prison warden "the Messiah". Inside the chocolate cake is a file containing the gang's secret plans to put "boots on the ground" and unilaterally invade the Middle East.

Wentworth: Extremely popular current Australian TV series set in Wentworth Prison, a harbourside electorate crammed full of a motley gang of gays, greenies, cis-genders, climate change activists, cyclists, latte sippers and a whole host of other touchy-feely miscreants. Although the original pilot show in 2009 — remembered for its sinister main character, an email forger called The Gretch — tanked spectacularly, there are high hopes that the

2015 re-make will run for at least ten years. Or even longer!

The Green Mile: Sickening melodrama in which a notorious gang of parliamentary luvvies led by "the PM" and his deputy "the Bishop" steal billions of taxpayers dollars and escape to Paris where they blow the lot on an elaborate Green scam known as "tackling climate change" and "saving the sinking atolls". Watch out for the clever sub-plot, in which the real deadly threat comes from a gang of "fundamentally weak" jihadists murdering everybody they possibly can.

Dead Man Walking: Desperately depressing film in which the main character, a notorious knife-wielding back-stabber played by Sean Penn, is condemned to wander from press conference to press conference uttering inane comments and unfunny zingers, all the while knowing he is doomed to meet a grisly fate at the forthcoming election. Susan Sarandon plays Tanya Pliberstab, a fantasist and high priestess of the Greens who appears to befriend him in his darkest hours, but in reality is secretly plotting to steal his job the moment he's in the chair.

Escape from Albanese: Classic escapist drama in which a hardcore left-winger tunnels onto The *Bolt Report* using nothing but his wits and a rusty switchblade where he passes himself off as a tough right-wing hardliner who wants to obliterate all Islamic terrorists and wipe the "scourge" of ISIS from the face of the earth whilst cunningly plunging the blade into the back of his uncharismatic and diminutive boss, Billy Shawshank (unfortunately not played by Clint Eastwood).

Broughbaker: Robert Redford plays this fictional shyster who encourages his accomplices to steal people's diaries in order to set them up for cabcharge fraud and drunken visits to Canberra wineries. In a novel twist, Broughbaker reveals himself to be the Minister for Integrity in the government who has actually come to clean up the entire joint. Critics (including the Prime Minister) were quick to dismiss Broughbaker as a complete farce.

Wyatt Twerp: A 15-year-old schoolkid pretends he is a federal politician and rides into town determined to make no impression whatsoever on anyone. In the end, he joins in with a desperate group of conspirators led by Arthur "Sin" O'Dinos who overthrow the Abbott government in the famous plot of 'iPhones at the OK Corral'. The film is a re-make of *Tombstone*, which pretty much sums up Twerp's career prospects.

Sleepers: Revenge movie in which a large fat billionaire only rarely turns up to parliament and when he does he promptly nods off. While he is asleep (which is most of the movie) he has wild dreams of rebuilding the Titanic and fantasises that one day a paying guest may actually book into his ridiculous dinosaur park. Released in China as *Take the Money and Run*, the film is regarded as one of Woody Allen's silliest comedies.

Papillon: Based on the notorious Dreyfus affair, in which shadow attorney general Mark "Papillon" Dreyfus tries in vain to catch his man, (see Broughbaker) this tense drama takes place on a remote desert island from which there is no escape, known as Labor's Future. In the end Papillon builds a light on a hill before the entire party jump off a cliff together and disappear under the waves of the 2016 election.

One flew over the Cuckoo's Nest: Tragic comedy in which a wild-eyed fanatic — known only as "the Prince" — escapes from an English lunatic asylum called "Buckingham Palace" where he has been incarcerated and kept under wraps for the past sixty-five years — and starts spouting complete gibberish.

The script writers famously tested the audience's ability to suspend disbelief, with classic lines such as "I want to be re-incarnated as a tampon" and "Islamic terrorism is all due to climate change".

❖

A former top Labor politician uses the International Day of Solidarity with the Palestinian People to accuse Israel of eliminating the Arab character of Jerusalem. And Mal Brough, one of the key organisers of the Turnbull coup, steps down.

Meanwhile, the Paris Climate Change conference manages to save the planet, with cash.

Allahu Bobkar

Financial Review
5/12/15

Former Labor stalwart "Allahu" Bobkar caused a furore this week with his explosive comments that a sinister group of Zionists and Jewish deli-owners have been responsible for the "Judaisation" of Melbourne. Speaking at a fundraiser for the Cutlery-Sharpeners and Suicide Vest-Manufacturers Association of Greater Bankstown, the former Labor titan "Allahu" Bobkar explained that the once great Arab city of M' el-Bourne has had its original Arab character entirely "eliminated" by a powerful group of lobbyists operating within a secret network operating out of Morty's Coffee and Bagel Emporium on Little Collins Street.

Said an outraged Mr Bobkar: "Street by street, deli by deli, shopping mall by shopping mall, we are seeing the very character, the soul, the essence, the nomenclature of this once noble and proud Arab city being changed before our very eyes."

Mr Bobkar drew sustained applause from his audience of knife-sharpeners and detonation experts when he went on (and on and on and on) pointing out the true story of how M' el-Bourne was once a thriving camel-trading post and date growing oasis in the middle of the Arabian desert.

Mr "Allahu" Bobkar backed up his claims by quoting a series of verses from biblical texts which clearly show that there were no Jews in M' el-Bourne prior to 1776. "This fabrication is a total disgrace!" the former Labor politician exploded in front of an ecstatic and ululating crowd. (Not literally, of course.)

Meanwhile, the world of advertising was shocked this week by the sudden demise of one of adland's most popular and enduring characters, the Malbrough Man. Speaking from his harbourside penthouse, the creative guru behind the hugely successful

Turnbull, Turnbull & Turnbull one man ad agency, Don "Mad Man" Turnbull, explained: "Unfortunately, the Malbrough Man has had its day. Yes, he was a very effective character in the past, and let's be honest, I wouldn't be where I am today without him, but unfortunately it has come to my attention that the Malbrough Man sets a bad example to the kiddies — Wyatt in particular — and it has also been shown time and time again over the past week that the Malbrough Man is highly toxic and going anywhere near him can prove extremely damaging to your polling numbers. Mine in particular."

In other news this week, the oceans began to recede and the planet began to heal thanks to the hugely successful Paris Climate Change Conference, in which the developed nations of the world made firm commitments to allow the undeveloped nations of the world to pollute their way to prosperity in order to avoid catastrophic climate change promises.

Said an ecstatic delegate: "What this new agreement does is allow the entire anglo-sphere to dramatically reduce our white, colonial guilt emissions at the same time as encouraging the rest of the world to boost their economies via renewables — meaning endlessly renewable pledges of hundreds of billions of dollars from us to them."

❖

A young MP and cabinet minister tells Sky News he doesn't remember whether or not he told Mr Ashby to copy his then boss's diary. "This is a conversation of years ago; I don't remember that specifically," the 25-year-old says. Meanwhile, the Leader of the Opposition is fined for texting whilst driving.

Alzheimers wyattitis

Financial Review
12/12/15

Health experts were shocked this week to learn of the onset of dementia in Australians of increasingly younger ages. According

2015 — The Year of Betrayal

to a report released in Canberra, a new strain of the disease, *Alzheimers wyattitis*, has been detected in young men barely out of their teens. The report's authors were devastated to find a young Queensland male holding down a highly responsible position within the federal cabinet who is barely capable of displaying any normal memory patterns.

Said a bewildered spokesperson: "What we found in this young man were these large sponge-like holes in the prefrontal cortex where normally you would expect to find typical highly emotional memories stored, which usually leave a strong impression on the adolescent brain. Yet when we fired random, trivial everyday questions at him — such as "where did you leave your diary?", "did you ask a friend to go and fetch your diary?", "was it someone else's diary?", "do you know anyone called Mal?" or even "is that bloke who works in whats-his-name's office really gay or is he just pretending?" — in every case this particular patient couldn't recall a single detail. To think that a young man in the prime of his life who has so little to offer the world could be so dramatically afflicted by such chronic memory loss is truly tragic."

One theory being put forward is that the young man's memory malfunction may have been caused by a significant trauma, such as being caught red-handed stabbing his leader in the back. "When such a despicable act of disloyalty is followed not by being punished — which is what you would expect — but in fact by being rewarded beyond his wildest dreams, this can have profoundly disturbing results on a developing brain. In this instance, the young man was suddenly promoted well above his proven abilities, which may have resulted in severe cognitive disturbance."

Said another expert: "We found numerous abnormalities in this individual's parietal lobe. Clearly, he is suffering from extremely debilitating delusions of grandeur, also known as *Arthur's syndrome*, which, as has been widely proven, frequently results in inexplicable memory loss." Experts believe the patient may carry on with normal bodily functions for many years to come, particularly given the lack of any serious challenges within his portfolio, but his long-term prospects are extremely limited. Meanwhile, in other news this week, police have released the transcripts of Bill Shorten's mobile phone calls, after he was photographed by a media outlet texting with both hands whilst driving at 40kph:

"Hey Albo u seen wot vat idiot Abbott has said now LOL"
"Sorry, who is this? I don't recognise the number"
"Haha LOL very funny anyway I gotta go call me asap"
"Hey Tanya hav u seen wot vat idiot Abbott has said now about how we should kick all the Mussies out of Austraya!!!!"
"Sorry Bill I'm in the middle of cleaning the oven can you call back later"
"Yeh OK LOL got anuvver urgent msg gotta go"
"Hey Chris maaaaate wot about how vat idiot Abbott wants to ban all Muftis!!!!"
"You have reached Chris Bowen's private message service I'm sorry I can't answer your text at the moment but your message is important to me please leave your details and I will get back to you as soon as I start counting numbers"
"LOL haha vats hilarious luv yr sense of humour m8 call me asap"
"Hey Burksie maaaaaaaaate wot about vat idiot Abbott wants to go to war wiv ISIS wot a dick!!!!"
"Sorry Bill I'm at a Friends of Peace-loving Jihadists meeting in Bankstown shoring up a few votes for my leadership bid, er, I mean for your continuing brilliant leadership let's speak soon, maybe after the Milad un Nabi hols in January insallah"
"LOL too funny maaaaaate luv it when yr taking the psss haha call me aarrrrgggghhhh...."

The rest of the transcript is unavailable due to an inexplicable collision through the front window of Mr Shorten's local pie shop. In other news this week, the Treasurer Scott Morrison, the most successful minister in the Abbott government and the man responsible for single-mindedly stopping the boats outlined his equally unambiguous and determined approach to reforming the tax system.

"Well, clearly, what we have agreed to today at COAG is that moving forward we as a collective of like-minded individuals from a variety of States each with its own critical requirements need to ascertain precisely those challenges which we consider appropriate under the circumstances requiring significant fiscal discipline yet notwithstanding an appreciation of all the stakeholders and by that I clearly consider the overarching need for innovation, in both an agile and a flexible (transcriber dozed off)."

❖

A castaway who claims to have survived at sea for 438 days is accused of eating his colleague's remains in order to survive, according to a $1 million lawsuit. Meanwhile, an ASIO director-general phones Coalition politicians to urge them to use the soothing language favoured by Malcolm Turnbull in any public discussion of Islam.

Cannibal

Financial Review
19/12/15

A castaway who was adrift in the wilderness for over six years has denied having survived by cannibalising his own captain. Salvador Turnbull astonished the world when he re-appeared on the remote shores of Lake Burley Griffin on September 14th this year looking fit and healthy despite having been all at sea since 2009, when his leadership mysteriously disappeared under a wave of unpopularity brought on by poor judgment and sinking opinion polls.

Unable to stomach being out of the limelight, the man survived on a diet of eco-friendly carbon emissions, drinking his own Ozemail shares and allowing nothing but waffle to pass his lips. He had drifted miles and miles away from his conservative moorings before his communications portfolio packed up completely, costing the taxpayer billions of dollars. Miraculously, he was then rescued by a cohort of 54 desperately nervous nellies who abandoned ship rather than show any signs of loyalty to their captain, whose rotting body and tarnished reputation they then dismembered and tipped overboard.

"I was going to top myself," an emotional Salvador said at the time from his impoverished harbourside village of Wentworthova, "but Lucy persuaded me all I had to do was believe in the almighty Arthur Sinodinos and my own awesome powers of persuasion and I'd be saved."

However, the family of the sunken vessel's Captain Pick, who mysteriously disappeared on that fateful voyage, now claim that he was in fact eaten alive by Señor Turnbull, whom they have branded a fraud who deliberately cannibalised his former colleague in order to avoid being humiliated by an inevitable Abbott victory at the Canning by-election.

Señor Turnbull denies the claims: "Even after he died, one part of my brain refused to accept Tony was dead, buried and cremated. So I laid him down on his side at the far end of the backbenches and carried on leaking against him."

In other news this week, the head of the Allied War effort, General Dunkin Donuts-Lewis, appealed for critics of the Third Reich to adopt a more soothing and non-inflammatory tone of voice when discussing matters connected to defeating Nazi aggression.

"To run around German-baiting is extremely dangerous," said an irate General Donuts. "Using offensive terminology like 'Bosch' or 'Hun' or 'Krauts' only serves to inflame tensions which risks offending and even radicalising young, vulnerable, impressionable members of the Hitler Jugend."

General Donuts is believed to have personally telephoned numerous rebel "conservative" members of the War Room to admonish them for their use of inflammatory and non-respectful language towards Germans. The phone calls are part of a broadbased effort by the Allied forces to influence how politicians, and indeed media commentators, speak about the Nazi war machine.

"I don't buy the idea that this so-called extremism is somehow fostered by or sponsored or supported by the writings of Adolf Hitler," the General claimed. "Nazism is a blasphemy of those benign lyrical verses of Mein Kampf that call for the subjugation of sub-humans and death to all Jews. National Socialism is, above all else, an ideology of peace."

The General's phone calls, believed to be at the specific behest of Mr Chamberlain, were viewed by some as a brazen attempt to "slap down" former Prime Minister Winston Abbott who in a recent editorial called for a "reformation" of the Wehrmacht.

Said the General: "This inflammatory language about fighting Germans on the beaches, on the seas and in the air is the worst sort of language and will only serve to inflame tensions and directly threaten our national security. Rather than fighting on the beaches, I would ask politicians to refer more respectfully to engaging in multi-faith dialogue and shared universal values on the beaches, on the seas and in the air."

Leaping to General Donuts' defence, Wing Commander 'Julie' Bishopsgate agreed: "The invasion of Europe is proceeding peacefully along soothing, compassionate, multicultural lines and the last thing we should be doing is inflaming tensions by using provocative language such as 'Muslim' or 'conquest' which can only have the undesirable effect of insulting those peaceful, law-abiding individuals currently involved in the, er, Muslim conquest of Europe."

2016 — The Year of Come Uppance

Politically, much of 2016 was a year of chooks coming home to roost. Having worked so assiduously to oust Tony Abbott and become Prime Minister, Malcolm Turnbull had no idea what he wanted to do with the job. During late 2015, Turnbull and his new Treasurer Scott Morrison made a great deal about things being "on and off the table", which became a euphemism for indecision. Instead of slogans, we got waffle, until people were so confused that the waffle was ditched in favour of new slogans. But instead of "stop the boats" — as unambiguous as you can get — the Australian voter had to get their head around "Continuity with change" and "Jobs and growth."

Meanwhile, as Turnbull trotted between his two harbourside mansions (the povo one belonging to the taxpayers, the glitzy one belonging to him), the rest of the world was going to hell in a handbasket.

Terrorism leapt out of alleyways across Europe and the world, brandishing a knife and screeching "Allahu Akbar", so often that it became almost routine and boring. (Nothing to do with Islam either, of course.) Europe sank under a flood of illegal immigrants who turned out to be not quite as cute and cuddly as Angela Merkel and others had promised. The Brits decided to bail out of the whole show with their Brexit vote, and the Americans opted for a politically incorrect real estate mogul and reality TV star for their next president.

And the more Turnbull dithered, the more Bill Shorten shone in the public's eye.

❖

Victorian prepackaged lettuce is recalled after a higher-than-usual number of salmonella cases were reported. Meanwhile, a famous rock group are threatened with a plagiarism law suit over their most famous song, the Treasurer dithers, and it is mooted (again) that Kevin Rudd wishes to run the UN.

Shortenella virus

Financial Review
6/2/16

Health authorities today released a nationwide alert warning of the risk of eating lettuce contaminated by the deadly *shortenella virus*, believed to be responsible for the poisoning of over 28 members of the shadow cabinet. The virus, which can lead to severe bouts of vomiting up endless commitments to Gonski and other such unaffordable spending promises has also been linked to confusion, amnesia and political paralysis.

Experts were at first puzzled as to the causes of the *shortenella* outbreak. "Then we heard numerous reports of an inconsequential little man surrounded by TV cameras wandering around supermarkets and fiddling with peoples' lettuce. He was even reaching into their shopping trolleys and picking it up and touching it! It was disgusting!" said a spokesperson for the Centre for Communicable Diseases. "When an individual displays symptoms of verbal diarrhea of this magnitude, then the risk of even the tiniest flecks of spittle spraying all over the place are lethal, particularly when he infects the language with unhygienic words like 'wiv', 'nuffink' and 'uvver'."

"*Shortenella* is a severe form of gastroenteritis, or gst for short, and occurs when the lettuce is covered in verbal excrement. We see a lot of this strain in Victoria, obviously, but now it's spreading. Bill has been spotted trawling through shopping malls across the country, desperately hoping to make intimate contact with everyday Australians."

All major supermarkets have warned shoppers to take every precaution to avoid being within proximity of Bill Salmonella anywhere near food counters or open microphones. "Anyone who suspects they might have come into contact with Bill should immediately throw him out, which is what we intend to do straight after we lose the next election," explained a spokesperson for cut-price retail politician Albo's.

In other news this week, famous rock group Led Morrison have been accused of filching their greatest hit, "The GST Remains the Same (or Maybe It Doesn't)", from the classic 2007 oldie "Stairway to Kevin". In documents tendered before the court, former prime minister Kevin Rudd claims the lyrics to the latest national conversation on the economy is a straight lift from his own folksy conversation on economic matters with the good burghers of Australia between 2007 and 2010.

Said a spokesperson: "If you compare the Morrison waffle with the Rudd jargon, they are uncannily similar. Both contain lots of long words, and lots of important-sounding promises but basically they never actually spell out what the message is — or indeed if there even is a message! In their total lack of any 'economic specificity' they are indistinguishable. Lay them on top of each other and you'll see the melodies are virtually identical, particularly the way they never resolve into any satisfactory conclusion and always leave the voter hanging in the air wondering what's coming next."

Experts believe that lead singer Scotty Morrison may have been influenced by sitting in parliament opposite Kevin Rudd for several years during his heyday and subconsciously (or otherwise) plagiarised the main riff. "Of course, Led Morrison's first hit, 'The Immigrant Song', is what made him incredibly famous in the first place, but now that he's the front man for the whole show he's completely lost it. Every time he gets up to perform it's just 'Dazed and Confused' or 'Ramble On' followed by 'Communication Breakdown'.

The case is expected to be settled in mid-May, with damages in the billions to be footed by the taxpayer.

Meanwhile, the Fin has obtained the first draft of a landmark speech scribbled on the back of a beer coaster in a New York lap-dancing club by newly-elected United Nation's Secretary-General Kevin Rudd outlining his modest plans for the year ahead.

1. *Fix Climate Change:* install pink floaties and free boogie boards in all low-lying atolls and sinking islands.

2. *Solve European financial crisis:* make speech explaining capitalism is finished then send 900 euro cheques to all Greeks, Italians, Spaniards, Portuguese etc (dead as well as living just to be sure).

3. *Bring peace to the Middle East:* set up free Assadwatch and Isiswatch websites allowing the user to compare sexual atrocities, beheadings, crucifixions and gassings in real time.

4. *Stop Iranian nuclear proliferation:* ditto with Ayatollahwatch website.

5. *Stop Chinese territorial aggression:* ratf—k 'em (in Mandarin).

6. *Solve third world illiteracy:* build Global Broadband Network bringing high speed internet to all third world villages (see detailed construction plans and costings for GBN on front of beer coaster).

7. *Inspirational ideas for future well-being of all mankind:* organise massive 2020 global ideas summit, guests: Bono, Cate, Angelina, Therese, Barack, Malcolm, Julie, ME.

8. *Solve Syrian refugee crisis:* open all borders, everywhere, now.

❖

Relations between Mr Turnbull and Mr Morrison become strained over successive failures to reform tax policy. Meanwhile, physicists announce the discovery of gravitational waves, ripples in the fabric of spacetime first anticipated by Einstein a century ago, whilst the CSIRO decides to sack a bunch of climate change scientists.

Gravitational waffle

Financial Review
13/2/16

In an announcement that has electrified the world of political science, a team of physicists has proven what Einstein predicted a century ago: the existence of gravitational waffle.

The discovery means that scientists have finally tapped into the deepest register of political implausibility at the heart of the Wentworth galaxy, where the weirdest and wildest implications of Arthur Einstein's Theory of Relative Popularity apply.

"Our understanding of the heavens has changed dramatically," said one scientist. "It is clear now that not only will there be no Big Bang economic reform, but we have conclusive proof that Malcolm is not God."

An all-star team of astrophysicists used a newly upgraded and excruciatingly sensitive $1.1 billion instrument known as the Liberal Government's Turn-Bulldust Interferometer, or LGTBI for short, to detect gravitational waffle from the distant crash of two massive black holes.

Said an excited spokesperson: "When two such vast objects collide, they send gravitational waffle right across the universe. In this instance, we detected the presence of two massive yet essentially vacuous entities, which we nicknamed 'Turnbull's Popularity' and 'Morrison's Budget', which are billions of light years apart and have been circling each other for months on end before they spectacularly collided in the middle of last week." At a news conference, the scientists played what they called a "twerp" — the faint signal they first heard on September 14, 2015. "To make sense of the raw data, we translated the waffle into sound. Any authentic or purposeful meaning was barely perceptible, even when enhanced by *Lateline*."

Scientists found indirect proof of the existence of gravitational waffle in the 1990s — computations that showed it dramatically altered the course of the Republican referendum and the Godwin Grech affair. Said one linguistics expert: "Gravitational waffle exists when you keep saying something over and over again with sufficient gravity even though it is essentially empty. It is the glue that holds our political universe together."

Said another expert: "It's one thing to know waffle exists

theoretically, but it's another to actually hear it in action. Take this classic example from last Wednesday, which we picked up on ABC radio, direct from Assistant Treasurer Kelly Hairdryer: 'I think you need to be able to make a really compelling argument for change — that's not to say I won't change my position if more compelling arguments are put on the table.' We've analysed it extensively but can detect nothing but pure, unadulterated waffle."

The expert claims Hairdryer, previously one of the brightest stars in the Liberal firmament, is clearly orbiting too close to the Morrison and Turnbull black holes and has been sucked in by an unstoppable force of gravitational waffle.

In other scientific news this week, the CSIRO have announced that the "science is finally settled" and that "97% of CSIRO scientists now agree in the likelihood that a large part of the global climate science scare is man-made."

Said a spokesperson: "It is now beyond doubt that the majority of the anthropogenic warming myth is in fact due entirely to human scientific invention. It is imperative that we reduce the number of CSIRO climate change scientists to at least pre-2000 levels, or at least by 50% if we want to avoid the results of a catastrophic build-up of toxic verbal pollutants."

When asked how the scientific community could best reduce its global warming research output, the spokesperson agreed that direct action was the most efficient way. "Basically, if we sack at least half the scientists then we can dramatically reduce their climate change output."

Experts are worried that the CSIRO risks reaching a "tipping point", where a build-up of dangerous levels of tiresome, repetitive climate change reports will require an urgent trip to the tip.

"Our modelling shows we've got tons and tons of this rubbish, mostly trashy research papers recycling that same 'the science is settled' garbage, and all of it costing the taxpayer billions of dollars in grants. We've tried to find some alternative use for it but all we can do is bury it in the ground. The alternative is incinerating the lot."

❖

The shine comes off the Turnbull team as the polls start to slip. And the punters are unimpressed when the Treasurer presents his economic narrative by including a "unicorn" in his spiel. Meanwhile, the new Star Wars *film gets poor reviews, with movie fans more interested in the low-key hit* Deadpool, *and John Cleese and Eric Idle team up in Sydney.*

Turnbull: The Force Awakens

Financial Review
20/2/16

The world of entertainment was stunned this week by news that the latest Hollywood blockbuster, *Turnbull: The Force Awakens*, which was supposed to be the biggest movie of all time, is in fact fading badly at the box office. After a remarkable run of five months, in which the Liberal's latest entertainment offering out-performed all its predecessors, it became clear last week from the numbers that the magic is no longer working and audiences are turning away in droves. If past blockbuster patterns are anything to go by, *Turnbull: The Force Awakens* appears destined to fall well short of its incredibly high expectations.

Experts believe the studio foolishly damaged the film's box office appeal by playing it ridiculously safe with the scripting. "There was nothing new in it, just a re-hash of all the old Abbott and Hockey story lines," said one Hollywood reporter. "We were promised this amazing new narrative, but the actors appear incapable of delivering it."

Other critics point to the woeful dialogue. "It's just waffle. In one scene, which seems to drone on for at least an hour, the hero strides up to the Podium at the National Press Club and delivers these cobbled-together lines about Elvis impersonators, Texakarna salesmen, Twenty20 cricket teams, stand-up comedians and 'backing innovation'... but then nothing actually happens. It's not only a complete anti-climax, even the die-hard fans are left totally bewildered and confused as to where the plot is going."

A further problem, according to an SFX expert, is that the film doesn't showcase any breakout technology. "They tried to introduce all these new gimmicks like raising the GST, scrapping negative gearing and raiding super, but at the end of the day audiences didn't buy it. There's nothing there to fire your imagination, particularly when you compare the lack of whizz-bang special effects to those classics of the past like 'Keating' and 'Costello'."

"Those films each offered things you've never seen before on screen," said another critic. "This new stuff just leaves you with an awful, sick empty feeling, like you've eaten way too much popcorn and drunk too much fizzy pop."

To be fair, *Turnbull: The Force Awakens* is a massive success by any metric. Before interest petered out, it smashed through a long list of early box office milestones. In inner-city, latte-serving cinemas, it topped Newspoll in just 21 hours back in mid-September, spawning a whole range of themed toys and video games around climate change, gay marriage, the Republic, Indigenous recognition and so on. "But then when you actually sat down and watched the film itself," complained one bitter fan, "none of that cool stuff ever appears in it."

On top of which, in recent weeks, *The Force Awakens* has lost business to Labor's surprise hit *Deadbill*, in which a hideously deformed and crippled Labor leader undergoes a violent shock treatment and comes back as a quirky mutant superhero, which is a far more engaging plot line for young audiences these days. Another surprise hit has been *The Revenant*, in which a desperate, foul-mouthed, ruddy-faced agrarian politician gets left for dead in the New England wilderness by his own Party but struggles valiantly against all the odds to survive and eventually comes back as leader of the Nationals and deputy PM.

But critics point to the final nail in the coffin for *Turnbull: The Force Awakens* being the fateful decision to make it more of a childish fantasy film than any of its predecessors. "It's that moment in the film when the unicorn appears out of nowhere that audiences really started to puke," said one former fan. "A unicorn? Are you kidding me? At that point you knew nobody on the Turnbull crew was taking our debt and deficit seriously, not even Mr Morrison."

In other entertainment news this week, the comedy duo behind the successful satirical TV show *Malcy Python's Wentworth Circus* teamed up in Sydney this week to launch their new two-man show, "Together In Power At Last — Forever". "Scott and I never really liked each other much before, but then we realised how powerful we'd be if we teamed up," said veteran funny man Malcy Bone-Idle. "Basically, we haven't bothered much with a proper script as such; it's easier just to make it up as we go along and say whatever the audiences want to hear.

"Some nights we just get up on stage and waffle on a bit... but of course we all know that the real reason the fans are here is to see us doing the 'Dead Abbott' sketch together.

"They love it. All I have to say is 'this Abbott is dead, buried and cremated', and it brings the house down."

❖

China attempts to reassure the world about its ongoing annexation of numerous remote islands.

Mee No Lie

Financial Review
27/2/16

In China this week, China's Minister for the Peaceful Annexation of Remote Chinese Islands, Mee No Lie, informed the world that China intends to continue its peaceful annexation of a remote artificial island comprising reefs and patches of sand that lies in disputed waters to its far south.

Said Lie: "It was just this useless patch of dirt floating in the middle of the ocean that nobody had any use for, so we thought we may as well grab Australia and do something with it. That's why we've bought up the farms, bought the mines, bought up the high-rises, bought up the dairies, bought up the IT industries, leased the naval base in Darwin and tried to snap up the nuclear missile testing range at Woomera. Our intentions are, of course, consistent with international law and entirely peaceful," he added, as his official translator collapsed in a fit of hysterical laughter and had to be executed.

❖

The PM and Treasurer decide to kiss and make up, whilst a political book is slammed for salacious gossip to do with the former PM and his Chief of Staff. Meanwhile, Iran's Foreign Minister comes to town, and the government spend millions on an ad campaign: "Welcome to the Ideas Boom".

A fork in a Chinese restaurant

Financial Review
12/3/16

The world of politics was rocked to its core this week by juicy revelations in an explosive tell-all book *Fifty Shades of Grey on the Road to Fiscal Ruin* by the Fin's leading columnist Nikki "Fair-suck-of-the" Saveloy. In an extract published exclusively here today, Ms Saveloy details the tempestuous relationship that undermined an entire government and brought down a popular Liberal prime minister.

> The whispers in the corridors of power were growing stronger every day, as the hot, steamy months of an unseasonably humid early autumn gave way to the cold, bitter winds of reality sweeping across the muddy waters of Lake Burley Griffin. Like the faint echoes of the ghost of

a lamented lover calling out in the night, two little words echoed through the Prime Minister's mind, over and over, as he tossed and turned clutching feverishly at his pillow, his passions and lusts unquenched even by the triumphs he had already enjoyed thus far. Two words played on his troubled soul, or maybe it was actually four. Budget Time. Double Dissolution.

Yet come the morning, Malcolm would leave the comforting yet empty confines of his marital bed and sneak off to an early-morning rendez-vous with 'The Other One', a sneering nickname given by his wife Lucy to the one person whose name she could no longer bring herself to utter:
Scott Morrison.

Staffers, whose names I won't reveal because they don't actually exist, have all told me in detail how they would feel uncomfortable in the presence of this fiery couple, Malcie and Scotty, as every gesture and nuance in their voices hinted at the unresolved tensions between them. Had two individuals ever been so totally dependent on each other, to the exclusion of all others? Was it sexual? Or was it more of a master-slave relationship? But who was the master? And who was the slave?

It was April 2016. They had assembled at the notorious Wild Duck restaurant, these two tormented souls, in order to wrestle with the diabolical dilemma that was torturing them both, tearing them apart, straining the very fibres of their beings. Questions that went to the very heart of their agonised relationship. When to release the budget? What on earth to put in it? Why did you torpedo the GST you psycho? Why did you torpedo negative gearing you psycho? What about super, Kelly says that's a "gift"! Shall we call a double dissolution? On what possible grounds? Why did you torpedo the ABCC legislation you psycho?

Those who were present at the table were shocked by the ferocity of the passion. They could see it in their eyes.

2016 — The Year of Come Uppance

The fear, the hatreds, the animosity, the terror.
The power couple chose, unwisely, to sit at the very table where rumours of the Turnbull affair had begun all those years ago, when Malcolm had been seduced by his previous paramour Clive into thinking all he needed to do was topple Tony and the world would be his aphrodisiac, um, oyster. On that occasion, Clive had ordered the Banquet (for himself) and Malcolm had settled for the dim sums.
But this time the atmosphere was different. Gone was the false bonhomie, the flirtatious smiles, the gentle ribbing and the mock affection. In its place, an icy silence settled over the table, staffers who don't actually exist have repeatedly told me. Too many decisions had to be made tonight. None of them pleasant. This time Scott wanted the dim sums but Malcolm ordered the sang choy bow, a favourite. "Are those dumplings as good as I remember?" whispered Malcolm, his hand uncomfortably close to Scott's. Scott smirked. "Here," he replied breathlessly, "why don't you try one for yourself?" The entire restaurant stared, horrified, as the Treasurer picked up his fork and spoon-fed the Prime Minister his dumplings. They couldn't believe their eyes! Who uses a fork in a Chinese restaurant?!

Meanwhile, in other news this week, Australia's foreign minister claimed success in her campaign to improve relations with Iran. Speaking from behind her new niqab, the minister, who has formed a close bond with her Iranian counterpart Omar Sharif who is visiting Australia this week, explained the enormous commercial opportunities now available to Australian firms, particularly in the manufacturing sectors. "Omar will be looking to Australian entrepreneurs to help him find innovative and agile ideas to take back to Iran, such as how to throw gays off buildings more efficiently, how to torture dissidents in a more flexible manner, how to use Aussie know-how to arm Hezbollah and Hamas and smuggle weapons into Yemen in a more agile way and how to re-arrange the world map more innovatively so it doesn't include Israel. This should make the Ideas Boom go off with a, er, boom!

❖

A controversial anti-bullying program encourages school children to experiment with being of a different gender.

All of Us

Financial Review
19/3/16

A new program to prevent bullying in the Federal parliament is to be introduced throughout the corridors of Canberra, known as the Safe Parliament "All of Us" program. Details of the controversial new program, to be funded by the taxpayer to the tune of $8 million, have been leaked to the Fin:

There are many types of politicians in Canberra, not just Liberal and Labor. The aim of this program is to make you understand what it is like to be of a different political persuasion altogether to the one you happen to think you are — in fact, there aren't just two political identities you can identify with, there are dozens!

In order to more fully understand them, you and your entire class should try the following creative exercises.

The Malcolm: In order to identify with being a Malcolm, tuck your penis between your legs and imagine that you have no testicles. Now you know what it feels like not to be able to make a decision about things like whether or not to raise the GST, whether or not to have negative gearing, or whether or not to steal people's superannuation. Then try walking quickly towards a double dissolution election and see what it feels like without any balls.

The Penny: In this exercise, you are asked to imagine that you have no genitalia. How would you dress? Try wearing a suit with trousers and an open collar that makes you look like a man, but then remember to wear a pair of earrings so you also look like a woman. People will be confused about what you stand for, but this is a good thing, because it allows you to lecture them shrilly about things like running a Safe Schools program designed to turn confused heteronormative kiddies into miserable fruitcakes.

2016 — The Year of Come Uppance

The Wyatt Twerp: Virginity is a subjective concept, and just because you think you are a political virgin that doesn't necessarily mean you really are one. There are all sorts of ways you can lose your political virginity, so why not imagine that you have hopped into bed with a disloyal Communications Minister and his friends at a house in Queanbeyan one night and been rewarded with a cabinet position well beyond your years or your talent? But don't worry — all you need to do is identify with being a cabinet minister, and then you are one!

The Cross-bencher: Dress up in whatever political clothes you feel like, even if they make you look a little strange because you have no idea how you actually won your seat and at first you feel a little uncomfortable. You can mix and match your policies as often as you like, change into new ones whenever you feel like it, or why not simply wander around without any policies on at all and enjoy the feeling of immense power and freedom that this gives you? But don't get too used it, however, because today's cross-benchers will be tomorrow's distant memory.

The Wee Willy Shorten: Bullies and other cruel people such as political satirists will often poke fun at people with a serious speech defect, but this is just typical nasty schoolyard bullying. In this exercise, you are asked to imagine that you have a problem saying words that have a "th" sound in them, such as "with", or "growth", or "nothing". Now get up in front of all your friends at the National Press Club and try and make a serious speech on your plans for the economy. The aim of the exercise is for the entire class to try and keep a straight face all the way through. Or should that be "frew"?

The Saveloy: Some people like to make up stories about other people's sexuality and enjoy harmlessly fantasising that one of them touched the other on the bottom or that one of them ate from the other's fork. This is perfectly normal behaviour during political puberty. Try imagining what it would be like if they were actually having sex! Then write down your wildest fantasies as a healthy way of experimenting with the truth and making a bloody fortune.

❖

The Treasurer is said to have been excluded from a key strategic cabinet meeting.

Deeper yet shallower

Financial Review
24/3/16

The beads of sweat glistened brightly on the smooth top of Arthur's shiny bald pate under the harsh halogens. He glanced around the room. This was it! The big DD Decision time. They were all here, all the critical players. Malcolm, Michaelia, Mathias and, er, Wyatt.

"OK team", Arthur said, "let's brainstorm."

Malcolm's leg was twitching excitedly. "No need! I've cracked it already!" said the prime minister, holding up his hand like a stop-go man at a crossing and grinning his trademark Cheshire cat smile, "Continuity AND change!"

"Huh?" said Arthur.

"It's our brand new slogan," said the PM smugly. "Lucy and I thought of it in the shower this morning. Or it might have been in the bathroom, or at least in the bedroom. Or maybe it was in the walk-in wardrobe. Or…"

"We don't do slogans, Malcolm," Arthur gently interrupted. "Three word slogans are out. 'Continuity and change'? That's three words. I'd strongly advise…"

"Well, it may be a three word slogan to you, Arthur," said the prime minister, smiling broadly. "But I see it as something far, far more — how shall I put it? — far deeper than that." The prime minister slowly took off his glasses and leaned back in his chair. Arthur's heart sank and he struggled to maintain his fixed grin. It was going to be a long evening.

" …deeper, yet shallower," said the PM, his hand expressively

2016 — The Year of Come Uppance

moulding thin air. "Profound yet obvious. Philosophical yet self-evident," he carried on. "I see 'continuity' as a nostalgic nod back down the road well travelled, a fond glance in the rear view mirror of life, yet at the same time 'change' offers a tantalising glimpse into the exciting, innovative future that awaits us on the long road ahead. Well, when I say long, I mean short. The short road ahead replete with long opportunities. Continuity and change."

Arthur reached for a napkin off the cheese platter and gently dabbed his forehead, not noticing he'd smeared camembert over his eyebrows. The PM's 'consiglieri' had long ago learned that the best way to cope with his boss's stream of consciousness meanderings, or 'waffle' as the satirists so cruelly called it, was to let it roll over you like a summer southerly and wait 'til it wore itself out.

The storm was in full gusto — a classic Turnbull buster. "Continuity and change. It says I can appreciate the... the roadways, the laneways, the byways, the highways, the streets even, and the footpaths we have all travelled down, and up, or along, and across, er... and yet, with both hands firmly on the wheel — well, not both hands, one perhaps tightly gripping the wheel and the other slightly looser, elegantly poised, allowing the driver to be both purposeful yet flexible, determined yet dexterous, sturdy yet nimble, pre-determined yet spontaneous, to the point where we can reach out and grasp the future with both hands...

"Not zo easy to reach out wiz both hands und have zem on ze wheel," muttered Mathias under his breath. Arthur scowled at him. Wyatt giggled nervously.

The PM carried on, "...and so we must be brave yet fearful, we must be cautious yet bold, we must be hungry yet satiated, we must be angry yet calm, we must be..."

Arthur felt his eyelids growing heavy. Suddenly an ear-piercing sound exploded in the room and shot him out of his reverie, scorching his eardrums. What on earth was that noise?

Fingernails down a blackboard? The screech of a power drill? A car crash on Capital Circuit? Then he realized it was just Michaelia speaking up.

"Lets foooiight the bloody Elekshun on Oooooiiiiiiii Arrrrrrrrr, Ooooiii reckun! Let's effin' shove it up them Soooiii Effffin' Emmm Eeeyyyy Ewww bastards!" shouted the Employment Minister feistily, her neat coiffure and elegant dress sense, Arthur always noted, providing a disarming contrast to her vocal manifestations.

"Well, of course, Michaelia is absolutely right," said the PM, without skipping a beat. "We can call a DD on the ABCC. IR is as much a positive as it is a negative, as much a threat as it is an opportunity, as much a strength as a weakness...."

"Eet eez more an egg-onomic issue zan a vorkplace vun," growled Mathias, struggling in vain to sound as little like Arnie Schwarzenegger as possible yet keen to keep the economic narrative firmly in his department's hands, rather than let it be snatched into the grasp of the incomprehensible screeching woman. "Ve must speak to Scott about zis," the Belgian said firmly.

"Who?" said the Prime Minister, puzzled.

"Scotty, old ScoMo," said Arthur quickly. "You know. The Treasurer."

"Oh him," said the PM, waving his glasses dismissively. "What's he got to do with our re-election plans?"

❖

As the government flounders around for an economic narrative, an Egypt Air plane is hijacked by a man in a fake suicide vest and one of the passengers/hostages grabs a selfie. Meanwhile, a university is accused of rewriting history after it encouraging students to use the term "invasion" for the British settlement of Australia.

Mustafa Tax Plan

Financial Review
2/4/16

The world of aviation was shocked to its core this week when a lone hijacker with a fake suicide vest managed to seize the economic reform agenda and force it to fly to a COAG meeting in Canberra. The mystery man, who surrendered to the inevitable, was later identified as Mustafa Tax-Plan, an oddball eccentric multi-millionaire from the small waterside village of Wentworth on the leafy shores of Sydney Harbour. The man, who was on a forlorn mission to save his prime ministership by delivering an economic narrative to the electorate, assembled his suicide agenda out of odd bits of leftover tax and federation policies that easily evaded detection by the economy's co-pilot, Mr Morrison, a former rug merchant from The Shire. "I didn't suspect a thing until, yet again, Mustafa pulled the rug from right out underneath me," said a distraught Mr Morrison, speaking from his home on the 'Outer Circle' of the Turnbull government.

During his flight from reality, a grinning Mustafa posed for selfies not only with himself but, amazingly, also with his hostages, a group of 54 red-faced Liberal MPs who lost their minds completely back in September and eagerly clambered on board and have been regretting it ever since. Said one, speaking on condition of complete anonymity (which is pretty much guaranteed after the next election): "He wasn't like those other hijackers Kevin and Julia. He had a really nice smile. I trusted him completely. He didn't force us to do anything against our will. We all went along for the ride but we've been going round and round in circles ever since on a headwind of nothing but hot air. It almost makes you long for the days of Captain Pick and Stewardess Peta."

No-one was injured in the incident, with authorities claiming Mustafa Tax-Plan appeared to be harmless and was simply "in love with himself". "He's been in an unstable psychological state since his polling figures crashed to earth. He's not an economic terrorist, he's just a waffler who's winging it."

In other news this week, historians at the University of New South Wales have unearthed the never-before-seen original diary notes for Captain James Cook's sinister New Holland invasion plans:

April 29, in the year of Our Lord, 1770

Woke up in the middle of a feverish night's sleep, dreams of conquest, bloodshed and mayhem surging through my mind, to see we have berthed in a large natural harbour. I decide to name it Battleship Bay after my plans for a full-scale naval assault but that lily-livered pansy Joseph Banks insists on calling it Botany Bay. What sort of a man, I ask myself, devotes his energy to looking for new kinds of blossom? Methinks he displays more the attributes of some cis-trans intersex gender fluid deviant than those of a virile heteronormative Englishman! But I digress. The bay is flat and wide and, disappointingly, nothing like the deep blue harbour to shelter a thousand Man O' Wars that I had hoped to find in these parts. Nonetheless, I comfort myself with the thought that it would make an excellent place for an airport some day, if only those layabouts Solander and Sporing would stop drawing daisies and start designing aircraft.

Peering through my telescope as I prepare my military strategy I note the enemy forces are aligned in plain sight along the beach, all seventeen of them by my latest count, where I see they are frantically collecting oyster shells and small little worm-like grubs, presumably as their main defensive weaponry of choice. My forces shall have to outflank them in a cunning pincer movement I have designed called 'The Yabbie', or perhaps I shall apply my strategic genius and get my men to build a giant wooden wombat with which to penetrate their inner fortifications. I am fully prepared to suffer many casualties during the landing, so we shall launch our armada under cover of darkness, with oars to muffle the sound of our approach. My second-in-command, Zachary Hicks, a baker's assistant from Stepney, believes we must engage the enemy at dawn, with the sun behind us, to maximise the element of surprise. Cunningly, I have advised my troops to also win the propaganda war, by writing to their loved ones back home about the beauty of this wild new land we have just discovered. To be sure, I have instructed them never to utter the world "invasion", but rather, refer to the "settlement" of the "colonies". We don't want to offend the natives, now do we? But... hark!

"What is that thumping sound?...who goes...?"

"Wake up! You were dreaming, sire! I've just been ashore and discovered these pretty little plants. I think I'll call them Banksias. Sooo divine."

❖

As Labor defy the odds and surge in the opinion polls, it is revealed the Leader of the Opposition has been employing a public speaking expert from a Victorian university to improve his communication skills.

All the Gonski that we can eat

Financial Review
15/4/16

The world of entertainment was rocked this week with the explosive news of a long-awaited remake of the 1960s smash hit movie *My Fair Billy*, starring newcomer Audrey Shorten. The updated version, being filmed currently at secret locations in Melbourne and Canberra, follows the familiar plot of a dysfunctional, down-and-out Opposition Leader — nicknamed "'E Lies And DoLittle" — undergoing intensive elocution lessons as part of a bet to see whether he can string two sentences together in a meaningful way before the federal election due on July 2.

The film opens with this waif-like, poorly-educated ex-union leader wandering the dirty streets trying to appeal to the lower classes by selling them the idea of a banking inquiry. "All I want is some class warfare, wiv me sitting in Malcolm's chair, oh wouldn't it be loverly? All the Gonski that we can eat, lots of coal making no more heat, Six point plans to make our steel, oh wouldn't it be loverly?" he laments wistfully.

Appalled by his mangled vowels and tortured syntax, he is spotted by an obscure voice coach and speech professor from Melbourne University, who takes him under his wing. "You see this creature," the professor boasts, "in six months I could pass him off as a future prime minister and leader of the country." At first Billy is suspicious, but every focus group tells him he would be better off if people could actually understand a word of what he said.

At their first elocution lesson, the professor instructs Billy: "Every night before you go to bed and say your prayers I want you to practice annunciating the following vowels and consonants at least fifty times over: C,F,M,E,U… C,F,M,E,U…"

To which Billy responds indignantly: "I do vat anyway! I'm a good boy I am!"

As well as Billy learning to "speak proper", much of the film's old-fashioned vaudeville humour comes from the interplay between the different classes, with Billy having to learn new etiquette and table manners, such as how to order a hot meat pie without swearing obscenities at the Chinese shop owner.

Billy struggles to escape from the expectations of his lowly Victorian-era birth and low status in life, preferring the company of corrupt truck drivers and "road safety" remuneration tribunals to whom he feels he owes his undying loyalty for having got him this far in life.

The film includes many of the Labor Party's traditional favourite songs, updated for a modern audience, including "Get Me To The Polls On Time", "Therese Rein Stays Mainly on the First Class Plane to Spain" and Billy's heartfelt "I'm An Ordinary Man" (to which the whole Party nods along in agreement) as well as his famous solo "Wiv A Little Bit of Luck".

"It's not 'wiv', it's 'with'," says the professor, wearily. "My dear boy, try and pronounce the following vowels and consonants slowly and clearly: "With a little bit of luck, the bogans will buy Billy's bank bashing balderdash."

One early scene leaked online shows Billy hilariously mixing up his aitches in the following tongue-twister: "In hospitals, health-care centres and homeless shelters, the HSU hardly ever comes." In another scene, the exasperated professor can barely hide his frustration: "If you're going to make a speech about all your new spending promises and say absolutely nothing about how you intend to pay for them, then at least say 'nothing', not 'nuffink'!" he shrieks. "But vat's wot Bowen and Tanya told me to say," protests Billy, "Vey said wotever you do, say nuffink!"
The action climaxes as the Opposition Leader finally "comes out" at a glittering double dissolution election attended by a colourful array of spivs, fakes and phoneys, including the sly barrow boy 'Albo', who doesn't bother hiding his own working class roots and is busily plotting Billy's downfall behind the scenes. Billy attempts to explain his economic policies to a bewildered electorate, employing a haphazard mashing of outdated ideas and meaningless focus group phrases. "We will pay for it all wiv a baccy tax, wiv a banking profits tax, wiv a super tax, wiv a carbon tax and wiv no more negative gear-wing," he explains in the film's most revealing scene.

"It's GEAR-ing! There is no 'W' in 'negative gearing'," shouts the professor. Albo grins slyly. "And not many votes, either," he quips.

In other disturbing news this week, an attractive blonde TV celebrity found herself imprisoned by the Lebanese following a failed kidnapping stunt. Said Julie Bishop, speaking on her cell from Beirut. "Thanks to those idiots at *60 Minutes* I am now held hostage and completely at the mercy of Hezbollah and Iran. They can demand whatever they want. I could be stuck negotiating with them for months, if not years."

❖

Labor announces plans for a Royal Commission into the banking industry.

Banking Royal Commission

Financial Review
23/4/16

Welcome to Day One of the Royal Commission into Banking Malfeasance and Financial Sector Corruption, or the Shorten Inquiry as it is known for, er, short. During the course of this Commission, established as the first priority of the new Shorten Government, the public will be shocked by the tragic tales of woe concerning the scandalous behaviour of the greedy, corrupt, money-grabbing banks and their lickspittles in the neo-con, capitalist finances sector. To this end, learned members of the gallery, we will hear from a randomly selected cross-selection of aggrieved, common-or-garden, everyday, union-affiliated, er, I mean hardworking Australians. Here are just some snippets from the avalanche of voluntary depositions already received.

Mr T, the Central Coast: Well, Your Honour the banks are all crooks for starters I mean I never did anything wrong but those bankers deliberately gave me this black credit card and stuck all these fake charges on it which had nothing to do with me whatsoever I swear Your Honour like a Double Thai Twins Massage with Happy Ending at Tiffany's and a Black on Blonde Girly Action at Loretta's which I never ordered anyway plus they forged my signature and charged me for two bottles of bubbly when I only ordered one and the thing is these banks can get away with making up whatever they want and they keep all your records even though Tiffany promised she'd destroyed them and it's that lack of respect for the privacy and dignity of my family that shows what crooks these bankers are.

JG of Adelaide: Well Oi've always said all along that these banks are completely untrustworthy Oi mean when Oi bought moi first house with moi boyfriend B — that's his sudo-noim — well we couldn't even get a doicent mortgage so B had to go all the woy over to WA and get the boys at the construction foim to cough up

2016 — The Year of Come Uppance

for some troining sessions and then Oi still didn't trust the banks so R — that's B's little rat-faced moit — R had to bury the spare cash in the back garden instead of putting it into moi Soivings Account which was a total rip-off and that meant Oi had to pay Con the Brickie, oops, Oi mean C-the-B in cash and Oi mean what sort of a country are we living in when you have to carry great wads of dosh around in a brown envelope stuffed down yer tracky daks?

BM of Long Bay: The thing about these bankers is that they're always on the take, I mean, I'll give you the classic example, I was keen to strike a Contra-Deal Bonus arrangement with one of my most valued suppliers, a gentleman and his glamourous wife who ran a boutique printing firm of the highest quality, specialising in premium business cards, embossed letterheads and the like but of course no sooner had I arranged a suitable Repayment Rewards Incentive Scheme than some impudent bank teller started asking intrusive personal questions like "sorry sir do you have an ABN number for this vast amount of cash?" which of course was the height of impertinence and made a mockery of my entrepreneurial attempts to incentivise my mistress, er, I mean my mate's wife.

M and K of Lover's Nest: Once upon a time we were a famous, high-flying couple, the darlings of the media, and feted at the highest levels of government. But now, thanks to the banks and the greed and incompetence of the financial sector — all of whom, to a man and a woman, kept insisting on being repaid squillions of arbitrary amounts of dollars before such and such a spurious date — we have lost our jobs, our livelihoods and our reputations and have had to fall back on the benevolence of one of our oldest and dearest friends whom we have known for at least six weeks and whose beach house we are currently forced to live in until we can flog it.

BS of Victoria: Wiv wot I've seen of these banks it's just one scandal after anuvver and nuffink ever changes I mean there was vis one time I went into a pie shop and they had all these weird flavours like chicken wiv asparagus and lamb wiv rosemary and all I wanted was a plain Aussie meat pie nuffink special so I could walk into the CFMEU wivout looking like a poof so I shouted at vis Asian woman and said why don't you sell a proper Aussie pie and ven she said she didn't take eftpos so I shouted at her why not and she said it was all the bank's fault! See! Told youse. Plus I agree totally wiv witness JG even vo I've no idea wot she said.

❖

The government announces plans to spend $50 billion on a fleet of French submarines to be partially built in South Australia. And the Prime Minister reveals that his father taught him how to roast tomatoes.

Whyalla submarine

Financial Review
30/4/16

Beatles fans were thrilled this week by the discovery of the original master tapes of a hitherto unknown film presumed to have been written by the fab four during their Australian tour and later discarded on an Adelaide nuclear waste tip. The film and album, originally entitled *Whyalla Submarine*, is a cartoon fantasy children's comedy about a group of French submarine manufacturers who travel to a psychedelic land at the bottom of the earth where half the people work hard to pay their taxes while the other half are on the dole or in the public service where they "live a life of ease, every one of us has all we need!" In this fantasy land, money grows on trees and shipbuilding jobs galore abound.

The film is based on the nonsensical and absurdist premise that the French must build twelve submarines in fifteen years out of nothing but solid Australian steel and using only Australian workers. On the way, the "fab Frenchies" must pass through a series of dangerous seas where they encounter all sorts of hilarious problems. These include the Sea of Holes (aka the May 3 Budget Song), the Sea of Waffle and the Sea of Money, where our hapless heroes almost drown in fifty billion dollars of hard-earned readies stolen from distraught taxpayers and showered all over them by the mysterious merchant banker Magic Malcolm waving a Cartier watch and singing "Baby I'm A Rich Man". But by far their biggest problem is the sinister gang of Blue Meanies, a group of hideously deformed union officials from the merged MUA and CFMEU who aren't even capable of "building a canoe" and are therefore jealously hell-bent on destroying the Whyalla submarines from the start. Working to a pre-ordained plan, the Meanies deliberately sabotage the French with an array of deadly weapons including watertight enterprise bargaining agreements, cost blowouts, scheduling over-runs, penalty rates and "sickies". Our put-upon submarine builders also encounter the invisible Nowhere Man, a former union official who has dreams of becoming a Labor Prime Minister. ("He's a real Nowhere Man, sitting in his Nowhere Land, making all his carbon tax plans for nobody" they chant.) In one of the film's most memorable scenes, Nowhere Man has a "bad trip" in a bakery, where he shouts at the terrified Chinese shopkeeper because she doesn't have any "marshmallow pies" as he taunts her with the psychedelic hit single 'Lucy in the Pie Shop wiv Donuts'.

Other highlights found on the Adelaide scrap heap include the original demo for the jaunty ballad about endless senate hearings and whining senate committees: "Penny Wong is in my ears, and in my eyes, there beneath the blue Canberran skies I sit, and meanwhile... Penny Wong."

The cartoon ends when the twelve Whyalla submarines finally "sink beneath the waves" — but unfortunately they don't come up again because Australian steel doesn't float.

In other news this week, the Prime Minister Malcolm Turnbull stunned voters on the eve of not only the most important federal budget in a decade but also the most important federal election in a generation with his frank and candid interview on Brisbane radio in which he revealed, er, his recipe for cooking Tomato Waffles.

PM: "Well, basically, my Dad taught me how to roast the tomatoes — well, when I say 'roast' you of course may prefer to 'grill', 'bake' or even 'pan-fry' them it's entirely up to you but I prefer to roast them — and may I point out that this is a very exciting time to be roasting tomatoes by the way, but let's... let's just step back here and look at the bigger picture — I mean tomatoes come in all shapes and sizes; on the one hand there are those small little cherry tomato things or on the other hand you can purchase in certain quality grocery shops those great big ox-heart ones; there are green tomatoes and even blackish purplish ones — so I mean it's not as if I am favouring one type of tomato over another, indeed, as far as I'm concerned so long as they are squishy and mushy and you can pulp them into this red little stew well that's all very well by me, I mean, the squishier the better, not that I have anything against firm tomatoes — and in fact it is an important fact that some people prefer their tomatoes to be firmer and I'm not in the business of arguing one way or the other about the hypothetical merits of firm tomatoes versus squishy tomatoes that's for others to comment on... and, er, sorry what was your question again?"

Interviewer: I said "what's the economic narrative for the budget?"

❖

As the Prime Minister reveals he spent $25,000 on a Cartier watch for his wife Lucy, the country still awaits a plausible economic narrative, following a Budget whose main features are a raid on self-funded retirees' superannuation and corporate tax cuts spread out over ten years. The Prime Minister stumbles badly in a Sky News TV interview attempting to explain the cost of his tax cuts, whilst two conmen are charged with forging a famous painter's paintings.

Malcolm's Fine Jewellery Emporium

Financial Review
7/5/16

One afternoon at Malcolm's Fine Jewellery Emporium in Double Bay.

Customer: Excuse me, sir, but how much does this Cartier watch cost?
Salesman (smiling broadly): Well, that's a very good question, and what you've got to understand is that the price, such as it is in nominal terms, will definitely come down in the long run, which is what is outlined here on this, er, price tag...
Customer: But how much does it cost?
Salesman (smiling broadly): Well, the... we have not... the... the watchmaker has not identified... the, er, the dollar cost of that particular item insomuch as... what you've got to remember is that what... what the price tag clearly sets out is a... a range of assumptions...
Customer (frustrated): But how much does it cost?
Salesman (smiling broadly): Well, it's... it's exactly what it says there on the price tag...
Customer (baffled): Where? It doesn't say anything. There isn't a price on the price tag.
Salesman (smiling broadly): Yes there is, er, right here. It says right here, in front of your eyes, it says: 'Finest Cartier Jewel-Encrusted Time Keeping Piece'. There you have it. Couldn't be more explicit...
Customer (attempting to remain composed): But that doesn't tell me how much it costs. How much does it cost?
Salesman (smiling broadly): Well, let me be totally clear... the cost of the watch is obviously a component of a number of arbitrary items which, when tallied together, over a specified period of time, that is to say, the cost is based on the assumptions that I have already outlined as per the watchmaker's specifications. I can't be any clearer than that!
Customer (through gritted teeth): But the cost?! What is the cost?!
Salesman (smiling broadly): Well, let's take a step back and look at the bigger picture. The...

Legal note: The Financial Review *would like to apologise to top entertainers David Speers and Malcolm Turnbull for any similarity between the above sketch and their brilliant comedy routine "How to Sell an Economic Narrative", as seen on Sky TV.*

In other news this week, a jury has been asked to determine whether a series of incredibly expensive works of art supposedly done by the famous painter Brett Costello are real or are in fact fakes. The works of art, described by experts as "obvious forgeries", were on display in a Canberra gallery this week under the title "The Liberal Party Budget 2016".

The prosecution alleges that although the pieces at first glance appear to be the work of a genuine conservative party, they are in fact clumsily executed fakes done in the style of the famous Treasurer Brett Costello but without any genuine merit and that they have little or no Liberal values in them at all.

The prosecution further alleges that the forgeries were done by two shonky dealers, Malcolm and Scotty, who had hoped to try and sell their fakes to a gullible public in order to stay in power.

The works of art, which spent the week on display in the parliamentary gallery, are known as "Big Blue on Super" and "Retirement at Bay". A further piece of work, "Retirement Plans out the Window", is also alleged to have been concocted by the dodgy duo as part of their scheme to rake in millions of dollars for themselves by stealing it from the over-50s who have always played by the rules. Critics have pointed out that not only are the budgetary strokes backdated, but that the way they look and even the way they are designed is completely at odds with the values, beliefs and style of Brett Costello, the famous Treasurer who tragically passed away back in 2007 after a fatal overdose of John Howard.

"Brett Costello had enormous talent," said his widower, Wendy, a self-funded retiree who wept in court as she stared in disbelief at her vanishing superannuation funds. "This Budget is an obscenity. Brett would never have done anything this bad."

The alleged forgers were both caught red-handed back in September stabbing their leader and stealing the conservative party. "They're a couple of frauds, really, and I wouldn't trust either of them as far as I could throw an onion," said one former acquaintance speaking on strict condition of anonymity from his electoral office on Sydney's northern beaches.

The forgeries first came to the attention of the public only minutes after being unveiled on Tuesday night. Said one irate Liberal victim, who is believed to have lost a fortune due to the changes to super: "There is no way this is even remotely like an original Costello budget. It's a complete fraud. I've been totally conned and had my life's savings ripped off by these two crooks and I'll never vote Liberal again."

❖

It gradually dawns on people that the Treasurer's proposed superannuation changes in the Budget are a disaster for self-funded retirees, small business people and other conservative voters. And the trailers for the new Star Trek *movie are released.*

Raiders of the Lost Super Nova

Financial Review
14/5/16

Star Trek 16: Raiders of the Lost Super Nova

The story so far:

Whilst the Starship Innovation (sister ship of the Starship Enterprise) circles the Western Galaxies seeking to rediscover a phantom positive Newspoll, Captain Kirkbull and his Team are stranded on an obscure and alien planet deep in the heartland of the Conservative Constellation populated by an irate tribe of self-funded retirees. Their mission? To boldly go where no conservative has gone before and suck the life force out of a gargantuan super nova through manipulating the time space continuum.

Captain Kirkbull: The natives seem restless, Arthur.
You told me they were normally a pretty docile lot.

Arthur: Until provoked, Captain. They do seem a trifle upset, it's true. We have to get back to the base, before it's too late.

Kirkbull: Unfortunately, I have no idea how to get in touch with the base. Why aren't the polls shifting, Mr Spock?

Spock: You have deliberately violated ze laws of quantum physics, Captain, when you said zat backdating our super coordinates to July 1, 2007 was not retrospective. That is not logical, Captain. How can backdating super changes by nine light years not be retrospective? It does not pass what you humans call ze sniff test, Captain, a local measure of logical thought. Now we cannot go forwards and we cannot go back. We are permanently stuck in zis illogical Budget stardate of May 3, 2016.

Kirkbull: Why the funny accent Spock? I thought you were a Vulcan.

Spock: I am actually Belgian, Captain. My name is Mathias.

Kirkbull: I see. So why am I calling you Spock? That's not logical.

Spock: It is entirely logical, Captain, in zis new universe you yourself have created where travelling backwards in time is not called retrospectivity, when of course it is. It is every bit as logical as you also saying your supernova changes only affect one per cent of ze population of zis planet, when of course, we can see by the murderous look in their eyes, zat every single one of them is drawn into its gravitational pull. They are suffering extreme fiscal anger, in a manner I believe only hard-working, conservative human beings know how to, Captain.

Kirkbull: Well, I wouldn't know anything about that. I've always been more of a lefty myself, Spock.

Spock: Yes, I know sir. We all do.

Kirkbull: Nothing wrong with a healthy dose of wealth re-distribution, I've always said, so long as it isn't mine.

Spock: Not to worry, sir, Sulu and Uhura managed to stash most of your Star Mining gold in ze Panama cluster.

2016 — The Year of Come Uppance

Kirkbull: Very good, Spock.

Spock: But, if you don't mind me pointing out Captain, your unusual social conscience on matters like ze Cosmic Republic, Same Species Marriage, and of course your firm belief in Intergalactic Climate Change, does make it illogical zat you are in charge of zis conservative Coalition ship when you clearly share different human values and belief systems.

Kirkbull: I was elected Captain. By the crew, Spock. It's my superior Communications skills. No-one else on the ship can put together a compelling economic narrative with quite my agility, my advocacy, my good humour, my clear-sightedness, my directness, my clarity of purpose, my panache, Mr Spock.

Spock: So I have observed, Captain.

Kirkbull: I even have a shiny new logo, just like my friend Captain Obama. I designed it myself. It's in a circle, and blue and yellow, with my name at the top...

Arthur (panicking): Quick Captain! We have to get out of this super worm hole right now! The Shortens are fighting amongst themselves! They want to open our borders and let in all the aliens! Their leader is completely exposed by his rebel candidates! And the Xenophons are threatening to take us hostage! Now is the time to strike with all our fire-power, sir! We must annihilate them all. There's not a moment to lose...!

Kirkbull: I'll be the judge of that. Beam us up, Scotty.

Scotty: I can't, Malcie. I've pulled all the levers. There's nothing left in the tank. I should have raised the GST like I wanted to, but now it's too late. Or adjusted the negative gearing on the forward thrusters. But now we're running on empty. I can't pull us out of this super nova even if I wanted to!

Spock: Excuse me, Captain, but we could always try and cut our spending. Zat would be logical. With a substantial reduction in welfare and other expenditure, we would be able to ditch ze super changes and keep ze base happy. Zat's the only logical way out of this mess, Captain.

Kirkbull: Cut spending, Spock? Are you completely out of your mind? We'd lose all our power!

❖

The annual Rich List is published.

Poor Me List

Financial Review
28/5/16

Following yesterday's Rich List, the Fin is proud to publish the 2016 Poor Me List, the definitive, must-read list of the top Poor Me people in Australia. The list is compiled exclusively from among the wealthiest or most celebrated individuals in Australia, who despite their great fortune and good luck, still bleat on about how hard done by they are. The judges' final decisions were based on the sincerity and heartfelt quality as well as the frequency with which the candidates have expressed the winning (and indeed whining) sentiment: "Poor me".

1. *Sheik Wahlid Logy:* A high rating member of every Poor Me List compiled since its inception yesterday morning, this much loved TV host, radio host, newspaper columnist, political commentator, terrorism expert, Boko Haram apologist, Hot Glossy Magazine Cover Boy and all round Top Dude who also happens to be married to a Hot Glossy Magazine Cover Headscarf-Wearing Top Chick has finally clawed his way to the very top of the Poor Me list. The judges were particularly moved by the way the tears flowed spectacularly in the audience during his Golden Ally Acceptance Speech as Mr Logy fought back his own tears and pointed out how horrendous and oppressive it is to be a Muslim in today's redneck, racist, xenophobic, Islamophobic, intolerant Australia.
Poor Me Rating: 11 stars.

2016 — The Year of Come Uppance

2. *Adrian Baddes:* This hugely talented sportsman and elite athlete soared to national prominence when a 5-year-old girl poked her tongue out at him and wiggled her fingers in front of her nose, thereby suggesting that Mr Baddes was descended from an obscure species of Bonobo that once thrived in the Serengeti (as indeed we all are). Not content with having the girl put under house arrest and humiliated for life, Mr Baddes was appointed Australian of the Century and National Treasure in quick succession. The judges were particularly impressed by Mr Baddes' heartfelt attempts to express goodwill and unite the nation by throwing imaginary spears at crowds of onlookers and by his speech in which he poured scorn on all privileged, white, male, anglo-saxon, non-indigenous Australians.
Poor Me Rating: 10 stars.

3. *Brigadier-General Major Captain Morriscorn:* Having toiled in the Australian Army in total obscurity for decades without having made any impression on anyone whatsoever, Leftie-Lieutenant Morriscorn was catapulted into national prominence when he went viral on YouTube after reading a speech written by somebody else. A keen *Star Wars* fan, the General's greatest military achievement was defeating the dreaded Jedi Council by firing every soldier who'd ever received a raunchy email, which rightly earned him the lucrative twin jobs of Diversity Guru National Treasure and Aussie of the Millenium. The judges were mightily impressed by his catch-phrase, "The salary you walk past is the salary you miss out on" and his speech in which he poured scorn on all privileged, white, male, anglo-saxon, non-indigenous, heteronormative, transphobic Australians. (something of a pattern developing here? - ed)
Poor Me Rating: 7 stars.

4. *Joanna Carrab:* Leading feminist, marketing guru, novelist, newspaper columnist, TV chat show personality and all-round Top Sheila, Ms Carrab earned the undying respect of the judges through her determination to endlessly complain that professional women in Australia suffer from endemic sexism and misogyny courtesy of privileged, white, males.

(OK, OK, we get it – ed.)
Poor Me Rating: 6 stars.

5. *Don "take-me-for" Granted:* A last minute entrant to the Poor Me List, Mr Granted has a genuinely impressive career and credentials as a top TV news reporter, both here and overseas. Mr Granted shot to long-overdue leftie prominence when, after decades of ignoring him, the Luvvies noticed he has aboriginal ancestry.
Poor Me Rating: 5 stars.

6. *Nonni Harris-Backbone:* Top Olympian and role-model to Indigenous girls, Ms Backbone was more surprised than anybody when former Prime Minister Julia "La" Grillard decided that as an indigenous female Ms Backbone should a) be catapulted into the Labor Party and b) be catapulted into the Senate despite having no interest in either. With Ms Backbone happily immersing herself in the senatorial lifestyle provided by mainstream taxpayers, the judges were hugely impressed by her tearful announcement that the only people worthy of criticising her are other Indigenous ex-Olympian senators.
Poor Me Rating: 8 stars.

7. *Julia "La" Grillard:* Patron saintess of the Poor Me Awards, this former lawyer and leading feminist struggled with her boyfriend to buy and renovate her own home before being catapulted to national fame by stabbing her male colleague in the back, stealing his job and then getting sacked because she was useless at it.
Poor Me Rating: 12 stars.

❖

A former General releases a politically correct video advising people how to behave appropriately in the workforce, including by not using the word "guys".

He, she or ze

Financial Review
4/6/16

In news this week, the former head of the armed forces released a widely-praised video in which he outlined how Australian Defence Forces' personnel should appropriately conduct themselves in the line of their duties.

"In the event of war," explained the former General who cannot be named for fear of being made a complete laughing stock, "the first priority of any soldier is to ensure that he or she — or indeed ze, as I prefer to address those of indeterminate or fluid gender preferences — does not risk causing offence to the opposing enemy forces in any direct conflict situation by denigrating them through the demeaning use of derogatory or sexist language in any shape or form. For instance, 'Die you slant-eyed bastard!' is a definite no-no, implying as it does that the individual concerned is of a non-caucasian background as well as drawing attention to a single-parent scenario which may be confronting and a clear form of unacceptable micro-aggression in a workplace environment such as when you are thrusting a bayonet into their spleen. Similarly, expressions such as 'where did you plant the bomb you sand-groping son of a bitch?' are to be avoided at all costs, lest the individual involved be made to feel of a lesser social status within the workplace hierarchy, not to mention the offensive depiction of their mother, or indeed their father, if he is a she, or a ze."

The video also advises issuing an appropriate trigger warning before shooting somebody in the head.

❖

Admitting that debt would be worse under his government, ("Labor will not have the same degree of fiscal contraction as the Liberals") the Leader of the Opposition claims the economy under Labor will return to health in ten years' time.

Fiscal contractions

Financial Review
11/6/16

The world of exotic diseases was rocked to its core this week following the sudden outbreak of a rare condition known as "fiscal contractions". Fiscal contractions, a parasitic virus linked to tissue inflammation and visual hallucinations, is unique in its ability to target all six components of the brain, leading to abnormalities affecting judgment, problem solving skills, speech, and memory. The virus is known to turn otherwise normal-looking individuals into gibbering idiots frothing economic nonsense from every orifice within a space of minutes.

The latest outbreak occurred during an early morning business breakfast in Brisbane, attended by opposition leader Bill Shorten, who displayed numerous signs of having caught the disease when he started promising "things will get worse" before everything gets better "in ten years' time".

"Fiscal contractions" have puzzled experts for centuries, but many believe the virus was first observed in Ancient Egypt, when the delusional Pharoah Bill Takelot the Last promised his nation "a full harvest in ten years' time" whilst plundering the royal treasures and splurging it all on extravagant indulgences demanded by his rapacious mistress Gonskititi. His empire disappeared into dust shortly afterwards.

The virus re-emerged some centuries later, shortly before the fall of the Roman Empire, when the diminutive Emperor Shortenus Minimus announced that he would return Rome to its former glories "ad finitum decadus". He perished shortly afterwards during an orgy of government spending, before being stabbed in the back by his closest friend, muttering "et tu Albo" as he lay bleeding on the steps of Capital Hill in Canberra.

During the Dark Ages, "fiscal contractions" were common throughout Europe, often mistaken for other less aggressive and contagious diseases, such as the common-or-garden bubonic plague. Sufferers, many of whom spent year after year denying that they were even infected by the virus, despite the evidence of the bloated, rotting fiscal corpses lying all around them, would often cover up their affliction by cunningly disguising themselves as "fiscal conservatives". This ruse worked in the early years — history records the almost messianic popularity of the charismatic false prophet Kevin Of Rudd in the Year Seven Oh Seven, whom many believe reintroduced the virus into the body politic — but by the time that an obscure charlatan known as Poxy Bill emerged from the mining pits of Beaconsfield offering his new "miracle cure", most sufferers recognised it was hopeless and there was no escaping the ravages of this deadly plague. Shortly after Poxy Bill nailed his brochure "My 10 Year Plan wiv a Plagued Economy" onto the church doors, he was torn limb from limb by two of his own grotesquely deformed disciples, Black Death Bowen and Bubonic Burke. Poxy Bill's discarded and putrefying remains are believed to have been fed to his demented flea-infested dogs (Tanya, Penny and Albo) on the morning of July 3rd in the Year of Our Lord Malcolm. However, it wasn't only the poor who suffered from the most virulent strains of "fiscal contractions". During the years leading up to the French Revolution, it was common for the members of the court of Billy the Sixteenth to have violent and spasmodic outbursts, leading to sufferers often defecating lavish promises out in the open electorates or behind the curtains in the flamboyant press galleries, leading to an intolerable stench of entitlements permeating throughout the entire Palais de Canberra.

Renowned British artist Hogarth chronicled the outbreak of "fiscal contractions" in the mid eighteenth century in his devastating prints "Industry and Idleness (Whyalla 2016)" and his engraving depicting the misery of life on welfare under a Shorten government — "Gin Lane" — in which a single mother is seen relaxing on her new sofa in front of her flat screen TV after pocketing another ten grand schoolkids bonus and spending it on the pokies, grog, and $40 packets of fags. Dickens, too, drew on victims of the virus for much of his grisly depictions of the worst excesses of the "Victorian Era". (Scholars define the Victorian Era as the miserable period under Premier Daniel Andrews, in which boys and girls as young as seven were sent to "safe schools" and forced to practice penis tucking and breast binding and share toilets in order to satisfy the perverse neo-Marxist fantasies of the teachers unions.)

Dickens' "Fiscal Contractions", the original title of his best-seller *Great Expectations*, follows the adventures of a young boy born in abject poverty, known only as Mal, who thanks to the devotions of a mysterious Australian multi-millionaire benefactor nicknamed "the Goanna", and egged on by a spoiled young rich girl called Lucy who has "great expectations" of him, realises he is destined to grow up and become prime minister without even bothering to cut any government spending and still return the country to surplus "in ten years' time".

❖

A few days after an Islamist terrorist commits the US's worst ever massacre at a gay club in Orlando, the Prime Minister invites representatives of the Islamic and other communities to a Ramadan 'iftar' dinner. Not all the guests meet with public, or indeed Prime Ministerial, approval. Meanwhile, the Prime Minister agrees Australia was invaded, whilst the Leader of the Opposition backs calls for an Aboriginal Treaty.

Islamohomophobia

Financial Review
18/6/16

In a landmark speech delivered last night at a gala dinner of attention-starved media celebrities, the Prime Minister of Australia spoke out harshly against rising Islamohomophobia.

"What we are seeing now in this country is a disturbing rise in truly despicable Islamohomophobic attacks," said the Prime Minister. "These verbal attacks upon innocent homophobic peace-loving individuals of one particular religous movement widely renowned for its kindness and tolerance — except, obviously, when it comes to gays, lesbians, transgenders, queers and so on — must be resisted at all costs."

Multicultural and diversity experts have identified "Islamohomophobes" as those individuals and groups within the community who are "frightened-of-Muslims-who-hate-homosexuals".

Said the Prime Minister: "Islamohomophobia is any and all criticism of those Muslims who (for purely harmless religious and academic reasons) happen to regard as inferior those within our vibrant and exciting community who (through no fault of their own not that there's anything wrong with it) self-identify as homosexual. It is up to each and every one of us to celebrate our shared humanity by recognising that there is a place in our rich, diverse, incredibly successful multicultural society for all of us, even for those who believe that homosexuals should be tossed off the nearest CBD high-rise. To say otherwise is obviously highly offensive and definitely Islamohomophobic."

Prime Minister M'ali Turnballah was speaking at a hastily-arranged dinner at K'irr- Ahbillah House on the shores of Sydney Harbour to celebrate the end of the month-long fast of what religious scholars refer to as the "never-ending ideas-free election campaign".

"It has been a long and wearying month," said the PM, "during which I have abstained from allowing any meaningful words to pass my lips, including any cuts whatsoever to government spending, and instead have had to rely for sustenance purely on my daily rations of pork-barrelling."

In order to celebrate the occasion, Mr Turnballah chose his favourite dish to share with his guests; an extra large serving of specially-prepared halal waffle.

Asked why no Muslim homosexuals had been invited to his celebration feast, Sheik Malcy explained that there aren't any gays in the Islamic Republic of Wentworth. "Well, at least not any who'll be voting for me anymore," he explained.

Way Beyond Satire

In other news this week, a draft Treaty was put forward by a group of Indigenous leaders following Opposition leader Bill Shorten's endorsement on the ABC's top-rating comedy show, *Q&A*, of the idea of an Australian-Aboriginal Treaty. The Fin has obtained a leaked copy:

> We, the undersigned, as custodians of this land for over 40,000 years (give or take the odd millennium) do hereby acknowledge this here-within-designated Official Peace Treaty with the White Invasion Forces of the Imperial Captain James Cook, Imperial Botanist Joseph Banks and, er, a couple of other blokes who were sketching seeds and stuff in their notebooks.
>
> In recognition of your right to trample all over our lands, ship in a bunch of convicts, chop down loads of trees, kill, maim and rape our peoples, steal our kids, breed sheep, breed whitefellas, dig up all the mineral deposits, flog the lot to the yellafellas over the seas and make a quid or two of the Crown's coinage so long as we get a decent cut of it, and moreover for allowing Rolf Harris anywhere near a didgeridoo, do demand by way of Final Reparations for these Egregious Grievances the following:
>
> Schools, tertiary education, the rule of law, equal rights for women, equal rights for homosexuals, equal rights for children, equal rights for the disabled, free medicine, free antibiotics, free flu vaccinations, free hip operations, decent plumbing, hot water on tap, cold beer on tap, shopper docker vouchers, laundromats, street lighting, twelve string guitars, Marshall stack amplifiers, cars, trucks, utes, diesel, roads, Uber, railways, airports, airplanes, frequent flyer points, business lounges, smoked salmon, matches, smokes, McDonalds, KFC, Coles, Woolies, Aldi (optional), Dan Murphy's (not optional), scholarships, mining internships, mining rights, land rights, Mabo, tent embassies, guaranteed top spots on Olympic podiums, ditto footy teams, ditto aussie rules, ditto hockey, ditto senate seats (plus senate seats for hockeyroos captains even if they don't want 'em), tourism dollars, bit parts in *Crocodile Dundee*, *Walkabout*

etc, starring roles in *Storm Boy*, *Jimmy Blacksmith*, *Redfern Now* (obviously), Bangarra gigs at the Opera House, Yothu Yindi recording contract, lotto, Dettol, Nurofen, Panadol, Mortein, Aerogard, iced Vo-vos, Tip Top bread, sourdough, cappuccinos, flat whites, decaf soy lattes, shrimps on the barbie, wagyu beef steaks on the barbie, honey and mustard glazing, tomato sauce, meat pies, Airbnb, microwaves, frozen veggies, ice cream, paddle pops, fruit loops, weet bix, denim, thongs, Adidas sneakers, silk ties, cotton shirts, stockings, ladders, electric drills, allen keys, Bunnings, plastic carrier bags, recyclable hessian carrier bags, sausage sizzles, fertiliser (cont'd for 240 years, er, pages)

❖

The endless eight week election campaign is livened up by Bill Shorten's claims that the Liberals intend to privatise Medicare. But is he lying?

Lie detector

Financial Review
25/6/16

"In order to conduct this lie detector test, Mr Shorten, we just need you first to answer a couple of straightforward questions. Your name please?"

"Well, wiv all due respect let me just say vis before I get onto vat and vat is vat wiv all honesty one fink for certain is vat my name is not Malcolm Turnbull and anuvver fink I can tell you wiv my hand on my heart is vat I am therefore not the man who is going to privatise Medi…"

"No, no. Just your name please. That's all. If you just say 'My name is Bill Shorten', that will be good enough."

"Well wiv all due respect vat might be good enuff for you, but it's simply not good enuff for me or the Party I lead which is committed to a fair go for all wivout privatising Medicare coz sumfink I am passionate about is being straight wiv the Australian people and one fink they know for sure about me is vat I will never privatise..."

"No, er, um, before we can test your actual lies, Mr Shorten, um... we just need a straightforward... um, what is your wife's name? Is it Chloe?"

"Wiv all due repect for your professionalism and I understand you have a job to do but what I don't see here wiv all these fancy wires stuck all over my body linked up to all these flashink lights and computers and stuff is Malcolm Turnbull. I mean you have a choice here between hooking up Malcolm Turnbull to a lie detector test and see how he goes wiv all his plans to privatise Medicare and wiv his plans to privatise all the hospitals and beds and bedpans and..."

"Yes, thank you, Mr Shorten, we've already done that and he passed wiv, I mean 'with' — sorry it's contagious — with flying colours. Well, on that question he did at least. It all got a bit crazy on climate change, same sex marriage, the republic and so on but that's another story. Now: Chloe? Is your wife's name Chloe, Mr Shorten?"

"Well if you'd stop interrupting me and let me finish the question wiv all due respect one fink I know for certain is vat my wife's name isn't Lucy which means she's not living in some harbourside mansion wiv all these servants and she's not married to a man who's so out of touch vat he's going to privatise..."

"Er, um. OK, OK, let's try this one — your current occupation? You are the Leader of the Opposition, is that correct?"

"Well vat is sumfink vat the Australian people will decide vis time next week wiv all due respect and vat is not sumfink vat I am going to speculate on because they have a clear choice which is do they want to see a fair go for all or do they want to see an American-style health..."

2016 — The Year of Come Uppance

"OK, OK. Let's try this. Um, does the sun rise in the east or the west?"

"Well, I'm glad you asked me vat question coz Labor believes in real diversity and same sex marriage wivout wasting billions of dollars on a plebiscite and it doesn't matter whevver your son wants to rise in the east or whevver he wants to rise in the west or whevver he wants to rise in uvver ways and express his sexuality..."

"No, no, the sun. You know, the big hot thing in the sky. Does it rise in the east or the west?"

"Well, fank you for clarifying that important point coz when it comes to catastroffic climate change one fink vat is crystal clear is vat Labor believes in climate change and vat it is real and wiv all due respect to your question it doesn't matter where the sun rises coz fanks to Mr Turnbull and Tony Abbott the Liberals have no clear plan to tackle..."

"OK, OK, we'll do all that in a minute. I just need, um... off the top off your head. Is fire hot or cold?"

"Well, I'm glad you asked me vat coz wiv all the bushfires we see these days fanks to catastroffic climate change which we were just talking about a moment ago we need our fireys to be protected under the full force of the law which is why my good friend Dan in Victoria is solving vis terrible dispute and making it fairer for the unions to kick out any volunteers who don't pay up..."

"Yes, yes thank you. Um, one last question. Did you knife Kevin Rudd and Julia Gillard in the back so you could grab the top job and will you stab Albo and Plibersek in the back the moment the election is over?"

"Yes, of course."

❖

Way Beyond Satire

The British vote to "Brexit" and quit Europe. In Australia, as election day arrives, a Sky News focus group reveals nobody has the faintest idea who the leader of the Greens is. And, dismayed by the Turnbull ascendancy, conservative "Del Cons" debate how they should vote.

How should I vote?

Financial Review
2/7/16

Confused about how to vote today? For the exclusive benefit of our readers, the Fin's favourite Agony Aunt offers her sage advice.

Dear Rowena,
Wiv the election I might find myself wiv a new job such as being Prime Minister in an Alliance or sumfink wiv the Greens and that gambling Greek midget who spells his name wiv an X instead of a proper Z but everybody reckons Malcolm's got it in the bag coz that useless Bowen bloke buggered up my budget big time like you wouldn't believe and now my bosses in the CFMEU are fretnink to kick me out so how do I stop everybody knifink me in the back on Monday?
Yours, anon.

Dear Bill,
I agree with every word you've written, not that I have the faintest idea what it is you wrote.

Dear Rowena,
In my former career I was a top player in advertising circles; in fact, I hate to boast, but I was single-handedly responsible for implementing one of Australia's most famous ad slogans, featuring the words "where", "bloody", "hell" and "are you" no less — a fact of which I am extremely proud! Also in that role I — somewhat selflessly — launched the glittering career of the talented screen goddess Lara Bingle. Then in my next job I became a top player in political circles where, yet again, I hate to boast, I was again single-handedly responsible for implementing another famous slogan, this one featuring the words "stop" and

"boats" — a fact of which I am also extremely proud! Yet again, in that role, I selflessly launched the equally glittering career of the equally talented Malcolm Turnbull. My problem is this: every time I do a sensational bloody good job somebody else ends up getting the credit! And I'm left out in the cold! What should I do?
Yours (name and address supplied).

Dear Mr, er, ScoMo,
Always the bridesmaid and never the groom, as we say in the agony aunt business. Why not just accept the inevitable and put your talents to good use? Apparently, there's a Julie B of Perth who's keen to have a quiet chat.

Dear Rowena,
Jolly well bugger and bollocks you wouldn't bloody well believe it! I go and pull off the greatest political referendum upset in the ruddy history of the poxy EU against all the odds and those ungrateful Tory Tossers toss me out on my ear! Any decent conservative gigs going down under?
Yours, Boris.

Dear BoJo,
I may have just the job. Ever done any same sex marriage plebiscites?

Dear Rowena,
Nobody has the faintest idea who I am. How, then, can they possibly vote for me?
Yours, anonymously (even though I'd rather not be).

Dear Dr Richard Di Natale,
Don't worry. Only people of severely limited intellect — or with a modern Australian tertiary degree in politics, the arts, enviro-eco-commerce or "communications" — would ever think of voting for your party, so whether they know your name or not is irrelevant; it being highly unlikely they could spell it in the first place.

Dear Rowena,
I am a happily married, retired former solicitor (among other things) living in a delightful home in leafy suburban Sydney. I have

voted Liberal all my life, but this year it doesn't feel quite right. My wife tells me I'm being silly and not to be such an old duffer, but I am concerned that if "The Turnbull Coalition Team" (as my former party of preference have brazenly re-branded themselves) are returned, what will happen to genuine conservatives like me? Let's not beat about the bush. This cad Turnbull is clearly a dyed-in-the-wool, tree-hugging, climate change fanatic who plans to ditch Her Majesty's Monarchy and bring in a Republic, probably with the ghastly Lucy as its President; thinks Australia was "invaded" by Captain Cook, two botanists and a galley cook; prances up and down Oxford Street with his tutu-wearing, anti-bullying, penis-tucking, dope-smoking Greenie mates and worse than all that put together he's gone and buggered up every decent hard-working Aussie retiree's superannuation! Even old Bernie next door reckons he's going to have to cancel his annual cruise to Vanuatu! When I think what the Liberal Party used to stand for in the good old days I want to weep into my well-thumbed copy of Menzies' Letters. It goes without saying that not in a million years would I vote for that lackey Shorten and his gang of grubby union vandals, and obviously only someone with serious cognitive deficiencies would ever vote for the Greens, but the question remains — who should I vote for?
Yours in dismay,
John.

Dear Mr Howard,
Yes, I see your problem. Buggered if I know.

❖

Despite a Liberal strategist suggesting "the base has nowhere else to go", nearly two million voters desert the party in favour of conservative alternatives. Meanwhile, despite nearly losing their entire majority, a senior minister labels the Liberal Party an "election winning machine".

Nowhere to go

Financial Review
9/7/16

This week, the Fin's expert political strategist traces the complex history and development of classic Liberal strategic political thinking.

"Imperium, the evidencus qualitatus is that Visigoths do not matter. The quantum of our centrally placed legions far outweighs any marginal losses they might inflictus upon us." — *Marcus Textorius, strategic and policy adviser to Turnbullus Augustus Caesar, last Emperor of Rome (fed to the lions).*

"But I assure you, mon Empereur. Mon qualitative evidence is zat ze sum of la Grande Armee far outweighs zis piddling Duke and his pissant army at Waterloo. Ignore 'im and 'e will have nowhere to go." — *Jean-Marc du Texteur, strategic adviser to the Napoleonic forces, Walloon (fate unknown).*

"It is abundantly clear to me that all the ferocious foot stomping and hysterical ululating is of little serious consequence and that we are safer here in the centre. There's no need to ever return to the base." — *The Marquis of Textor, Rourke's Drift (last recorded diary entry).*

"Fear not, men. My qualitative evidence is that there's a thousand miles of scorching impassable desert between us and the so-called mujahadeen. The sum of our advanced weaponry and, of course, of my superior strategic planning far outweig... ugggghhh." — *T.E. Mark of Arabia, Khartoum (head last seen on a pike).*

"The qualitative evidence is that these alleged sniffles will soon pass. The sum of a few sneezes far outweighs any harm done by the loss of a so-called handkerchief." — *Senor Marco Tequsta, public health adviser to the Spanish authorities, 1918 (applying for sick leave).*

"Ja mein Fuhrer! Ve haf studied all ze unzugänglich Normandy beaches und ist klar zey do not matter vun little bit. Ze strength of ze wehrmacht means even if zey land some boats, so vot? Zey haf nowhere else to go!" — *Unterleutnant Marcus von Textherr, qualitative strategic adviser to the Third Reich (shot at dawn).*

"Yes Mr President, I've plotted out the most qualitatively secure route — we sneak past that grassy little knoll over there then duck down past the book depository, which leaves any potential shooter nowhere to aim at, sir." — *Mark Texas, strategic security adviser to the Democrat Motorcade Fleet, Dallas branch (DOA).*

"Houston, my qualitative advice is that we don't have a problem. They're just these insignificant little rubber washer wotsits that will quickly expand in the centre to outweigh any theoretical loss of compression. The nitrogen has nowhere else to go."
— *Dr Dexter Marks, Head of Strategic Propulsion Planning, NASA (incinerated).*

"The qualitative evidence is that marginal hypothermia doesn't matter. The central summit approach outweighs any loss of ground to the right, so there's no need to get back to the base."
— *Sherpa Textzing Markay (embalmed in ice).*

"The qualitative evidence is that conservatives don't matter. The sum of a more centrist approach outweighs any alleged marginal loss of so-called base voters." — *Marked with a texta on the strategic planning whiteboard of The Turnbull Coalition Team, 2016.*

Also this week, our innovation expert traces the history of the world's most successful machines.

Khristophepine's Locust Culling Machine: Invented on September 14th, 2015 BC, this mechanism was designed to stave off an electoral loss of Biblical proportions but was abandoned some months later after a plague of disgruntled conservatives wiped out most of the Pharoah's much-needed parliamentary supplies.

2016 — The Year of Come Uppance

Christos Pynus's Volcanic Seismic Advance Detection Machine: Invented circa AD 79, the original designs and prototype of Pynus's ingenious machine and its inventor were found centuries later in pristine condition perfectly preserved in pumice in the southern precincts of Pompeii.

Count Kristos von Pynhof's Aerial Flotation Machine: Built entirely of South Australian steel, and powered by copious amounts of hot air stored in gigantic "waffles", Pynhof's machine was last sighted heading out over Lake Burley Griffin where it disappeared into an electoral fog. An eccentric farmer by the name of Bobkatter who washed up onto the shores of parliament is believed to be the only known survivor.

C. Pinenut III's Wall Street Share Market Profit Guarantee Machine: Invented by a boastful young bedwetting shoeshine boy known as "The Fixer" working in downtown New York in early October 1929, this spinning machine was especially designed to print any results upside down, so that a massive loss (of seats in an election campaign, for example), would immediately look like a win! Still in use in South Australia today.

Pyne's Election Winning Machine: Designed by an obscure South Australian submarine enthusiast in the garage of his friend's harbourside mansion, this clunky voting machine chewed up billions of taxpayers' dollars financed by plundering self-funded retirees superannuation before abruptly wiping out the government's entire majority.

❖

The world is entranced by a bizarre new virtual reality game called Pokémon Go!, and Malcolm Turnbull, claiming victory, prepares for a cabinet reshuffle, as a young girl visiting the PM's office boasts to him that she once met Tony Abbott.

Malcémon Go!

Financial Review
16/7/16

A new augmented reality game called *Malcémon Go!* is taking the Liberal party by storm. The game, due to be officially launched on Monday morning at a special "party" room meeting in Canberra, requires players to imagine that they are in a fantasy political landscape populated by pocket monsters who only appear when the Prime Minister isn't looking at them.

In the imaginary landscape, which is based on real life Google maps landmarks such as the backrooms of Capitol Hill or Peter Hendy's home in Queanbeyan, but which otherwise bears no resemblance to reality, players get to pretend that they have just won a magnificent victory and are celebrating by forming a popularly-elected government with a massive majority. In this fantasy landscape — which can only be accessed via your innovative smartphone or your agile iPad — there are literally hundreds of loyal MPs that the Prime Minister can choose from for his imaginary new cabinet.

The aim of the game is to not get "caught out" by the Prime Minister. This can happen in many unexpected ways, such as by Malcémon throwing a trick question at you (e.g. "did you like my round Turnbull Team logo?") or by complaining how woeful you thought his "jobs and growth" mantra really was. Instead, players must win "brownie points" by praising their leader's insightful "forget the conservatives" strategy and by encouraging Malcémon to believe that they will remain "loyal" to him throughout the rest of the term, er, game.

Several functions on the *Malcémon Go!* app allow you to accrue bonus "loyalty points" which keep your longterm career prospects alive and boost the likelihood of you being selected for a cushy "job" in the PM's fantasy cabinet at some point in the future.

Gamers can also gain additional points by using the following tactics: never mentioning Tony Abbott; never mentioning the little girl who mentioned Tony Abbott; never mentioning the newspaper reports that mentioned the little girl that mentioned Tony Abbott; never mentioning the brilliant strategic advice that the "base have nowhere else to go".

Players can also buy special *Malcémon Go!* coins from the Prime Minister's Million Dollar Malcémon Donation Fund in order to keep the game going even when the Party itself is flat broke.

Malcémon Go! was designed by Nuttendo to boost their flagging fortunes. The genius of the idea is that it combines the modern era of innovative and agile technology with many of the cuddly nostalgic characters from when the game was at the height of its popularity over a decade ago. Indeed, most 20-30 year olds have extremely happy memories of that period, known fondly as The Howard Years.

Below is a list of the most highly prized and sought-after Malcémon monsters you can collect.

ScoMo: Originally a terrifying tiger-like monster famous for stopping anyone who tried to sneak into the game on a boat, Nuttendo's designers changed their mind and turned him into a toothless pussycat who rolls over and has his tummy tickled when you call him "Treasurer".

JuBi: Ferocious female Malcémon with huge staring eyes and razor sharp claws, this firebird is at its most dangerous just after it pledges its "undying loyalty" to you. Likes to fly a lot (First Class, preferably).

SuperAnnuate: An ugly little critter with long arms and even longer fingers designed to reach deep into old people's purses and wallets when they least expect it and steal all their money.

RetroSpectiv: Created in 2007, this ingenious offshoot of SuperAnnuate can travel back in time and steal even more money from when the old people were young!

ChriPy: Creepy indeed, this dandy-like creature has a squeaky voice and laugh that sound like fingers on a blackboard which it uses to great effect as a "fixer" to "fix things" within the game. ChriPy also invented the Malcémon Election Winning App.

SinoDinosaur: With its bright shiny head and piercing blue eyes this charming little gnome spends its time wandering around hatching plots. Very fond of water, which it tries to turn into money.

BradHarrizard: Former Attorney General of New South Wales.

WyaTwerp: Deleted.

Textaurus: The least valuable of all the Malcémon monsters, this one tries to trick you into believing that you don't need to collect any conservative monsters because they have no other games to play in. Not worth bothering with.

CoryBern: It's unclear whether CoryBern actually exists in *Malcémon Go*, or whether every single monster you encounter is actually him in a clever disguise. Points for messing with your mind. (Rumours are CoryBern will be used to launch a sequel later in the year.)

PetaChu: By far the most exciting, clever, formidable and collectible of all the *Malcémon Go!* characters. Such a pity she's no longer in the game.

❖

On the ABC's popular Q&A show, a senator reveals he is a Muslim and asks Pauline Hanson — repeatedly — whether he should have been banned from coming into the country as a 5-year-old immigrant.

2016 — The Year of Come Uppance

The Diary of Sam Dastardly, age 5 and a half (with apols to Sue Townsend)

Financial Review
23/7/16

First day at my new school since we arrived as Reffos in Australia last week after escaping from the Eye of the Tollahs in Iran. Mum says we mustn't let anyone know we are Muslims coz then they might try and send us back. Mr Jones is the headmaster and every Monday he does Q&A where everybody gets to ask anybody else any question they like so long as Mr Jones gets to approve it first, otherwise he calls it a Comment which means it doesn't count.

Pauline's sitting next to me. I really like her coz she's got red hair. She was the first to put her hand up and she asked me if I'm a Muslim and why did they let me in if I'm a Muslim and did I swear on the Koran during Assembly instead of the Bible and I didn't know what to say coz Dad made me promise to keep my trap shut about that stuff, (Dad's always telling me to keep my trap shut so nothing new there.) Then Sonia who's really pretty put her hand up and said that all Muslims should be in a band which I think is a great idea so I'm going to learn the guitar.

But then Pauline said she had a Premonition that when I grow up I'm going to be running around with a great big knife stabbing everybody and I said you mean I'm going to be a Terrorist and she said no you're going to join the Labor party.

Kevin gave me this really strange look. He's got blond hair and blue eyes and sits in the front row eating stuff from his ears and telling everybody that one day he's going to be the King of the Whole Wide World which everybody else thinks is a really dumb idea apart from Julie who says he'd be good at it so she'd like to nominate him which everybody said is typical Julie sucking up. Dad was really worried when I told him Julie is in my class coz he reckons she's good friends with the Eye of the Tollahs and even wants to let them make a bomb to blow up Israel. (I haven't met Israel yet but nobody likes him anyway.)

Way Beyond Satire

My friend Larissa is saving the planet by turning hot air (mostly mine) into electricity and said that Pauline thinks Muslims have got three heads. So during Recess I went into the Girl's Toilets to check — coz this is a Safe School and you're allowed to go into any Toilet you like so long as you tuck in your penis first even though back in Iran they'd throw you off the top of the Bike Sheds if you did that — and when I looked in the mirror I could only count two heads (including the one on the top of my neck) so I think maybe I'm not a Muslim after all, which solves that problem.

Then Mr Jones said he wanted to get a question from his Teacher's Pet called Elomar who really is a Muslim and was sitting quietly and peacefully at the back of the class doing some peaceful drawings on his peace-loving Facebook page which had this blue star with six points dripping blood and stuff and some squiggly peaceful writing about pigs which looked weird but only in a very peace-loving kind of way.

Elomar explained that he has an 11-year-old son who he sits with peacefully and watches videos of Pauline which I thought sounded a bit creepy but everybody else started booing Pauline instead so I guess I still have a lot to learn about the culture of this place.

At Lunch Break I asked Pauline if she wanted to share my Halal Snack Pack with me but she politely declined, and explained that we shouldn't get too friendly coz when we grow up we're going to be in the Senate together which sounds like fun. I asked her what we will be doing there and she said that it will be our job to stop Malcolm from being Malcolm, which doesn't sound hard.

Then Malcolm came over and bragged that he'd just been made Class Captain, even though hardly anybody voted for him, and gave us some Party Waffles.

Just before the bell, Scotty and Kelly snuck up from behind and nicked all my pocket money which I'd been saving for a rainy day! When I yelled out that that was illegal they just laughed and said one day they'd make a Retrospective Law to let them steal as much of other peoples' money as they felt like.

A TV documentary showing a young man in a restraining chair and spit hood in detention in the Northern territory prompts the Prime Minister to immediately call a Royal Commission. Meanwhile, the Pope decides we are at war with Islam before changing his mind.

Bag on head

Financial Review
30/7/16

The world wasn't at all shocked by graphic images on a current affairs programme this week of Australian juveniles being forced to wear bags on their heads. The footage, described as being reminiscent of the notorious Abu Dhabi Shopping and Leisure Centre, revealed a number of unidentified girls as young as thirteen strolling through western Sydney covered from head to toe in a large cloth bag, with a special mesh covering to allow normal breathing. Experts believe the chilling imagery was filmed with a hidden camera and smuggled out of Lakemba's Broadway Plaza, and that the perpetrators of the enforced "bag-wearing" have never been called to account.

The disturbing documentary also claimed juveniles were often forced to sit for hours on end, or even made to squat face down on the floor, listening to strange monotonous ramblings from ancient bloodthirsty texts about decapitations and amputations.

A shocked Prime Minister Turnbull, in one of the most dramatic interventions of his leadership, was quick to announce that there was no need whatsoever for a Royal Commission into such archaic and medieval practices. "Like everybody else, I am completely disinterested in the fact that some people might well describe it as 'torture' or even 'barbaric' to have to wander around on a stifling hot summer's day, when all the other girls are in short skirts and tee-shirts, or even go to the beach where all the other girls are in bikinis, dressed in a large bag-like outfit that was designed in the Middle Ages for the express purpose of keeping women and girls as chattels. That is of no concern to me whatsoever and shouldn't be of any concern to anybody else either, which is why I won't be doing anything about it."

The Prime Minister cut short his press conference as he was running late for a special multicultural Eid celebration dinner. In other news this week, the shocking transcript of a secretly-taped confessional was smuggled out of the Vatican and leaked to the world's press:

"Oops. Forgive me Father, for I made a bit of a boo-boo yesterday on the Holy Plane on the way back home. Because I was feeling somewhat jet-lagged after a couple of refreshing chardy's up the Papal Pointy End but also because I was feeling 30,000 feet closer than normal to Your Divine Presence I happened to wander down to steerage looking for the rest of the bottle when I bumped into some friendly members of Your Flock brandishing cameras and microphones who asked me about the murder of that French priest so I took the Divine Opportunity to declare that World War III had just begun and that this war is The Holy War against the Mohammedans which I thought you'd be Almightily impressed with. But just as I was getting warmed up some PR johnnies dragged me back behind the curtain and told me that a Holy War wasn't on Your Earthly Agenda anymore and that it had never really researched all that well in focus groups anyway and that Your Divineness would be far happier with a War on Poverty like Brother Bono has always banged on about or a War on Climate Change like Brother Al made his Oscar-winning film about or a War on Corruption like, er, well, we won't go into all that again but anyway I'm sorry if I caused Your Graciousness any embarrassment up there. I hope you'll forgive me, actually, scratch that, I know you will forgive me. Now, where did they hide that cheeky little red?"

❖

Plagued by a near-death experience at the election, chronic indecision and poor polling, many begin to wonder how long Malcolm Turnbull will last. And another Hollywood blockbuster comes out to poor reviews.

Suicide Squad

Financial Review
6/8/16

Movie buffs and film critics alike have been quick to slam the latest Hollywood blockbuster, *Suicide Squad*, out in cinemas today. The film is a dark and disturbing remake of a popular comic book released on September 14th last year, in which a team of supervillains are assembled from some of the worst misfits on the political scene in order to overthrow the government. But then, one by one, the plotters are themselves completely obliterated — hence the film's title.

Much of the hype surrounds the fact that this is the first time an entire front bench has been made with anti-heroes and supervillains as the main characters. The plot revolves around Lucy Waffler, an ambitious, cut-throat puppet-master and former Mayor of Gotham City who assembles her Suicide Squad out of a miserable group of talentless backbenchers, disgruntled senators and rank opportunists in order to turn her millionaire husband into the Prime Minister. But it all goes horribly wrong and they end up installing the grinning, cartoonish Joker instead.

Every member of the suicide squad holds a personal vendetta against the film's only hero, Onionman, because it was he who was responsible for getting them their jobs in the first place. Onionman wears red speedos and can stop boats, strike free trade deals and destroy carbon taxes with just his onion breath. Despite his heroic deeds featuring heavily in the films PR campaign, Onionman never gets to sit in the front rows, er, bench.

But after a dramatic opening scene in which the Joker declares "This is the most exciting time to be alive" the plotters and most of the supervillains end up back on the scrap-heap themselves, having failed abysmally to get re-elected, leaving the Joker sitting awkwardly on a razor's-edge.

Wyatt Twerp, aka The Milky Bar Kid, is the most innovative of the supervillains, so much so that he gets to innovate himself straight into a twilight zone of total obscurity from whence he is never heard of again.

More successful is Hendyman, aka the Queanbeyan Night Prowler, who meets a grisly death at the hands of his electorate but magically re-appears in the next scene as Economic Guru, an arch manipulator who can turn a complete lack of talent into a massive box office payrise.

Malbrough Man, aka the Slipper Stalker, has a unique super power of being able to implode himself at will, which he does repeatedly throughout his career.

Sinister Dino, aka the Water Man, almost drowned as a high powered corporate executive at a water company when he fell into a deep pool of deadly eye cack. Stripped of all integrity, the Water Man has learned to drown others in order to keep himself afloat.

Laundry Man, aka Bogan Craig, is so slippery he can wriggle himself straight into cabinet, despite holding odious views on Israel. Defying all credibility, he actually survives.

Loyal Deputy, aka the Samurai Assassin, is by far the most complex supervillain in the story, with her deadly laser stare and her ability to smile with a fixed grin at the camera whilst unsheathing her katana blade behind your back. But by joining the plotters she ends up committing harikari on her own leadership ambitions.

"Suicide Squad is bad," one critic declared. "Not fun bad. Not redeemable bad. Not the kind of bad that is the unfortunate result of politicians honourably striving for something ambitious and falling short. Suicide Squad is just bad."

Said another: "Nothing happens. Despite all the pre-release hype, the film feels like it runs for about eleven months. It just meanders aimlessly all over the place. It's like the actors were desperate to make a film but when they got on the set they had no idea what to do."

One newspaper said the film recalled too many governments in the climate science fiction and economic fantasy genres: "It's just Rudd vs Gillard all over again. More CSIRO climate scientists, same sex marriage, Indigenous royal commissions and all these art house themes which the public are largely disinterested in are conservative box office poison," lamented one critic. "Where's all the good Liberal blockbuster stuff? Where are the deep spending cuts, the slashing of bloated welfare, the battling and fighting for free speech? This stuff is for latte sippers. They never should've got rid of Onionman."

One critic cites the film's "lousy script" and lack of "satisfying storytelling". "The economic ideas roll on and off the table, but there's never any proper narrative or philosophical underpinnings," he complained.

But other critics disagree. "There's a fantastic cameo by Super Annuation, aka ScoMo, who comes in and wipes out all the old people's savings and then obliterates the government's entire majority in one swift blow," said an excited fan on Twitter.

❖

The Australian Bureau of Statistics 2016 Census, the first online census of its kind, runs into trouble when its computer system has to be shut down on the night of the Census because so many people are using it, as they were told to. And the Olympic swimming pools in Rio turn green overnight.

ABS Innovations

Financial Review
13/8/16

Here at ABS Innovations Pty Ltd, our crack team of agile innovators (motto: "there's never been a more exciting time to be a statistic") are delighted to share with you some of our recent successes:

The ABS Australian Census Website.

Our ten million dollar data collecting system which we developed under the helpful guidance of specialist design team Hawke, O'Dwyer, MacCormack, Kalish & Turnbull for the Australian 2016 Census is already proving a huge success. Built entirely around our unique, patented and ground breaking Collection, Retrieval, Analysis, Privacy system (CRAP), the website has already revolutionised the way your personal data is safely collated and your elephant penis jedi Hitler Elvis dung faeces fascist scumbag Pauline Hanson is right er, hang on there appears to be a slight glitch somewhere.

UPDATE: ABS Innovations apologise for any inconvenience due to a temporary malfunction of the site. Rest assured heads will roll (but definitely not the ones that should).

The ABS Olympic Swimming Pool Hygienic Chlorination System.

Our twenty million US dollar water purification system which we developed under the special supervision of eco-designers Kalisch, MacCormack & Turnbull is already proving a huge success at the Rio 2016 Olympic Games. Built entirely around our unique, patented and ground breaking Pool Innovative Sanitation Services system (PISS), the mechanism has already revolutionised the way the world's top swimmers can express their individual talents and enjoy the purity and visual delights of crystal clear cough splutter gurgle shit my eyes are stinging help I can't see a thing I can't breathe I've gone blind where are my bloody goggles scratch that where's my bloody lawyer?

UPDATE: ABS Innovations apologise for any inconvenience due to a temporary malfunction of the service. Rest assured heads will roll (if they haven't already choked).

The ABS Badgery's Creek International Airport.

Our eight billion dollar aeronautical navigation system which we developed under the special supervision of top design team Baird, Hockey & Turnbull is already proving a huge success in international aviation circles. Built entirely around our unique, patented and ground breaking Flight, Orientation, Gridlock system (FOG), the facility has already revolutionised Sydney's overcrowded air traffic control and transportation hubs allowing a more flexible approach to runway six sorry no did you say six or five I can't see a bloody thing in this soup bowl hello I can't hear what's that an approaching aircraft where what side hello hello.

UPDATE: ABS Innovations apologise for any inconvenience due to a temporary loss of altitude. Rest assured heads will roll (all the way down the runway).

The ABS Submarine fleet.

Our 50 billion dollar submarine navigation and propulsion system which we developed with the expertise of world class submariner designers Pyne, Morrison & Turnbull for the Australian navy is already proving a huge success. Built entirely around our unique, patented and ground breaking Submersible Innovation and Nautical Know-how system (SINK), the device has already revolutionised the way the Australian taxpayer can feel safe and secure in the knowledge that every possible component made here in Australia has been thoroughly tested and constructed to assemble must need you Allan key box inside screwdriver before put part A inside slot B important do NOT get device wet.

UPDATE: ABS Innovations apologise for any inconvenience due to a temporary loss of oxygen. Rest assured heads will drown.

The ABS Ausgrid Privatisation system.

Our 10 billion Keeping NSW Afloat system developed at the last minute by designers Xenophon, Hanson, Morrison & Turnbull is already proving a huge success. Built entirely around our unique, patented and ground breaking Radical Activation of Commercial Interests in Sustaining Turnbull programme (RACIST), the system has already revolutionised the way Alan Jones can scare the bejesus out of Malcolm.

UPDATE: ABS Innovations apologise for any loss of face. Rest assured heads will roll (when the Red Army invade).

The ABS Self-funded Retirees Superannuation system.

Our 1.6 million dollar secure retirement system which we developed under the genius of economic design team Morrison, O'Dwyer & Turnbull for the 2016 Federal Budget is already proving a huge success. Built around our unique, patented and ground breaking Superannuant's Transition to Enjoyable Aging Lifestyle system (STEAL), the programme has already revolutionised the way every honest, decent, hardworking, taxpaying small business man and woman can look forward to many years of retirement bliss secure in the knowledge that you've got to be joking interest rates are WHAT?! I can't even afford to feed myself let alone pay the bloody electricity bills you bastards I'm never voting Liberal again.

UPDATE: ABS Innovations apologise for any inconvenience due to a permanent loss of income. Rest assured heads will roll (yours, actually).

❖

The inquest into the Sydney Lindt café siege uncovers some unusual police priorities and practices, including missing emails and text messages on the night of the siege.

SWAT Teams

Financial Review
20/8/16

In this day and age of nasty things like extreme violence perpetrated by unknown individuals of indeterminate ethnicity or religion for reasons that are almost impossible to fathom and are manifestly psychological in nature, the job of being a SWAT Team Leader is harder than ever before. On top of that, everybody in the outside world has this ludicrous and completely impractical idea that the so-called Police Force would just "barge in" and "shoot the baddies" and "rescue all the hostages alive" as if we were in a Bruce Willis movie. Nothing could be further from the truth.

2016 — The Year of Come Uppance

For this reason, we in the high command segment of the NSW Police Response And Tactical Services (PRATS) have decided to update our Siege and Hostage Interception Response Kit (SHIRK) to help all members of the force know the correct way to behave should they confront any difficult situations in the future.

Emergency response: Normally the first persons who are aware of the threat of a hostage or siege situation are sitting in a café or some such multicultural communal environment enjoying everyday life in our harmonious, diverse community when another person, or a group of persons of indeterminate cultural identity bursts in and starts shooting everybody or threatening them with lots of guns and bombs or even a machete. Sometimes this Aggrieved Person may be shouting words over and over again in a strange guttural language or waving a black piece of cloth with squiggly white writing on it. This can be very confronting, and may lead one or more people present to dial 000 on their iPhones, where of course their details will be taken down in a sensitive and compassionate fashion in line with community expectations and the highly trained Answering Person will assess whether the person who is shrieking at them down the phone in such a rude and inappropriate fashion may actually just be suffering from depression and needs to be referred to the appropriate Helpline or whether they are in fact just a bunch of drug-crazed teenage pranksters ordering a pizza and the call will be put on hold.

Rapid Deployment: On the rare occasions that an event of extreme violence is being perpetrated, it is imperative to deploy all available resources as quickly as possible to determine the best mode of response. This involves rapidly assembling a crack team of Public Relations experts, spin doctors, and media spokespersons, all of whom must immediately gather at the designated Crisis Point no matter how busy they are on other important matters, such as explaining our transgender diversity program to kindergarten kids or assisting with selecting appropriate, telegenic community representatives for next year's Kirribilli Ramadan iftar dinner celebrations.

Identifying the threat: It is critical that all relevant intelligence concerning the event — such as how soon it is until the next State election, how long until the Boss resigns, who is up to replace him or her, and all the latest focus group approval ratings — is quickly put up on a large whiteboard so that it can be closely analysed to help frame the tactical response to the event and then just as quickly be rubbed out again.

Understanding the Motivation: People do all sorts of unpleasant things for all sorts of reasons that are impossible to discern, but are almost certainly the result of a troubled cultural background where they have been subject to systemic racism, Islamophobia, and manifold expressions of white cultural oppression and privilege. Do NOT jump to conclusions: just because they are shouting Allahu Akbar at the top of their voice as they chop peoples' heads off in no way infers they are acting out of religious motivation.

Observing legalities: Even though you have three trained snipers all with clear lines of sight and ample opportunity to pull the trigger, this does not mean you can abuse another person's inalienable human rights by putting a bullet in their skull.

Keeping calm: No matter how tense the situation, it is critical that as a Senior Commanding Officer you keep calm at all times. The best way to do this is to go home, turn off your phone, have a nice dinner, watch the telly (a romantic comedy should do the trick), and get a good night's kip.

Lines of communication: Decision-making can get very messy and confusing in the midst of a siege. On the one hand, you may have Tony Abbott on the phone offering to send in the army, but on another line you may have an army of PR experts advising you that that would be the very worst thing you could do for your reputation. Think carefully.

Neutralising the threat: After it's over, wipe out all your texts and delete all your emails as fast as you can.

❖

A seemingly never-ending spate of random killings by men of the Islamic faith screaming "Allahu Akbar" are dismissed as being the result of mental or psychological problems, including the slaying of a young backpacker girl in Queensland.

Mental health epidemic

Financial Review
27/8/16

The world of mental health and wellbeing has been rocked to its core by a bizarre global outbreak of inexplicable nervous breakdowns. Researchers are struggling to find a common cause or factor that may link or in some way help explain what is behind this mysterious epidemic of mental, or psychiatric, illnesses. Thus far experts remain baffled as to any similarities between the cases, which to date have been reported with their own specific medical terminology.

Homophobicus orlanditis: In this disturbing case, a young man from an ethnically diverse and culturally rich background that co-incidentally has strong traditional taboos against such modern practices as man on man copulation or woman on woman coupling and yet who exhibited no previous symptoms of any mental disorder whatsoever mysteriously suffered an acute breakdown of his nervous system (or *homophobicus orlanditis*), when he found himself inexplicably confronted by a tutu-wearing group of cavorting drag queens in a 'gays only' nightclub in an American tourist resort. Symptoms of the mysterious breakdown included loudly and repetitively shouting out guttural slogans with strong flat vowel sounds whilst expressing his neurological disturbances via the means of shooting everybody dead. Diagnosis: Unknown mental illness.

Catholicus intoleranza: In this extremely rare case, a young man and his associate, both from ethnically diverse and culturally rich heritages that co-incidentally hold strong traditional taboos against the faith-expression practices of so-called "non-believers" and yet who exhibited no previous symptoms of any mental disorders mysteriously suffered an acute and simultaneous breakdown of their nervous systems (suspected *catholicus intoleranza*) when they found themselves accidentally confronted by on old priest and two nuns swinging a bowl of incense in front of their faces in a French medieval town. Symptoms of this unusual twinned nervous breakdown include both individuals simultaneously breaking into guttural verbal manifestations with unusual linguistic quirks whilst displaying signs of acute psychological disturbances via the means of slitting the priest's throat. Diagnosis: Unknown mental illness.

Backpackeritis stabbata: In this recent case, a young man from an ethnically diverse and culturally rich background which co-incidentally has strong ritualised practices of encouraging females to behave as 'personal property' and dress in large black traditional coverings (or 'sacks') and yet who exhibited no recognisable symptoms of mental disorder whatsoever oddly suffered an acute breakdown of his entire nervous system (common-or-garden *backpackeritis stabbata*), when he found himself confronted by a young girl heading off to the beach in a tee shirt and denim shorts. Symptoms of the mysterious breakdown included an inability to express his pain via any means other than verbal excretions of repetitive foreign-sounding two-word phrases whilst his mental anxieties manifested themselves via the means of stabbing her to death. Diagnosis: Unknown mental illness.

Colognosis gropitis: First detected on New Year's Eve in a northern German town when a series of young men across a wide demographic sphere drawn from a multitude of diverse and ethnically rich backgrounds (i.e. no discernible commonality) many of which co-incidentally hold strong traditional cultural mores on the appropriate behaviour of young women inexplicably and spontaneously found themselves unable to control normal motor functions and muscle control in a crowded situation (extreme *colognosis gropitis*). Symptoms of the mysterious mass nervous disorders include reflex thrusting of hands (for warmth, perhaps?) down the pants and up the skirts of any female they happen to encounter. Diagnosis: Unknown mass mental illness.

2016 — The Year of Come Uppance

Yehudinis mortis: In this unprecedented case, a young man from an ethnically diverse and culturally rich background that co-incidentally has strong traditional taboos against such chronically disturbing practices as being Jewish and proud of it and yet who exhibited no previous symptoms of mental disorders whatsoever mysteriously suffered a breakdown of his nervous system and mental equilibrium (or acute *yehudinis mortis*), when he found himself unfairly confronted by a man in a black hat with curly black bits of hair hanging down the side. Symptoms of the patient's complete psychological breakdown included loudly and repetitively shouting out incomprehnsible phrasings whilst expressing his neurological disturbances via the means of chopping the man to death with a machete. Diagnosis: Unknown mental illness.

Hostagitis chocolatitis: In this unusual case, a man from a culturally rich background that co-incidentally has strong traditional taboos against drinking hot chocolate on the way to work and yet who exhibited no previous symptoms of mental disorders whatsoever apart from murdering his wife and sending abusive letters to dead soldiers mysteriously suffered a nervous breakdown (or *hostagitis chocolatiti*), when he found himself alone in a Sydney café with eighteen hostages and a gun. Symptoms of the patient's psychological disorder manifested themselves in the ritual holding up of a black flag in the window. Diagnosis: Unknown mental illness. Treatment: Ignore hostages and concentrate on prevent non-existent imaginary backlash against people of diverse cultural backgrounds.

❖

A Labor Senator is ensnared in a donations scandal, when it becomes known that a Chinese businessman paid for his excess travel expenses, as well as him being gifted a trip to the Chinese Film Festival. Meanwhile, the anniversary of the Turnbull coup coincides with the re-enactment of a murder on a beach in Bali.

Chinatown

Financial Review
3/9/16

Dear Chinese Film Buffs,
Welcome to your accommodation here at the Crown, Melbourne, for this year's star-studded Chinese Film Festival, hosted by legendary Hollywood heartthrob Sam Dastardly. We trust you shall find our hospitality to your liking, and should you wish for any assistance whatsoever during your stay your personal valet Dr Minschen Myname will personally attend to your every need, including picking up the tab for any old travel expenses you may have lying around.

The highlights of this week's festival include:

Take the Money and Rong: In this hilarious comedy mockumentary, Sam Dastardly plays a petty crook who aspires to the good life by joining the Sussex Street mobster gang, stealing a plush red seat in the Senate, and then plotting a major bank heist disguised as a royal commission. Along the way he stabs two prime ministers in the back with a pair of chopsticks but ironically Dastardly only ends up getting caught when he helps himself to a dodgy Chinese takeaway.

The China Syndrome: In this terrifying thriller, which won veteran Hollywood funnyman Sam "Dastardly" Lemmon a Best Actor nomination in the twilight of his career, a political donations scandal sends off mysterious "vibrations" in which Canberra comes perilously close to a nuclear meltdown, where the body politic melts all the way down to China, hitting the major parties and forever contaminating the surrounding groundwater of Lake Burley Griffin.

Mr Bean: Hilarious slapstick comedy where veteran British comedian Rowan "Sam" Dastardly goes through the entire film without muttering a single word, as he refuses to explain how he came to be lining his pockets courtesy of a foreign communist power. Highlights include Mr Bean, described by Dastardly as "a

2016 — The Year of Come Uppance

child in a grown man's body", attempting to fix various problems presented by everyday expenses scandals and yet always tripping over himself, stumbling around pretending to be morally superior.

Chinatown: In this classic neo-noir film from the '70s, which made an instant superstar of the young actor Sam "Dastardly" Nicholson, a sinister world of political donations and communist infiltrators is exposed after a seemingly innocuous sixteen hundred dollars of "travel expenses" mysteriously turns up in a Chinatown calligraphy studio.

Shanghai Noon: Hilarious slapstick comedy where veteran martial arts actor Jackie Chan plays a Chinese calligrapher who travels to Canberra to rescue its politicians from penury. After teaming up with a union gangster, played by hunky Sam Dastardly, the unlikely duo are given two free bottles of wine by the Woo Hoo group.

The Killing Season: In which Sam Dastardly plays himself, on the phone.

In other news this week, the world of forensic evidence was rocked to its core as police forced an Australian couple to re-enact the bloody night in which they are alleged to have slain an innocent man in mysterious circumstances.

The Australian woman "was definitely involved" in last year's slaying of a politician on the shores of Lake Burley Griffin, police said yesterday, after she and her politically gridlocked boyfriend Malcy were required to re-enact the assault step by step.

Queanbeyan police chief Mr Hendy Withaknife said the purpose of the reconstruction was to resolve the different accounts provided by Mr Malcy and Ms Julie.

Ms Julie had earlier told investigators she tried to separate Mr Malcy and Mr Speedo after a fight broke out between them over who should lead the Liberal party, and that she had tried repeatedly to warn Mr Abbott of the mortal danger he was facing by being seen as Peta Credlin's "handbag".

But during the reconstruction, Ms Julie acted out a scene where she appeared to be on top of Mr Speedo, straddling him as he was lying face down on the party room floor, while hitting him again and again over the head with his royal knighthood. The policeman playing the role of Mr Speedo then mimed biting Ms Julie on the thigh, mistaking her flesh for the flesh of a juicy brown onion.

"Ms Julie was definitely involved in the assault. She even hit the victim with accusations of winking during a radio interview," investigators were quoted as saying.

In a surprising twist Ms Julie's lawyer said his client had never actually been to the house in Queanbeyan herself, but on that fateful night had sent her Chief of Staff instead. "There was no actual physical contact ever made with any of the sharp implements. Julie was forced to re-enact her part in a knifing which she never took part in," her lawyer, Mr Sinodinogar complained. But Mr Malcy insists the couple "did it together", Mr Hendy Withaknife told reporters.

However forensic tests clearly show Ms Julie with bloodstains still visible on her hands. "The base never forgets. Unfortunately, it's a lifelong sentence," her lawyers admitted.

❖

When Malcolm Turnbull makes his maiden speech at the United Nations, guess who pops up to steal the limelight, and the Sky News interview? One of our many deposed PMs, of course.

Giblets

Financial Review
24/9/2016

In a revealing interview this week with top Sky News political journalist Kieran Giblets, former Australian prime minister Kevin Rudd outlined his vision for making the United Nations far more effective and proactive at solving global problems and international conflict.

Kieran Giblets: So tell me, Mr Rudd, what's wrong with the UN and how would you, er, I mean, how should whoever the next Secretary-General happens to be go about fixing the clear lack of your, I mean of somebody-or-other's brilliant leadership in this woeful organisation?

Kevin Rudd: Well, let me just say this, Kieran, if I may, and I thank you for your interest in this critical topic. Number One: let me point out to your erudite viewers that it's not as if I've just spent the last three years as the President of the Peace Institute's National Knowledge Building and Territorial Treaties Society (PINKBATTS) committee twiddling my thumbs here in New York, Vienna, Copenhagen, Geneva, Hong Kong and London. Number Two: As is clear, K Rudd has been working tirelessly and relentlessly on behalf of the good burghers of this planet solving the world's most intractable problems such as climate change, the Middle East, global poverty, child slavery, drug cartels and international arms smuggling to name just a few off the top of my head. Number Three: Working with a small staff of around fifty dedicated experts, my sole job is one of programmatic analysis and collegiate resolution. Basically, I analyse each problem, solve it, and then tell the others what our decision is.

Kieran: So, in a nutshell, how would you, er, I mean how would whoever is in charge of the United Nations fix up the world?

Kevin: Well, Kieran, Number One: I believe strongly in personal interaction and individual charisma. In my capacity as Chair of the Regional Asian Trade and Foreign Key Relations Security (RATFKRS) committee I have established warm and respectful relations with all the good folk of the Great Global Powers, and Number Two: I have actually addressed many of the world's leaders on an informal but intimate basis without a translator as it happens thanks to my gift for languages, which clearly puts me ahead of the rest of the rat, I mean, er, pack when it comes to these sorts of delicate diplomatic relationships.

Kieran: And how would you, I mean, er, how should a future Secretary-General, whoever that might be, approach the thorny yet interrelated problems of, for example, Syria, Isis, Russia, Turkey, the Kurds, Iranian nuclear weapons and the broader Middle East conflict?

Kevin: Well, Kieran, Number One: in my capacity as Global CEO of the East Asian Resistance to War and Xenophobia (EARWAX) organisation, it is well documented that I like to keep my ears open and I have never hesitated to repeatedly put my finger in and have a good dig around any sticky problem before sinking my teeth into whatever comes out and then digesting it all before starting the whole process all over again.

Kieran: Thank you Mr Secretary-Gen... er, I mean Mr Rudd.

Meanwhile, also in New York, Prime Minister Malcolm Turnbull delivered his first address on the world stage where he outlined his inspirational "Three Pillars" policy.

Speaking to an empty General Assembly Hall, Mr Turnbull addressed his wife Lucy and a couple of Muslim janitors: "We must be clear that there is only one way to solve the Syrian conflict and to prevent Europe from being inundated by refugees," he told his enrapt audience, over the loud din of two industrial-strength vacuum cleaners. "The First Pillar is making sure you win a huge majority under your predecessor, get him to stop the boats, get him to secure your borders, and get him to bomb ISIS and shirt-front Vladimir Putin. The Second Pillar is toppling your predecessor by telling the bed-wetters that he is an onion-munching winker who will lose the next election. The Third Pillar is narrowly scraping in and then pretending to be just like your predecessor except in an orange tie instead of a blue one."

In other news this week, the campaign director of the Liberal party, Mr Nutty Tone, explained to a packed audience of newshounds how successful his election strategy for the 2016 federal election campaign had been.

"I'm delighted to be here at the National Press Club to explain my brilliant electoral strategy, but, to be honest, I am not at all surprised that you all turned up here this afternoon because, as my genius campaign strategist Mark Textor explained to me this morning, 'don't worry about the Press Gallery showing up, they have nowhere else to go'. Anyway... Hello? Hello? Is this microphone actually on? Sorry, is there anyone out there...? Where is everybody?"

❖

The Australian Financial Review *releases their Power Play list of the most powerful people in the nation. And the lights go out in South Australia when the windfarms all fail because there's too much wind.*

Powerless

Financial Review
1/10/2016

Feeling sick to the stomach and green with envy that you didn't make it into the Fin's annual Power Play issue of the most powerful people in the land? Help is at hand, with our "2016 Powerless Play" list, compiled by our most powerless columnist Rowena Stricktlyinitforthecash.

Sneaking in just hours before entries closed, our panel had no choice but to give the coveted Most Powerless Award for 2016 to *the entire state of South Australia*. The judges were particularly impressed by the way the state's Premier Jay Weathervane has worked tirelessly for years to ensure the state now operates solely at the mercy of Wind Powerlessness and Solar Powerlessness, ensuring that when there is no wind, a bit of wind, too much wind, gale force winds, a bit of rain, drizzle, torrential downpours, a few clouds, twilight, or dark, (or any combination of the above) $1.7 million Aussies are completely, well, powerless.

Wyatt Twerp: Another late entry, but a firm favourite with the judges, Mr Twerp is a young, agile, innovative and flexible member of Generation ADHD who has devoted his considerable skills to stripping away all power from everybody he meets, including himself. "Mr Twerp's CV," says Rowena, "reads like a classic rags-to-riches Power Play, except in reverse." Starting at the very top, as a 12-year-old MP elected into Parliament entirely on the coat-tails of Tony Abbott, Mr Twerp devoted all his energies to scheming behind the scenes to betray his boss. Rewarded for his treachery with a cabinet post, Mr Twerp then set about introducing his "innovation agenda", which quickly became a laughing stock that helped wipe out the government's credibility, its majority, nearly wiped out Mr Turnbull, and of course completely wiped himself out of parliament. Mr Twerp is currently assisting the Peshmerga to be wiped out in Iraq.

The entire academic staff of Sydney University: Once one of the most powerful and respected universities in the country, if not the world, Sydney University has recently indulged a hardcore leftwing rump of fifth-rate academics and anti-semitic socialist hacks in their impressive and highly effective "march through the institution" to render the university completely powerless to promote itself as a place of serious academic value or professional credibility. The judges were particularly impressed by the fact that no fewer than 130 so-called "academics" proved just how powerless, ineffectual and intellectually-bereft their credentials are by putting their names to a letter objecting to the university's decision to award a doctorate to John Howard.

Bill Powershortage: The judges believe this candidate's entry form speaks for itself: "Wiv my brilliant strategy to reject the gay marriage plibersik so vat I can become Prime Minister instead of Albo I reckon vat I should be in power wivin the next twelve or sumfink months so vat we can have 100 per cent renewable power and save the planet coz nuffink matters more than that and — hey you! How come vis pie is stone bloody cold? — I said just stick it in the effin' oven — wot do you mean there's a blackout?"

Mike Buried: Former Golden-Eyed Boy of NSW, Mr Buried impressed the judges with his lightning speed at losing power by winning the race to the bottom of the polls. Likening him to a sleek greyhound, the judges noted that as recently as last year the odds on Mr Buried ever becoming powerless were the longest in the Premier Stakes. However, at a disastrous meet on July 6, Mr Buried shot out of the gates with a bizarre Facebook posting that destroyed the livelihoods, lives and passions of thousands of battlers and he's been in front of the powerless pack ever since. Experts believe Mr Buried was live baited with forced council amalgamations and lock-out laws and that he has now lost so much power he'll have to be put down.

Self-funded retirees: The judges were impressed by the fact that despite having very little power of their own thanks to exorbitant electricity bills, an army of self-funded retirees, small business people, hard-working, decent taxpayers and others regarded as the "backbone of the Coalition" have been stripped of their aspirations, dreams, hopes, years of planning, security and above all of their own money by a spendthrift, inept, so-called "Liberal" Treasurer. "I've always been powerless," said Mrs Kafoops of Kanga Retirement Villas, "now I'm penniless too."

Special commendation: The judges were impressed by an early entry for the 2056 Powerless Awards: "The $50 billion South Australian-built Submarine Fleet which not only lost all power when we ripped out the nuclear engines and replaced then with steam, er, diesel ones, but the propellers were never installed because we kept having all these blackouts."

❖

Renewable energy targets come under attack as South Australia's Labor government tries to pin the blame for their blackout on climate change and freak storms.

South Australia

Financial Review
8/10/2016

Welcome to South Australia, home of Sustainable Renewable Energy. Here are a few handy hints prepared by Tourism SA to help you enjoy your stay, with our brilliant selection of exciting things to do and, er, not see.

Spin the bottle: Loads of fun when the lights go out (which is pretty much the moment you arrive, if they aren't out already) especially for single adults and divorcees. Place an empty bottle of Barossa's finest on the floor, sit around in a circle, and give it a good spin. When the bottle stops, kiss whoever it's pointing at. No need to worry about gender choices either, because you can't actually see each other! Those sweet tasting lips belong to whatever gender your fluidity chooses to imagine. For an added spark of electricity, wire the spinning bottle up to a small generator and do what the locals do — generate yourself a bit of reliable baseload power. Every bit as efficient as our famous local windmills.

Pin the Tail on the Donkey: South Australia's favourite past-time. And the best bit is you don't even need a blindfold! Simply hold your arms out in front of you and stumble around your hotel room navigating only by touch. For added excitement, pretend you're looking for where you left the spare bloody batteries for the bloody torch ouch! &*#%^ who left that bloody cupboard door open?!

Learn Braille: These days, most South Australians prefer to read in the dark. So why not try your hand at it too? Simply run your fingers over the bumps and see if you can make out the letters and numbers that we find on everyday items. Practice with something nice and large to begin with, such as your daily electricity bill! Clue for beginners: that squiggly "S" symbol is a dollar sign and all the little bumps after it are zeros and commas.

Wine tasting: South Australia is famous for its blind wine tastings. Partly this is because we have such a rich variety of vintages and varietals to choose from, and party because most South Australian wine tastings are by necessity carried out in the pitch black. Your olfactory senses will become highly developed as they compensate for your lack of vision. Join a large tour group in savouring the delightful aromas and mysterious flavours from our greatest vineyards. Just be careful you don't swig from the spit bucket by mistake!

2016 — The Year of Come Uppance

Calligraphy classes: Nowadays, most South Australians prefer to communicate important documents and other critical information with each other via the most modern, efficient, reliable, speediest and sustainably renewable means available, i.e. pen and paper.

Basket-weaving: It's only in recent times that we've seen a surge in popularity for this delightful local past-time, as unemployed Holden assembly-line workers, out-of-work Arnotts Iced VoVo cookie cutters, on-the-dole Caroma cabinet makers, redundant Mitsubishi hub-cab designers and a plethora of other highly skilled South Australians turn their talents to the one manufacturing task they can deliver on time, within budget, and without electricity.

Glow-in-the-dark: When four-wheel driving through the magisterial magnificence of the South Australian outback, you'll marvel at the beautiful, amazing and miraculous glow that lights up the night sky coming from the canopy of stars over... er, sorry, scratch that, it's actually our nuclear waste dump better chuck a u-ie quick!

Submarine-building: As the quaint old South Australian slogan proudly emblazoned above the gates to our state-of-the-art $50 billion taxpayer-funded Christopher Pyne-endowed nautical manufacturing plant says, "We couldn't even build a canoe". Which is why it's lucky we're concentrating on sustainable renewable two-stroke diesel "Victa-class" submarine re-fits instead.

No problem gambling: Thanks to the tireless work of our wonderful SA politicians including the indefatigable local heart-throb Senator Nick Xenopoke, you can enjoy all the delights of our problem-free gambling venues! Spend as many hours as you like sitting in front of an entire bank of pokies and you won't lose a cent (because there's no electricity to switch them on with).

Hang gliding: For thrill seekers only! Hop into one of our downtown office lifts just before the weather sets in and you'll be left hanging there in the dark for hours! Scary stuff!

Weather-watching: Here in the Climate Change capital of the World, you can watch the climate change in front of your very own eyes! Experience our shocking once-in-a-lifetime ill weather events (known colloquially as weatherills) that are so ferocious they bring the entire state to its knees. These include: cloudy with gentle breezes, overcast with slight drizzle, early morning showers, late afternoon breeze, chance of rain, mild south-easterly winds, howling westerly gales, heavy rainfall, north-easterly gusts, drought, floods, snow, sleet, hail, full sun, moonless night (full list of once-in-a-lifetime weatherills available from weather-ill@climatechange.completecon).

❖

UNESCO decides that some Jewish historic places have nothing to do with the Jews. Yep, the United Nations, as usual, stretch the very limits of credibility — and even satire.

Unesco

Financial Review
15/10/2016

In a major victory for the United Nations and the freedom-loving, peace-loving, sharia-dominated democracies of the world, the United Nations Educational, Scientific and Cultural Organization (UNESCO) on Thursday passed a resolution sponsored by a majority of peace-loving Islamic states that denies any Jewish connection whatsoever to a range of Jewish icons. These include the Temple Mount, the Western Wall in Jerusalem, Jerusalem itself, the Holy City of King David, the Temple of Solomon, the Dead Sea Scrolls, the Psalms of David, the Valley of Death, Goliath's old stomping ground, a leather sling with a pebble in it, that bit of the Red Sea which parted so Moses could cut through it, a large pillar of salt in the middle of the desert somewhere, some bullrushes on the Nile, ten plagues, a burned bush, two stone tablets, Bob Dylan, Larry David, *Seinfeld* series 1 to 9, the cast of *Seinfeld*, the writers of *Seinfeld*, the camera crew of *Seinfeld*, Mel Brookes, *The Producers*, *Blazing Saddles*, New York, the Upper West Side, South Brooklyn, the Bronx, Woody Allen, all of Woody Allen's movies but particularly *Annie Hall* and *Hannah and her Sisters*, Intel processors, Steven Spielberg, jeans, *Fiddler on the Roof*, bagels, ballpoint pens, pickled herrings, pacemakers, defibrillators, smoked salmon, kidney dialysis, Google, the raid on Entebbe, Leonard Bernstein, Barbra Streisand, lipstick, Albert Einstein (full list of Jewish icons with absolutely no connection whatsoever to the perfidious Jews available from antisemites@unesco.isis).

❖

And just in time to make it into this book, the Australian Human Rights Commission manage to completely prove the absurdity of their organisation by announcing they are investigating one of Australia's greatest satirical minds, the cartoonist Bill Leak, for "racial hatred". Why? Because of a complaint they received after the Race Commissioner published the cartoon on social media and asked people to complain about it.

I can't find any racism

Financial Review
22/10/2016

Rowena's Agony Aunt Column, where even the most vexing problems are solved:

Dear Rowena,
I'm a highly paid Race Discrimination Commissioner in a multi-million dollar taxpayer-funded organisation that pays me hundreds of thousands of dollars more than I'd probably earn in the private sector. My worry is that in order to stay in my rather cushy job surely I have to keep finding examples of racism? But what if I can't find any?! I might end up on the scrap heap and actually have to go and find another job! Where can I find some examples of racism so that I can appear to look busy?
Yours, (name and address provided but far too long and complicated to fit into this space).

Way Beyond Satire

Dear Anon,
Fear not. Help is at hand. Despite the depressing (from your point of view) fact that here in this wonderful land of ours it is extremely hard to find genuine examples of racism; because apart from a few boofheads who get blotto on a Friday night at the footy and call each other silly names, and then wake up the next morning with a broken nose, we are actually one of the world's most racially tolerant nations. (Obviously, you wouldn't have to look hard to find a decent slab of "racist" or indeed "anti-semitic" behaviour if you chose to hang out in specific large, segregated establishments favoured by a certain major religion, noted for its peace-loving and tolerant ways, but we won't go there!) But here's a handy tip to keep you busy. Go grab your nearest newspaper and find a cartoon. Cartoonists are different to most people in newspapers because rather than using words they use pictures, and it's far easier to cry "Racism!" at a drawing than at a word. For example, if I wrote "the problem with Indigenous delinquency is often the lack of proper parenting" you would be hard-pressed to describe that as racist — in fact, you'd probably get a grant to go and do a study on it. However, imagine if instead of using words I drew a picture (because that's what cartoonists do) and, say for example, I drew a caricature of a black guy with black skin and a black kid standing in front of him and a black cop and made a gag in the speech bubble about how the Dad didn't even know his own son's name then... Bingo! You'd have a field day! I might even put a beer in his hand, and make him look a bit slovenly because that's what cartoonists do! Then all you have to do is put the cartoon on your Facebook page and ask any Aboriginal people if they are offended by it and tell them to complain to your organisation if they are! You'll be inundated! Problem solved!

Dear Rowena,
I am a highly paid Human Rights Commissioner in a multi-million dollar taxpayer-funded organisation that pays me hundreds of thousands of dollars. My worry is that in order to stay in my rather cushy job surely I have to keep finding examples of human rights abuses? But what if I can't find any?! I might end up on the scrap heap and have to find another job! Where can I find some examples of human rights abuses so that I can appear to look busy?

Yours, (name and address withheld by the sub-editor,
who took it out of context)

Dear Anon,
Fear not. Help is at hand. Despite the depressing (from your point of view) fact that here in this wonderful land of ours it is extremely hard to find genuine examples of human rights abuses; because apart from a few boofheads who get blotto on a Friday night after the footy and king hit each other, we are actually one of the world's most non-violent and non-abusive nations. (Obviously, you wouldn't have to look hard to find a decent slab of human rights abuses if you chose to hang out in virtually any of the scores of nations dominated by a certain major religion, noted for its peace-loving and tolerant ways, but we won't go there!) But here's a handy tip to keep you busy. Switch on the ABC and watch something called a "current affairs doco". (Don't mix it up with the fictional drama shows, although they're hard to tell apart.) The ABC is taxpayer-funded to the tune of many millions of dollars (see, you already have something in common!) and their producers love to use pictures, often sourced from such visually-rich areas as Youtube in order to make their point, rather than rely on what some might call "facts". The morning after the show has aired you'll be inundated by outraged viewers! Bingo! Problem solved!

❖

As Halloween approaches, the controversy over the investigation of cartoonist Bill Leak continues throughout the media, with — in particular — the role of the Human Rights Commission coming under deserved scrutiny.

Halloween

Financial Review
29/10/2016

It's time to scare the kiddies senseless with the Fin's Handy Halloween Guide. In it you'll find all the tips for games and costumes to make sure this All Hallow's Eve is hours of terrifying fun for the whole family.

Trigg or treat: This year, get the kids to dress up as their favourite Human Rights Commissioner (yikes! spooky stuff!) and go around the neighbourhood knocking on peoples' doors in the middle of the night when they least expect it and scaring them witless! Here's how it works: When the person (preferably a cartoonist, journalist or uni student — but it could be anybody at all!) answers the door, you immediately threaten them with the ancient cry of "Trigg or treat?" They then have a choice: either to hand you a lolly bag stuffed with candy money and other goodies (five grand in cash will usually do the trick) to make you go away or else, if they don't cough up, you get to play a Trigg on them. The Trigg can be as mischievous or as monstrous as you like — we are celebrating the night of the living dead after all! Why not say you are investigating them for "racial hatred" because of some innocuous drawing they did or comment they made about segregation on Facebook? Hours of fun — sorry, scratch that — years of fun for the whole Commission!

Carve your own soutpumpkinase: For the superstitious only! This is an ancient Halloween custom believed to ward off evil spirits, such as being falsely accused of racism, sexism or homophobia. First, buy a large round pumpkin from your local green grocers. The rounder the better. You'll also need some black tufts of string (for the hair!) as well as any other props you fancy, such as a pair of cartoony black horn-rimmed glasses. Hollow out the "brains" of the pumpkin — this shouldn't take long — and then carve out the features onto the face of the pumpkin to resemble your favourite Human Rights Commissioner! See if you can capture that truly scary look of self-righteous, sanctimonious taxpayer-funded self-importance and sneering pomposity. Carefully place a small candle into the empty space where the brains were — or weren't — and then pop your soutpumpkinase in the window! For even more fun, take a photo of it and pop it onto your Facebook page and ask people to contact you if they are "offended" by it! Then, if you're truly feeling supercilious, sorry, we mean superstitious, you get to completely destroy their lives by investigating them for "racial hatred"!

Witch dunking: In medieval times, witch-hunters would spend Halloween trying to determine who was a witch and who wasn't by grabbing unpopular women and dunking them into the local pond. If they drowned it meant they were innocent, but if they didn't drown it meant they were guilty and had to be burned at the stake! Either way, they met a suitably grisly end simply by being accused of the crime of witchcraft by anybody in the village who didn't like them! These days, we have perfected the system and we are even more barbaric but just as effective — we use 18C. Punishment guaranteed, even when you're innocent!

Fantasise your own horror stories: Halloween wouldn't be the same without terrifying stories about all the dreadful things that people like to imagine really go on in the world. So why not make up your own scary yarns? For example, you could pretend that those outrageous comments you made in a taped interview were "inserted by the sub-editors". Or you could tell terrifying tales about kids in detention being sick when they're not, about guards carrying guns who don't, about never meeting Labor ministers to discuss an inquiry when you did, about executions being linked to border policies when they weren't etc (full list available from talltales@trigg.comm).

Write your own tales from the crypt: First, don a scary Hallowed Waleed mask then write a piece for a major international newspaper claiming that Australians are torturers sacrificing innocent lives! It's Halloween, so some people might actually believe you!

Horror ride: Organise your annual general meeting to take place just hours after a horrific fatal tragedy. Then announce that it's back to business-as-usual with unseemly haste. Then announce a massive bonus for the CEO. You, your brand and your PR firm will be haunted by it for years to come!

Things that go bump in the night: There's nothing scarier than being stranded all alone in the dark; no light, no electricity, no TV, no internet, no business, no customers, no working lifts, no emergency equipment — just the eerie sound of ghoulish weatherills wailing in the blackness! So for a truly terrifying Halloween, go to South Australia!

A Federal Circuit Court judge throws out the 18C case against three Queensland University of Technology students accused of "racial vilification". There are calls for the President of the Human Rights Commission to be sacked.

Triggology

Financial Review
5/11/2016

Welcome to the Queensland University of Triggology, where you will find a plethora of challenging courses that will prepare you for a (very) lucrative career in the dynamic field of contemporary Human Rights. Courses include:

Triggonometry: The study of this intriguing branch of mathematics goes back to ancient times, and relies on three specific points in order to calculate the difference between a typically funny cartoon and an outrageous example of extreme racial hatred. Greek astronomers discovered that if you have a fixed lunar leftie (often referred to as an obtuse angle) you can measure the distance from reality to insanity based solely upon the skin colour of the complainant as well as the ethnicity of the cartoonist or university student being complained about.

Triggle-down economics: This purely theoretical branch of economics is widely used to characterise those economic policies that favour extreme wealth, power and outlandish privilege at the expense of the everyday taxpayer. For example, if you run a $21 million government-mandated quango, or star chamber, answerable to nobody but yourself, you can afford to pay its top executives vast sums of money that far exceed anything that you, or they, could ever hope to earn in the so-called "real" world.

Psychiatrigg studies: Mental health experts today recognise that extreme psychological trauma can be "triggered" simply by an innocent individual being investigated by an out-of-control government quango fixated with its own ideological mission to uncover rampant "racism" and punish people for the imaginary crimes of "causing offence" and being "insulting". In this three year (minimum) course, students get to explore first-hand the overwhelming sense of injustice that this process creates, with experts admitting that many victims will suffer extreme feelings of persecution and paranoia, not to mention severe poverty, as they are hounded by a sinister star chamber for months, or even years, on end. Once they have completed their diploma, students will have learned that even when innocent they are guilty.

TrigAdvisor: For those who love to travel, first-class preferably, this is the ideal course for you to take so you can land a really cushy job that requires no specific skillset. TrigAdvisor is one of the original social media platforms that relies solely on user-generated content, so after you complete this course you'll be an expert in encouraging people to generate content on your behalf. For example, why not put up a cartoon on the TrigAdvisor Facebook page and ask Aboriginal Australians if they find it offensive? You're bound to generate at least one comment that you can then rely on to further your own career. But be warned: some TrigAdvisor comments are completely fictitious, particularly the negative ones, which people make simply to denigrate those they don't particularly like.

Trigger warnings: In this exciting new branch of contemporary linguistic studies, you learn what words, ideas and thoughts are so outrageous that they require trigger warnings to prevent people from being offended or insulted by them. During the course, students will be encouraged to avoid certain ideas altogether, which we do by not allowing them to be exposed to them in the first place. The following are a random selection of typical words or ideas that students learn they must detest unequivocally if they wish to succeed in the brave new world of modern "progressive" academe: free, speech, Bill, Leak, cartoon, John, Stuart, Mill, conservative, Tony, Abbott, Donald, Trump, Brexit, Israel, settlements, Cory, Bernardi (full list of trigger warning words no longer available as they have all been deleted from our University mainframe).

Sub-triggiting: In this exciting journalism course, you learn to report a hugely embarrassing interview and transcribe it word for word exactly as it happened.

Trigglycerides: There are many different types of dangerous fatty acids, but this course focuses on those which synthesise to form a noxious component within the bloodstream known by the latin term "sanctimonio pompositus" or "Commissioner's disease". Once they make their way into the brain, these trigglycerides can block up normal pathways to free expression and rational thought, resulting in severe ideological seizures and fantasies of self-importance.

Trigg and field: This university prides itself on its athletic prowess, no more so than when it comes to the races. In this popular extra-curricular activity, students are encouraged to "identify" as being of one particular race and their opponent must "identify" as being of a different race. Competitors then run around in circles pretending to be "offended" or "insulted" by something someone on the other team said, did, or even drew, and financial compensation is immediately demanded. It is then up to the opposing player to "prove" that what they said is "genuine", "in good faith", "fair comment" and "not racist". Winners can get up to $250,000. Losers go straight to hell.

❖

Against the expectations of most of the media and political pundits (myself and a couple of others excepted), Donald Trump wins the White House. The Left go nuts.

The ABC's guide on how to survive the next four years

Financial Review
12/11/2016

Dear loyal ABC viewers,
It will have come as a major shock to you all on Wednesday

2016 — The Year of Come Uppance

November 9 when normal scheduled programming was interrupted by a mysterious malfunction which our technicians have subsequently identified as a freak once-in-a-lifetime cataclysmic event known as the "Trump election victory disaster".

We apologise sincerely to all our regular customers that the narrative during the course of this particular televised event did not go strictly as foretold. Indeed, as the nation's most respected and experienced broadcaster, it is fair to say that not a single one of our valued employees could possibly have foreseen events unfolding in such an unsatisfactory and unfathomable manner.

For those regular viewers who experienced violent cognitive dissociation and nervous exhaustion brought about by the unseemly and unedifying manner in which we allowed our airwaves to be polluted by revolting and unacceptable images beamed at us from overseas networks over which we have no control (predominantly in the United States) we accept full responsibility for any mental trauma which may have resulted and we urge you to contact completelyfreakedout@yourabc to lodge a formal complaint in order that we can compensate you as soon as possible (at full taxpayers' expense) for having to suffer this ordeal.

Many viewers have already written to us to point out the error in our live broadcast, in which we accompanied images of the celebration victory party of President Hillary Clinton with old footage of a failed New York real estate mogul from the early '80s.

Rest assured, here at the ABC we will do everything within our power to restore your normal mental equilibrium and cultural viewing habits. Indeed, we are proud to announce next months' ABC highlights:

Four Corners: In which our intrepid reporters expose the corruptness at the heart of the US electoral system and the torture and forcible detention of the so-called voting public. In this highly disturbing expose of mental abuse within the

American heartland, we reveal the sinister truth in which millions of white Americans were strapped down by the ankles and wrists in chairs in dark rooms with hoods over their heads and forced to endure hour upon hour of a shock reality TV show called *The Apprentice* (featuring a racist, misogynist, sexist, crotch-groping, moronic white billionaire) whilst being force-fed bucket loads of fried chicken before being made to stand for hours on end in a long queue and ordered to fill in a so-called ballot paper. The results are too terrifying to detail here.

Q&A: This week's Special US Election Coverage edition of *Q&A* will be filmed live in the hallowed grounds of Sydney University, where host Tony Jones will interview the brightest minds of an American think tank, who will explain in detail how the average US voter's ignorance is so utterly profound these days because they never read any of the many hundreds of papers the think tank churns out every year.

7.30: In this ground-breaking interview, top investigative journalist and host Leigh Fails interviews the entire staff of the billion-dollar-taxpayer-funded ABC from the janitors to the chief executives in search of one single conservative-thinking individual who was even capable of imagining let alone predicting let alone supporting a President Trump. As the title of the show suggests, Leigh fails.

The Killing Season: In this gripping investigative follow-up to last year's warts 'n' all diagnosis of the horrendous Rudd-Gillard fiascos, we explore how Rudd and Gillard gave away hundreds of millions of Australian taxpayers' dollars to the Clinton Foundation in order to... er, um, hang on, any chance we can get any of it back?

Lateline: In which top investigative host Emma Over-twitchy explains how the Hillary Clinton presidency will unfold, from the cracking of the glass ceiling through to the inevitability of a second term, followed by the strong likelihood of Michelle Obama succeeding President Clinton for another eight years of enlightened feminist rule, after which Chelsea Clinton will be a clear favourite to continue the inspiring Clinton legacy. Not tobe missed.

Tuesday Book Club: This week our panel discusses the most popular books currently cluttering up the remainders bins: *Madam President, The Clinton Dynasty, Smashing the Glass Ceiling, It Takes A Village* etc.

Pointless: In which the hard-working Aussie taxpayer ponders the meaning of subsidising to the tune of over a billion dollars a year a public broadcaster completely out of touch with the real world.

The author of this book urges all Australians to demand the repeal of section 18C of the Racial Discrimination Act before we lose our liberty, our freedom to express ourselves creatively, politically and satirically, our beloved Aussie larrikin sense of humour — and our souls. The criminalisation of free thoughts and creative expression for supposedly causing offense and insult is, quite frankly, way beyond satire.